~~~ckburn

Two internationally distinguisheu
improbable saga of English in time a
guage from its obscure beginnings over ⌐   ...₁ ₒᵣ dialects
spoken by marauding, illiterate tribes. The   ...ᵥᵥ ᴛne geographical spread
of the language in its increasing diversity has made English into an international
language of unprecedented range and variety. They look at the present state of
English as a global language and the problems, pressures and uncertainties of its
future. They argue that, in spite of the amazing variety and plurality of English,
it remains a single language.

English – One Tongue, Many Voices tells its story with the help of maps, diagrams
and pictures. The text is interspersed with panels focusing on particular topics
of interest, and is followed by notes that give the sources of information, as well
as detailed references and indexes.

A book for students and their teachers, and for anyone who wants a broad and
authoritative introduction to the phenomenon of English worldwide.

Jan Svartvik, the distinguished Scandinavian scholar of English language, is
now Emeritus Professor at the University of Lund, Sweden. He is co-author of
Engelsk universitetsgrammatik (with Olof Sager, 1977) and *Handbok i engelska*
(with Rikard Svartvik, 2001), and author, co-author or editor of some 35 books
and 75 papers or articles on varied aspects of English linguistics, contrastive
grammar and nautical terminology. He is a Member of the Royal Swedish
Academy of Sciences, The Royal Academy of Letters, History and Antiquities
and Academia Europaea.

Geoffrey Leech has recently retired as Research Professor of Linguistics at
Lancaster University, UK. Author, co-author, or co-editor of 25 books and
100 papers or articles on varied aspects of linguistics and the English language,
he is a Fellow of the British Academy and a Member of Academia Europaea. He
is co-author with Margaret Deuchar and Robert Hoogenraad of *English Grammar
for Today: A New Introduction*, now in its second edition.

Together with Randolph Quirk and Sidney Greenbaum, Jan Svartvik and
Geoffrey Leech co-authored the 'Quirk grammars': *A Grammar of Contemporary
English* (1972) and *A Comprehensive Grammar of the English Language* (1985).
They are co-authors of *A Communicative Grammar of English*, which went into its
third edition in 2002.

English

One Tongue, Many Voices

Jan Svartvik

and

First published in 2006 by
PALGRAVE MACMILLAN
Houndmills, Basingstoke, Hampshire RG21 6XS and
175 Fifth Avenue, New York, N.Y. 10010
Companies and representatives throughout the world.

PALGRAVE MACMILLAN is the global academic imprint of the Palgrave Macmillan division of St. Martin's Press, LLC and of Palgrave Macmillan Ltd. Macmillan® is a registered trademark in the United States, United Kingdom and other countries. Palgrave is a registered trademark in the European Union and other countries.

ISBN-13: 978–1–4039–1829–1 hardback
ISBN-10: 1–4039–1829–5 hardback
ISBN-13: 978–1–4039–1830–7 paperback
ISBN-10: 1–4039–1830–9 paperback

This book is printed on paper suitable for recycling and made from fully managed and sustained forest sources.

A catalogue record for this book is available from the British Library.

Library of Congress Cataloging-in-Publication Data

Svartvik, Jan.
    [Engelska. English]
    English : one tongue, many voices / Jan Svartvik, Geoffrey Leech.
        p. cm.
    Rev. and updated ed. of: Engelska : öspråk, världsspråk, trendspråk. c1999.
    Includes bibliographical references and index.
    ISBN 1–4039–1829–5 (cloth)—ISBN 1–4039–1830–9 (pbk.)
      1. English language – History. 2. English language – Variation – English-
speaking countries. 3. English language – Variation – Foreign countries.
    4. Globalization. 5. Communication, International. 6. Culture and globalization.
    I. Leech, Geoffrey N. II. Title.

PE1700.S83 2006
420.9—dc22   2006041002

10 9 8 7 6 5 4 3 2 1
15 14 13 12 11 10 09 08 07 06

Printed and bound in Great Britain by
Antony Rowe Ltd, Chippenham and Eastbourne

For Gunilla and Fanny

Contents

List of Figures

Acknowledgements

We gratefully acknowledge permission from the following sources to reproduce illustrations and other copyright material. Every effort has been made to contact copyright holders, but if we have failed to find the copyright holder, or if any have been inadvertently overlooked, the publisher will be pleased to make amends at the earliest opportunity.

Illustrations

Figure 2.3   Runes, reproduced from Dennis Freeborn, *From Old English to Standard English*, 2nd edition 1998; Palgrave Macmillan.

Figure 3.1   A scene from the Bayeux tapestry, 'Beachhead 1' from the replica of the tapestry in the Reading Museum © Reading Museum Service (Reading Borough Council). All rights reserved.

Figure 3.2   The opening lines of Chaucer's Canterbury Tales, from Caxton's early printed version (1478). Reproduced by courtesy of the University Librarian and Director, The John Rylands Library, The University of Manchester.

Figure 4.2   The Swan Theatre; sketch by Arent van Buchell (Arnoldus Buchelius, 1565–1641) after a lost original of *ca.* 1597 by Johannes de Witt (1566–1622), Utrecht University Library, MS 842, fol. 132r.

Figure 12.3   Northern Cities Shift, adapted from *A National Map of the Regional Dialects of American English*, by William Labov, Charles Boberg and Sharon Ash at the following website: http://www.ling.upenn.edu/phono_atlas/NationalMap/NationalMap.html.

Text materials

Pages 161–3   Edward Olson, 'Differences in the UK and US Versions of four *Harry Potter* books, FAST US-1, Introduction to American English, Department of Translation Studies, University of Tampere, Finland, at the following website: http://www.uta.fi/FAST/US1/REF/potter.html.

Page 180   'Sweet and Dandy' by Frederick 'Toots' Hibbert; of Toots and the Maytals, reproduced with permission, transcribed and annotated by Peter L. Patrick, *Jamaican Creole Texts*, on his website: http://privatewww.essex.ac.uk/~patrickp/JCtexts.html.

List of Abbreviations and Special Symbols

AAVE	African American Vernacular English (see p. 169)
AmE	American English
AustE	Australian English
BBC	British Broadcasting Corporation
BrE	British English
EE	Estuary English (see p. 130)
EFL	English as a foreign language
ELF	English as a lingua franca (see p. 232)
EU	European Union
GA	General American (pronunciation) (see p. 81)
NZE	New Zealand English
RP	Received Pronunciation (see p. 125)
ScotE	Scottish English
UK	United Kingdom
US, USA	United States (of America)
WAPE	West African Pidgin English (see p. 185)
WSE	World Standard English (see p. 225)
WSSE	World Spoken Standard English (see p. 227)

Pronunciation

Symbols used in transcription are explained on pp. 286–7, at the back of the book.

Stressed syllables are represented (in transcription) by:
' (primary stress) or ˌ (secondary stress) preceding the syllable:
    as in 'government, be'tween, ˌinter'national.
Or alternatively stressed syllables are represented (in the text) by underlining:
    as in government, between, international.

Long vowels are represented by : placed after the vowel symbol:
    as in /kɑː/ for the RP pronunciation of car.

Preface

This book began in 2000 when one of the authors – Jan Svartvik – presented to the other author – Geoffrey Leech – a copy of his book in Swedish *Engelska – öspråk, världsspråk, trendspråk*, which translates as 'English – island language, world language, trend language'. Geoffrey Leech, in spite of his severely restricted reading knowledge of Swedish, was impressed by the overall content, shape and appeal of the book, and was further impressed to learn that it had received the August Prize for the best non-fiction title published in Swedish in 1999. It seemed to both of us that the book would benefit a wider audience, and would indeed appeal to students and teachers of English as well as to other people throughout the world with an interest in the English language.

The Swedish publisher Norstedts Ordbok very kindly allowed as to adapt and develop our book from the original Swedish version. However, producing an international edition of the book was not easy. It was not just a matter of translating the Swedish into English. It was necessary to edit out some of the Scandinavian focus of the original (for example, the Vikings, understandably, had more than their fair share of the Swedish book). As we worked together on the English version, we had to take account of new developments and worldwide perspectives. In fact, we had to rethink and redraft the book from beginning to end. The result, we hope, is an up-to-date and wide-ranging historical and geographical survey of English divided into three parts:

Part I: History of an Island Language (Chapters 2–4) covers how it evolved from its beginnings as a separate language.
Part II: The Spread of English round the World (Chapters 5–9) tells the unprecedented story of the worldwide spread and diversification of a single language.
Part III: A Changing Language in a Changing World (Chapters 10–12) examines English as it is today, and speculates on its twenty-first century prospects as a global language.

Arguably, English has so many different incarnations in different parts of the world that it is no longer a single language, but some kind of plurality of languages. As the original title of the book did not translate easily into English, we chose a title that emphasized this mixture of unity and plurality that is the present day English language: *English – One Tongue, Many Voices*.

We are especially grateful to Rikard Svartvik for his indispensable contribution to the book in the form of partial translation and historical comments. We also owe an enormous debt of gratitude to Gunnel Tottie, who put at our

disposal her breadth of knowledge, particularly on American English as compared with British English, and generously gave time to a thorough reading and
insightful commentary on our drafts. More specific, but hardly less valued, were
the comments of Susan Dray on Caribbean English, pidgins and creoles,
Graeme Kennedy on New Zealand English, Vivian de Klerk on South African
English, Ian Lancashire on Canadian English, Pam Peters on Australian English
and Toshihiko Suzuki on Japanese. David Britain acted as the publisher's
clearance reader, and we valued his expert and well-targeted comments. Julia
Youst MacRae commented on some chapters from the point of view of a speaker
of American English, and we appreciated being able to make use of her vivid
comments on certain areas of usage – see particularly the quotations on
pp. 153–4 and 211–13. We end with the conventional (but genuine) caveat that
none of these friendly commentators can be held responsible for any errors in
the book in its final form.

The work on this book has been a great pleasure and source of inspiration.
Our professional lives have been devoted to the English language, and this
represents our latest undertaking in a co-authorship habit which extends over a
period of more than 30 years.

Jan Svartvik, Lund University, Sweden
Geoffrey Leech, Lancaster University, England

1
English – the Working Tongue of the Global Village

English, no longer an English language, now grows from many roots.

Salman Rushdie,
The Times, 3 July 1982

Ahead of his time, the Canadian writer Marshall McLuhan predicted that electronically connected media would eventually transform the world into a huge 'global village'. English has become the working tongue of that village.

It is a new feature in the history of languages and language learning that this demand for English comes largely from the grass roots, not from society's elite, as was the case with Latin forced down the throats of previous generations of school pupils, or as the English language itself was imposed in earlier times on speakers of Celtic, Bantu or many other languages. The most remarkable thing about English today is not that it is the mother tongue of over 320 million people, but that it is used as an additional language by so many more people all around the globe. Non-native speakers in fact outnumber native speakers – probably a unique situation in language history. There are estimates suggesting that about a quarter of the world's population know, or think they know, some English. But, of course, sheer numbers mean little here – the expression 'know English' has plenty of latitude.

According to Ethnologue, a database maintained by the Summer Institute of Linguistics in Dallas, Texas, there are today about 6,800 distinct languages in the world. Yet just five languages – Chinese, English, Spanish, Russian and Hindi – are spoken by more than half of the world's population. And English cannot claim the highest number of native speakers; Chinese has about three times as many. What gives English its special status is its unrivalled position as a means of international communication. Most other languages are primarily communicative channels within, rather than across, national borders. Today, English is big business and the most commonly taught foreign language all over the world.

So why this demand for English among language learners around the world? The reason is not that the language is easy, beautiful or superior in linguistic qualities. Most people who want to learn it do so because they need it to function in the world at large. Young people, finding it both practical and cool, are attracted by things they can do with English, such as listening to music, watching films and surfing the web. For scientists and scholars, English is a necessity for reaching out to colleagues around the globe, publishing results from their research and taking part in international conferences. For tourists, English is the most useful tool for getting around and communicating with people all over the world.

English is spoken in circles

The Indian-American scholar Braj Kachru has taught us to think of English, as used around the world, in the form of three concentric circles (see Figure 1.1). The Inner Circle represents a handful of countries where most of the inhabitants speak English as a first language. The Outer Circle includes a larger number of countries where English is a second, often official or semi-official, language, but where most users of the language are not native speakers. Beyond the Inner and Outer Circles, English is learned and used as a foreign language in the huge Expanding Circle, which in fact includes most countries in the world.

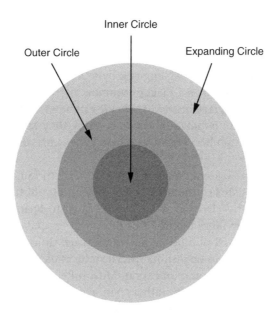

Figure 1.1   The three concentric circles of English worldwide

The Inner Circle

The Inner Circle includes, above all, three geographical blocs: the United States, Canada and the West Indies in the New World; Britain and Ireland in Europe; Australia, New Zealand and South Africa in the Southern Hemisphere. In these eight regions there are over 320 million people speaking English as a first language, and two out of three of them live in North America.

In some countries there are different figures for population and speakers of English as a first language (see box below). For some 40 million Americans the first language is Spanish – in fact, Hispanics have now replaced African Americans as the largest minority group of the United States. Canada is officially a bilingual country where almost a quarter of the population report French to be their mother tongue. In addition, native Canadians speak various indigenous languages. The Republic of Ireland has two official languages, Irish Gaelic and English, but only a small proportion of the population use Gaelic. In Britain and Ireland, English is the first language of over 60 million inhabitants. What many people find surprising is that neither in the United States nor in Britain, the two countries that seem to have imposed their language on the world, has English ever been formally declared the official language.

In the Southern Hemisphere, English is spoken by almost 20 million Australians and New Zealanders. While this is a modest figure compared with the number of native speakers in North America and Europe, English is an important means of communication around the expansive Pacific basin. South Africa is a special case with eleven official languages, one of which is English. It stands astride the boundary between the Inner and Outer Circles. English is not its primary language: among the population, English has a first language share of less than 10 per cent – in South Africa, English has always been a minority language, yet its population of native speakers is comparable in size to those of Ireland and New Zealand. In South Africa today, English retains a dominant position: it is the language most commonly used in Parliament and the main medium of instruction in higher education.

Countries in the Inner Circle		
Countries	**English as a first language**	**Population**
United States	215 million	278 million
United Kingdom	58 million	60 million
Canada	20 million	32 million
Australia	15 million	19 million
Caribbean	6 million	6 million
Ireland	4 million	4 million
New Zealand	4 million	4 million
South Africa	4 million	44 million
Totals	**326 million**	**447 million**

People who happen to be born in the Inner Circle of course enjoy a privilege since they learn, for free (more or less), to speak this global language with a native accent. Their language gives them a certain global reach and an advantage in many walks of life, whereas those who happen to be born into the Outer and Expanding Circles have to put years of time and effort into attaining some mastery of the language. For obvious reasons, in English-speaking communities there is a widespread lack of enthusiasm for learning other languages. But life in this 'fast language lane' of native English speakers comes at a price. Having English as your mother tongue means you lose out in the direct experience of feeling at home in other cultures and life-styles. You view the world through English-tinted glasses. The other side of this coin is that, among speakers of the world's other languages, there are fears that the pervasive influence of English will undermine their own cultural and linguistic identities.

The Outer Circle

In countries outside the Inner Circle, English has different societal functions, and it is therefore practical to place these countries in two different circles: the Outer Circle and the Expanding Circle. Yet there are linguists who argue that, today, a distinction between English as a second and a foreign language is not relevant. In their view, it doesn't really matter whether you learn English in, say, Nigeria or Japan. Recently English linguistic influences have been penetrating further into countries like China, Mexico and Norway, for which it has always been a foreign tongue.

In the Outer Circle we mostly find people who live in former British colonies, such as Kenya and Tanzania in Africa, and India, Pakistan, Malaysia and Singapore in Asia. In many of these countries, English is an official language and widely used in administration, education and the media. India is a striking example of the spread and importance of English in the Outer Circle. In this country with more than a billion inhabitants and 200 languages, English has held its position and is widely used in government administration, the law courts, secondary and higher education, the armed forces, the media, commerce and tourism. Estimates suggest that some 4 per cent of the population – more than 40 million people – now make regular use of English. Going further than this, David Crystal's book *English as a Global Language* gives the figure of 200 million for the number of Indian second-language users of English. Whichever of these figures we accept – and such estimates are bound to be hazy – India is among the leading English-using nations in the world.

However, as we shall see, the question of whether a country belongs to one circle or another – like the question of what makes a speaker a native speaker of English – is trickier than one may think.

The Expanding Circle

The Expanding Circle encompasses large parts of the world where English is learned as a foreign language because it is found useful, or indeed indispensable, for international contacts in such areas as industry, business, politics, diplomacy, education, research, technology, sports, entertainment and tourism. Today there are hundreds of millions of people who, though not living in an English-speaking country, have acquired a good working knowledge of English. This circle now seems to be ever-expanding, strengthening the claims of English as the international language of today. Is this expansion of world English going to reach saturation point? Arguably it is, and in the not too distant future, it will be appropriate to rename the 'Expanding Circle' the 'Expanded Circle'.

Do we need a world language?

In the history of the world up to now, there has never been a situation where one language could claim global currency. There have been languages, like Latin during the Roman Empire, that gained widespread international currency through military might or economic influence. But this was not a worldwide conquest: even in Roman times there were barbarian hordes living beyond the empire, and there were vast tracts of the world that the Roman legions never reached. So why should we now think in terms of a world language? Is there any need for one?

The answer to such questions, above all in the globalized society we live in today, must be 'Yes'. To overcome the confusion of tongues, people have tried in the past to make up artificial international languages, such as Esperanto, Ido, Volapük, Novial, Interglossa, Interlingua. The most successful of these has been Esperanto, yet, despite the high hopes of previous generations that Esperanto would take over the world, artificial languages have met with little success. It is true that the grammar of artificial languages has been planned to be regular and easy to learn and their vocabulary combines elements from different languages. Yet somehow, these advantages have not weighed against the built-in advantages of a natural language which already has a head start in the international language stakes. English already had this head start, and gradually extended its hegemony through the twentieth century.

As a bonus, a natural language also offers a cultural milieu and a rich canon of literature. In the case of English, this literary canon originates both in the Inner and Outer Circles: embracing not only Jane Austen, Ernest Hemingway, Patrick White and William Butler Yeats, but also Arundhati Roy, Wole Soyinka, Ngugi Wa Thiong'o and Derek Walcott.

Why English?

English did not become a world language on its linguistic merits. The pronunciation of English words is irritatingly often at odds with their spelling, the vocabulary is enormous and the grammar less learner-friendly than is generally assumed. There are people who think it is much to be regretted that some other language, like Italian or Spanish with their pure vowel sounds and regular spellings, did not achieve the status of lingua franca. David Abercrombie, a well-known Scots phonetician with a keen interest in English teaching, once suggested that spoken Scottish English, not English English, should be used internationally because of its superior clarity. In fact, foreigners often find Scottish English with its clear *r*'s easier to pronounce and understand than Southern British English with its *r*'s either not pronounced (as in *girl*) or obscurely pronounced (as in *right*) – see p. 125, 142. Also, with few diphthongs, Scottish vowels are similar to those widely heard throughout the world, including on the European Continent.

True, English grammar has few inflectional endings compared to languages like German, Latin or Russian, but its syntax is no less complex than that of other languages. A comprehensive grammar of English is definitely no shorter than, say, a grammar of French or German, as has recently been demonstrated by Rodney Huddleston and Geoffrey K. Pullum's *Cambridge Grammar of the English Language* with more than 1,800 pages. So it is totally wrong to suppose, as some native speakers actually do, that English has no grammar. The grammar of English not only exists, but has been subjected to more detailed study than that of any other language.

As everybody knows, the English word stock is vast. Any major dictionary of the English language has over a 100,000 headwords, and the most comprehensive of them all, the *Oxford English Dictionary*, defines a total of over 600,000 words. With its 20 volumes this lexical whopper occupies a great deal of shelf space but, fortunately, is now available in electronic form. The third edition now in progress, and to be completed in another 20 or so years, will be 'an *OED* so massive as perhaps only to be amenable to use on-line'. Yet, while all these words exist in the dictionary, no native English speaker knows them all. The average native speaker probably uses no more words than a speaker of any other major language.

So what made English the world language? Behind its success story there are two main factors: first, the expansion and influence of British colonial power – by the late nineteenth century the British Empire covered a considerable part of the earth's land surface, and subjects of the British monarch totalled nearly a fourth of the world's population; second, the status of the United States of America as the leading economic, military and scientific power of the twentieth century.

And there are yet other contributing factors. One is the increasing need for international communication as a result of modern technology: such innovations as the telephone, radio, television, jetliner transport and computers each introduced a step-change in the potential for international communication. Air traffic controllers all over the world use English when talking to pilots, whether Russian or Danish or Chinese, and whether at Kennedy or Schiphol or Narita airport. And, of course, in information technology, American English is king.

Yet another factor: in countries or groups of countries where people have several or many different first languages, English may be the preferred lingua franca because it is felt to be neutral ground. In the global economy, many multinationals have adopted English as the workplace vernacular. Half of all Russian business is said to be conducted in English. In the European Union, the practical 'working language' in communication across language barriers is usually English, often reluctantly adopted as the only language that is sufficiently widely used. Across the Union (excluding the British Isles), nine out of ten students choose to study English as a foreign language. English is said to permeate EU institutional activities and many areas of cultural and economic life more and more thoroughly. Today, it is hardly possible to pursue an international career without English. As a window on the world, English is looked upon as the best means to achieving economic, social and political success.

The aim of this book is to explore this astonishing global phenomenon. The history of English as a separate language started about CE 500, when its ancestor was a collection of dialects spoken by marauding Germanic tribes who settled in the part of the British Isles nearest the European continent. In those distant days, this proto-English was spoken by less than half a million illiterate people. Compared with the prestigious Latin language which had dominated the western Roman Empire up to that time, it was a totally insignificant tongue. In the 1,500 years since then, the English language has come heavily under the influence of other languages, especially Old Norse, French, Latin and Greek. Eight hundred years ago it was a humble medley of native dialects in a country where the rulers spoke French. Yet it somehow survived as a basically Germanic language, and has now come to be known to something like 1½ billion people.

This fantastic story needs to be told, and so, in Chapters 2–6, we look back and trace the history of English as it developed in the British Isles and later in territories conquered and settled through the growing British maritime and commercial power. But when we reach the last two centuries, the story of English becomes international and worldwide. Around 1880 the United States became the leading English-speaking nation, in both population and wealth. Chapters 7–8 tell the story of how the English language has evolved today in the British Isles and the United States, building on the historical foundation already described. Chapters 9–10 deal with pidgins, creoles and standard language.

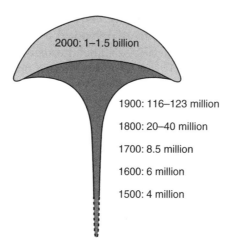

Figure 1.2   The mushroom of English

Over the centuries, the number of users of the English language can be seen as forming a mushroom with a slim base and a huge cap. These statistics, necessarily approximate of course, derive from Otto Jespersen's *Growth and Structure of the English Language* (pp. 233–4) and David Crystal's *English as a Global Language* (pp. 62–5). Yet what can be stated with some certainty is that, in the long history of the English language, the mushrooming effect is of quite recent date. In the 1936 edition of *The American Language*, H. L. Mencken gave 174 million as the estimated number of native speakers. As for speakers outside what we have called the Inner Circle, he wrote: 'it is probable that English is now spoken as a second language by at least 20,000,000 persons throughout the world – very often, to be sure, badly, but neverthess understandably' (p. 592). How things have changed!

Chapter 11 describes some of the on-going changes in the current English language. Finally, Chapter 12 looks to the future: all languages being works in progress, what will happen to English? Will it split into mutually incomprehensible languages, as Latin did? Or will it remain a single language, in spite of all the variety of its manifestations around the world? Will it remain the leading language of international communication? Or will it be overtaken by another language? We don't know the answers to these questions, yet they are worth asking and debating in an informed way.

One or two explanations

First, why are three chapters (2–4) of this book devoted to what happened in remote periods of history? The answer is simple. What the English language looks and sounds like today is fundamentally due to distant events: the Germanic migrations and invasions, the Norman Conquest, the introduction of printing, the Renaissance. Recent centuries have brought their own story of the growing international dispersion of English, but this story builds crucially on more ancient foundations.

Second, we try hard to avoid confusion between describing linguistic realities (which we aim to do) and making value judgements (which we do not). As David Crystal remarked in the preface to his book *English as a Global Language*: 'It is difficult to write a book on this topic without it being interpreted as a political statement.' It is easy to fall into the trap of considering English a successful language because of its inherent qualities as Melvyn Bragg arguably does in his book *The Adventure of English*, rhapsodizing over the Elizabethan age of English: 'English was now poised to grow into a richness, a subtlety and complexity which would enable it to become a world language.'

There is no room in this story for triumphalism. On the other hand, it is easy to fall into the opposite trap of seeing the spread of English on a global scale as a linguistic form of imperialism, as has been argued by Robert Phillipson in his book *Linguistic Imperialism*. We believe it is better to see the rise of English in more objective terms. It has won out in the linguistic ecology of the twentieth century rather as dinosaurs won out in the battle for survival above other species in the Jurassic period, or as *homo sapiens* is dominating other species in the survival battle of the present age. But there is a crucial difference: the English language has won out, at least for the present, because of the political, economic and military success, at a crucial period, of the people who were its speakers, not because of the features of the language itself. This is an amazing story to tell, but if we give any impression of glorifying English or the English, this is far from our intention.

The avoidance of value judgements is important, too, in discussing the different kinds of English – the many *varieties* of the language, as they are called. We have inherited a tradition of such judgements, for example, in the assumptions that some kinds of grammar are 'correct' and others 'incorrect'; that standard language is somehow superior to non-standard dialects; that English as a mother tongue is somehow superior to the English of non-native speakers. It would be foolish to lay much store by such traditional attitudes. It is worthwhile reminding ourselves that non-natives speakers of English in the world now outnumber native speakers by at least three to one. Further, it is quite possible – and is seriously argued today – that the future of English will be more determined by the majority of its users – those in the Outer Circle and the Expanding Circle – than by the Inner Circle, the traditional heartland of English. We return to this discussion in our last chapter.

Part I
History of an Island Language

2
The First 500 Years

Your Roman-Saxon-Danish-Norman English.
Daniel Defoe, *The True-born Englishman* (1701)

We cannot understand what a language is until we know its history. More than for most subjects, history is the key to language, because the very fabric of a language – its vocabulary, its grammar, its spelling, and so on – is a living record of its past.

So in the light of history, how can we begin to explain how English came to be what it is in the twenty-first century? How did it come about that this language, once a tongue spoken by only a small number of people in a rather small island, has become the most powerful international language in the world's history? English is said to be a Germanic language, but why is it that more than half of its words are of Latin or Romance origin? Why do we sometimes have a wide choice of words to express more or less the same thing? And what is to blame for the chaotic English spelling? In the next few chapters we turn to history to find the answer to these and other questions.

In a satire on eighteenth-century Englishmen's beliefs in national superiority, Daniel Defoe, probably best known as the creator of *Robinson Crusoe*, described his mother tongue as 'Roman-Saxon-Danish-Norman English'. To Defoe, English was but a mixture of the tongues spoken by different peoples who, in the course of history, had invaded what is present-day England. Although he was being sarcastic, he did have a point. Put simply, the making of English is a story of successive invasions. But this is, of course, not the whole story. English, like any other language, is rich and varied, but constantly changing – a tapestry with many strands. Yet we can point to some crucial events, such as the coming of Christianity or the Norman invasion, and study texts from these and other periods to find a pattern in the weave of the language.

So where do we begin? Surely, we must take a broader stance than Defoe's. Long before any Roman legions sailed across what we now know as the Straits of Dover, the British Isles were inhabited by various Celtic tribes.

Roman Britain

English was not always spoken in these islands. During the first millennium BCE, Celtic tribes settled here, as they did virtually in all of western Europe, in successive waves of migration. Although they were actually a mix of peoples speaking related languages, we will refer to them collectively as Celts. It is important, though, that the Celts spoke a group of Celtic languages, and were not a single national or ethnic group.

Some 2,500 years ago, Celtic languages were spoken widely across Europe. On the European mainland, however, they were gradually replaced by other

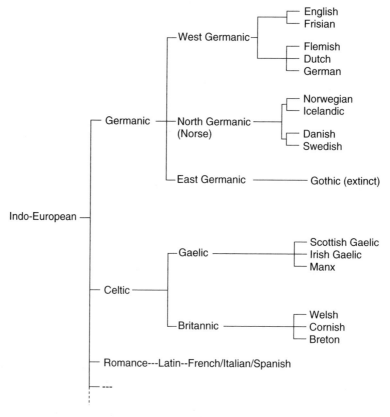

Figure 2.1   Diagram of Germanic and Celtic languages within the Indo-European family

languages – for example, the Romance family of languages, including French, Spanish and Italian. On a rough estimate, Celtic languages are today spoken only by some one million people in the world. In the British Isles, the Celtic languages, which now survive as modern Welsh, Irish and Scottish Gaelic, have long been fighting a rearguard action against English. The most viable of these survivors is Welsh – also known as Cymraeg – with about half a million speakers in Wales, where the vast majority of the population also know English. In some western parts of the Republic of Ireland, efforts are made to sustain and revive Irish Gaelic and, in the highlands of Scotland, Scottish Gaelic, but these efforts are having to fight hard to survive against the insidious influence of English.

Over 2,000 years ago, the Roman general Julius Caesar led two expeditions to what he called Britannia, the land of the Britons. Although Caesar's most

---

What's in a name?

This most remote province of the Roman Empire was called Britannia and its people Britanni, from which come the modern forms *Britain* and *British*. *Caledonia* was the Roman name for Scotland and, although outside the Empire, it was seen by the Romans as a sphere of their influence. *Hibernia*, the Roman name for present-day Ireland, was never part of the Roman Empire.

In 1707 the nation of *Great Britain* was formed by the Act of Union between England, Scotland and Wales. The *United Kingdom of Great Britain and Northern Ireland* was formed in 1921 when the *Irish Free State* – later named the *Republic of Ireland* – became a separate nation. *The United Kingdom* (or *UK* for short) includes the island of Great Britain, comprising England, Scotland and Wales and, in addition, Northern Ireland, occupying the north-east corner of the island of Ireland. Unofficially, the UK is often simply called *Britain*, and its people are called *British*.

The British Isles is an unofficial but convenient geographical name. It refers to the two large islands of Great Britain and Ireland, together with several islands and island groups, such as the Isle of Man and the Orkney Islands. Many Irish people consider this term *British Isles* a misnomer. For them, Ireland is not, nor should it be, in any sense 'British'.

The people of the United Kingdom of Great Britain and Northern Ireland are British citizens (see Figure 2.2). Not everybody likes the modern label *Briton* or *Britons*, although this is the correct way of referring to the ancient Celtic people of Britannia. Still, it is short and practical to use in headlines:

BRITONS FLOCK TO THE SEASIDE

Brit is informal and can be derogatory. In older American slang the British are called *Limeys*, a term originally applied to English sailors who were routinely supplied with limes to prevent scurvy. In Australian and New Zealand slang *Pom* and *Pommy* are common but can be offensive. It seems there is no neutral way of referring to the inhabitants of the United Kingdom!

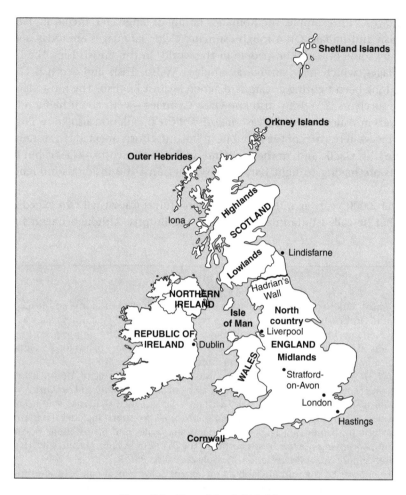

Figure 2.2   Map of the British Isles

famous utterance was '*Veni, vidi, vici*' ('I came, I saw, I conquered'), this certainly did not apply to his visits to Britannia: he soon went home and never returned. The inhabitants of Britannia, collectively called Britanni by the Romans, kept their political freedom and were not again troubled by Roman legions for almost 100 years. It was later, in 43 CE, that Emperor Claudius ordered the invasion of Britain. Gradually the Roman legions moved their frontiers further north and west, bringing almost all of what is now England under Roman rule. During most of the period of occupation, the effective northern frontier was Hadrian's Wall (named after the Roman Emperor Hadrian 76–138 CE), stretching between the present-day northern English cities of Carlisle and Newcastle. Designated a World Heritage Site in 1987, the remains of Hadrian's Wall, also known as the Roman Wall, proudly rank alongside the Taj Mahal and other treasures among the great wonders of the world.

In Roman Britain, towns grew up for a variety of reasons. The earliest settlements were built by the army. In place-names like *Lancaster, Leicester, Chester, Manchester* and *Winchester*, the element spelled *caster, cester* or *chester* is derived from the Roman word *castra*, meaning 'camp'. The Romans brought a wide range of innovations to their British province, changing its landscape for ever. Roman roads still criss-cross the landscape of England. The Latin word for a Roman road was *via strata* 'paved road', which is the origin of English *street*, German *Strasse* and Italian *strada*. But, even though Britannia was under Roman rule for nearly 400 years, the Roman occupation left hardly any lasting linguistic legacy. This is because the English language has its roots in the next invasion, beginning in the fifth century, when Germanic tribes settled in the country. Unlike the Romans they stayed for good and, in due course, they were to call their language *English*.

Ships are sighted with English in embryo on board

Like other parts of the Empire, Roman Britain had long been subject to attacks from external enemies or 'barbarians' and, by the early fifth century, Roman legions were withdrawn and Britannia was left to defend herself. According to later sources, in this desperate situation one of the Celtic leaders enlisted the help of Germanic peoples who lived just across the North Sea on the European mainland. It is reported that these semi-pirates expelled the enemies of the Britons, but then turned their weapons against their hosts. Once settled, the newcomers supposedly invited other continental tribesmen who arrived with swords at the ready.

This story rings true. Befriending one band of enemies to ward off another was an old Roman tactic which the Britons no doubt adopted. But we shall probably never know exactly what happened. It is clear, though, that from the middle of the fifth century and for the next 100 years or so waves of migrating tribes from beyond the North Sea brought their Germanic dialects to Britain. These tribes are traditionally identified as Angles, Saxons and Jutes. Archaeology confirms that objects found in English graves are comparable to those from what is now north Germany and the southern half of the Danish peninsula. To this list of tribes we should add Frisians who, to this day, speak the continental language considered to be closest to English. Still, there is no need to be concerned about the exact ethnic mix of these new settlers: more important for us were the immense future consequences.

There was no sense of national identity among all these tribes, but they spoke neighbouring Germanic dialects and were no doubt able to communicate with each other. For centuries there was no collective name for the Germanic peoples who settled in Britain. The term **Anglo-Saxon** is sometimes used to denote anything connected with English soil – language, people, culture – before the Norman Conquest. But this is reconstruction, a convenient but vague label, used in contradistinction to **Old Saxons** who remained on the continent. The settlers called the native population *wealas* 'foreigners' (from which the name *Welsh* is derived), while the Celts called the newcomers *Saxons*, regardless of their tribe. This term today appears in the modern Welsh words *Saeson* 'the English (people)', and *Saesneg* 'the English language'.

Very few old Celtic words survived the invasions to leave their imprint on modern English. The main survivors were the names of places and rivers. Place-names, such as *Dover, Cardiff, Carlisle, Glasgow* and *London*, and river-names, such as the *Avon*, the *Clyde*, the *Severn* and the *Thames*, all have some distant Celtic link. This scarce linguistic evidence has been used in support of the idea that all Celts were driven out or killed. Most scholars however agree that the word 'genocide' is out of place here, and that 'ethnic cleansing' may have been more applicable. There was, after all, no love lost between rival tribes of Celts and Anglo-Saxons. Many of the Celtic-speaking Britons retreated into the more remote and rugged regions that we now know as Cornwall, Wales, Cumbria and the Scottish borders. Some of the Britons even emigrated across the Channel to Armorica, as reflected in its present-day name Brittany, but the bulk of the British population probably continued to live meagrely under Germanic rule and to speak their own language. Though atrocities did occur, there can hardly have been a mass expulsion. A more likely scenario is that the Britons, losing their Roman affiliation, gradually became absorbed into the Germanic population and eventually gave up their own language. This process has continued to the present day. Cornish, the Celtic language of Cornwall, passed into history in the late eighteenth century. The Celtic language of the Isle of Man, Manx, gradually gave way to English in the nineteenth century, and the last Manx speaker is said to have died in the 1970s. (See Figure 2.2, p. 16.) The tragic issue of 'language death' is highly topical today, and these languages are now being revived by enthusiastic antiquarians.

Old English (as we call the language of the Anglo-Saxons) was not very hospitable to foreign loans, which make up less than 5 per cent of the recorded Old English words. But the traditionally held view that the Celtic languages made virtually no impact on the language spoken by the Anglo-Saxons has recently been questioned. Some linguists argue that, so far, Old English has been traced in a purely Germanic context and that the social context in which English emerged has been overlooked. All Indo-European language families, Celtic being one of them, share similarities, and where people intermingle it is realistic to consider multiple origins of words or of other language features.

Bilingualism is a recurrent theme in the history of the English language. It existed not only at the time of the Germanic settlements but also later at the time of the Scandinavian and Norman conquests. If these later invasions had not taken place, the English language today might have sounded not unlike Frisian, the European language most similar to English. A few examples of the similarities between Modern English and other related languages (all are Germanic languages, except Welsh) are shown in the box.

English	Frisian	German	Swedish	Danish	Welsh
boat	boat	Boot	båt	båd	bad
cat	kat	Katz	katt	kat	cath
cow	ko	Kuh	ko	ko	buwch
dream	dream	Traum	dröm	drøm	breuddwyd
green	grien	grün	grön	grøn	glas
house	hus	Haus	hus	hus	tŷ
lamb	lam	Lamm	lamm	lam	oen
mother	mem	Mutter	moder	moder	mam
ox	okse	Ochs	oxe	okse	ych
sheep	skiep	Schaf	får	får	dafad
three	trije	drei	tre	tre	tri, tair

Christianity in the Isles

Roman Britain has been described as 'a religious kaleidoscope'. Christianity was introduced into Britain in Roman times and, by the third century, British bishops were regularly attending Church Councils. Constantine the Great, who was to convert the Roman Empire officially to Christianity, was actually acclaimed emperor at York (then known as Eboracum) in 306. The Germanic tribes, however, were pagans, worshipping their own gods, whose names, incidentally, survive in *Tuesday, Wednesday, Thursday* and *Friday*. After the Germanic invasions, the Christian faith was kept up only in Celtic areas such as present-day Cornwall and Wales. From Celtic Britain it was introduced, in the fifth century, into Ireland where it developed in cultural and artistic isolation for nearly 200 years. From this Celtic Church, Christianity was carried to the island of Iona on the west coast of Scotland and, later, to the northern English kingdom of Northumbria (see Figure 2.3, p. 20).

In 596 Pope Gregory I sent a group of missionaries, headed by a monk named Augustine, to the former Roman province of Britannia with instructions to convert the Anglo-Saxons to Christianity. The kingdom of Kent, nearest to the continent, was swiftly converted and Augustine became the first Archbishop of Canterbury. Since then Canterbury has remained the ecclesiastical capital of England.

Figure 2.3   Map of the main Anglo-Saxon kingdoms (early 8th century)

However, the missionaries from the south did not have it all their own way. The mission that came from Iona to the Northumbrians (the Anglo-Saxons living north of the River Humber) brought the Irish strain of Christianity, rich in a tradition which inspired the wonderful artistry of the Lindisfarne Gospels (dating from *c.* 700), a richly illuminated holy book that can be seen in the British Library today. Not long after its conversion, the north of England in the early eighth century became a hive of Christian culture and scholarship whose influence spread far and wide into continental Europe. Apart from the Lindisfarne Gospels, two remarkable monuments of that 'Northumbrian School' are the Anglo-Saxon monk and historian Bede's *Ecclesiastical History*, a feat of historical scholarship unrivalled at the time, and the Ruthwell Cross, a stone cross, intricately carved and bearing extracts from a great poem in the dialect of Northumbria, known as *The Dream of the Rood*. The Ruthwell Cross actually stands in southern Scotland, showing that the English language had, already in those days, strayed into what is today Scottish territory (see Figure 7.4, p. 139).

What did all this mean for the history of the English language? Latin was the language of the Church, and Bede naturally used Latin as the language of his great historical work. The missionaries promoted literacy and, more importantly for our story, promoted translations from Latin into the native tongue. A number of Christian ideas needed to be explained in simple terms to the new converts, and Old English native words were applied to these new concepts: the Latin *euangelium* (from Greek *evangelion*) was rendered as *gōdspell* 'good news', later shortened to *gospel*; *Dominus* was rendered as *hlāfweard*, literally 'guardian of the loaf', from which we derive *Lord*; the Latin *Infernum* was rendered as *Hell*, an old Germanic word meaning 'hidden place'. In this way, the language extended its own wordstock to meet new cultural needs.

But in other cases the translators found it easier to borrow words direct from Latin. Altogether, there have been recorded some 400 Latin words in Old English introduced as a result of the spread of Christianity. However, many of these loanwords, such as *cugele* which gave us *cowl*, 'a monk's hood', were not in general use and only a few of them actually survive in modern English. The survivors are typically connected with religion or the services of the Church, such as these:

Latin	Old English	Modern English
abbas	abbod, abbud	abbot
apostolus	apostol	apostle
candela	candel	candle
cyriacum	cyrice	church
diabolus	dēofol	devil
discipulus	discipul	disciple
episcopus	biscop	bishop
martyr	martir	martyr
monachus	munuc	monk
nonna	nunne	nun
papa	papa	pope
presbyter	prēost	priest
templum	tempel	temple

While most of these words were originally Greek, they were adopted into English from their Latin forms. Latin loanwords have been taken into English in virtually all periods of its history. It is sometimes difficult to separate loanwords that were common Germanic from those that came directly into English. For example, the Latin *scōla* was most likely borrowed into prehistoric West Germanic on the European mainland, as it has since evolved into German *Schule*, Dutch *school*, Swedish *skola* and Danish *skole*, as well as English *school*.

Most Latin words we find in Old English were introduced considerably later, in the tenth century, through the great revitalizing of church life and learning known as the Benedictine Revival. Many names of animals, plants and trees entered the language this way: for example, *cypress, ginger, lily, lobster, parsley, plant, purple* and *radish*.

The Viking age

One summer day in the year 793, while the monks at the wealthy monastery of Lindisfarne on Holy Island off the Northumbrian coast might have been gathering hay, strange-looking ships were sighted out on the North Sea (see Figure 2.3, p. 20). We imagine the monks leaving their work and scurrying down to the shore to see who these strangers might be. Later, they would become all too well known and feared as the Vikings. The famous monastery was plundered and those who survived the attack were sold into slavery. This is how the *Anglo-Saxon Chronicle* recorded the event:

> In this year dire portents appeared over Northumbria and sorely frightened the people. They consisted of immense whirlwinds and flashes of lightning, and fiery dragons were seen flying in the air. A great famine immediately followed these signs and a little after in the same year, on 8 June, the ravages of heathen men miserably destroyed God's church on Lindisfarne, with plunder and slaughter.

The *Anglo-Saxon Chronicle* is an early record in Old English of events in England from the beginning of the Christian era to 1154. Yet we must try to assess those who wrote history as much as those who made history. The damage caused by the Vikings may well have been exaggerated by the scribes of the period. Since the Vikings failed to produce their own historian, their deeds are known only through the eyes of chroniclers who were on the receiving end. In the longer run, recent scholarship tends to emphasize the long-term peaceful benefits of the Norse landings. The Scandinavians made their mark in the British Isles not only as raiders and conquerors but also as traders and colonists. Still, it is impossible to deny the evidence: three Anglo-Saxon kingdoms destroyed; great monasteries, innumerable towns, farmsteads and villages plundered; charters and documents lost.

The origin of the word *Viking* remains a puzzle. In the Old Norse sagas, committed to parchment in the twelfth and thirteenth centuries, the word *viking* (Old Norse *víkingr*) is generally restricted to brutal and unpleasant characters. It was as late as the nineteenth century that the word became the standard term for Scandinavian invaders. In the *Anglo-Saxon Chronicle* there are only five occurrences of the term *wicing*. Contemporary chroniclers called them by many names, including 'heathens' and 'pagans', but they were generally referred to as either 'Northmen' or 'Danes'.

The Viking raids and subsequent invasions took many forms and reached out in many directions. Generally speaking, adventurers from the western part of Scandinavia sought pillage and conquest in the west. Sailing south from Jutland, plundering along the Frisian coast, the Danes raided the British Isles and the Carolingian Empire. Others, mainly people from present-day Norway, sailed round the north of Scotland via the Shetlands and the Orkneys and southwards to the Isle of Man, Ireland and north-west England. For three generations after the raids began, the bands of Vikings arrived mostly as separate and small-scale undertakings, not as royal expeditions or large invasions. There were at least three phases of Viking activities, stretching over some 250 years: sporadic raids, permanent colonization and political supremacy (see map, p. 26).

In the first phase, from the late eighth century, the attacks were basically hit-and-run affairs, as in the case of the Lindisfarne raid, but from 835 raids became more intense. For three decades the attacks came almost yearly with pillaging of the very heartland of Anglo-Saxon kingdoms.

In the second phase, from 865 to 896, casual plundering gave way to permanent colonization. Until the mid-tenth century there was no unified English monarchy but, in the mid-ninth century, there were still four recognizable Anglo-Saxon kingdoms: East Anglia, Mercia, Northumbria and Wessex (see Figure 2.3, p. 20). By the early 870s only the kingdom of Wessex (roughly corresponding to present-day England south of the Thames but excluding Kent and Cornwall) remained intact. In Wessex the opposition was better organized than in the other kingdoms. King Alfred of Wessex succeeded to the throne at the time of acute danger from Danish invasion but, through a mixture of military success, tactful diplomacy and good luck, he managed to roll back the Danish tide. Before Alfred's death in 899, he reached an agreement with the Viking leader Guthrum to confine the Danes to the north and east of a diagonal line stretching roughly from London to Chester, an area later known as the *Danelaw*, where Danish customs prevailed in contrast to the areas of Anglo-Saxon law to the south and west. Guthrum agreed to leave Wessex alone and even accepted Christian baptism, taking the English name of Athelstan – a truly humbling fate for a Viking chieftain.

King Alfred the Great

King Alfred is the only English monarch ever to be given the title 'Great', and justly so, since he not only stemmed the Viking invasions, but laid the ground for a re-conquest, so that his heirs eventually became kings of England. The West Saxon monarchs who succeeded him gradually took over the Danelaw, paving the way for the unification of all England towards the end of the tenth century. Under King Edgar, the country enjoyed two decades of peace up to the 970s.

Alfred longed to improve the education of his people and set up what today might be called 'a crash programme in education'. He started a court school and invited scholars from abroad, arranged for the translation of Latin texts into English, and employed learned churchmen to strengthen royal authority and establish a system of law. He and his team of scholars were the founding fathers of English prose. If it had not been for Alfred, the history of the English language might have taken quite a different turn – the standard language of Great Britain might actually have been a Scandinavian tongue.

However, this legacy of Alfred had a sad ending during the long inglorious reign of King Ethelred, nicknamed 'the Unready'. In the years up to 1014, Viking activities entered the third and final phase of political conquest, when King Sveinn of Denmark arrived with a Viking army, not for the extortion of tribute, as was customary towards the end of the tenth century, but for the conquest of the kingdom. After his death, the throne of England eventually passed to his son Cnut, the 'King Canute' who, according to legend, sat on the shore and tried to stem the rising flow of the tides. Actually a wise and effective ruler, Cnut was reconciled with the English, supported the Church and maintained peace in the country. After his death in 1035, Denmark and England again became separate kingdoms, and in 1042 the old House of Wessex was able to return to power. Politically, but not linguistically, this was the end of Scandinavian influence in England.

Both the impact and scale of Viking colonization have been much discussed. It is uncertain how many Scandinavians became settlers in the lands where they had first appeared as marauders. The Vikings spoke dialects of **Old Norse**, the parent language of modern Danish, Swedish, Norwegian and Icelandic (see the diagram on p. 14). The Anglo-Saxons spoke dialects of **Old English**, which is the name we give to the language from the middle of the fifth to the beginning of the twelfth century. Old English and Old Norse were related Germanic languages, and many words were identical (*folc/folk, hus* 'house', *sorg* 'sorrow') or similar (Old English *fæder* 'father', *græs* 'grass', *wīf* 'woman' corresponding to Old Norse words *faðir, gras, víf*).

About 1000 words in modern English can be traced back to Old Norse origins. The impact was particularly great in English varieties spoken in northern England and in Scotland, where today we meet dialect words such as these (for comparison, modern Danish words are given in brackets): *gate* (*gade*) 'street, road', *ken* (*kende*) 'know', *lake* (*lege*) 'play', *neb* (*næb*) 'beak, nose'. The borrowings from Old Norse belong to the language of everyday life, reflecting close social contacts between the two peoples. As the great Danish scholar, Otto Jespersen, once observed: 'An Englishman cannot *thrive* or be *ill* or *die* without Scandinavian words; they are to the language what bread and *eggs* are to the daily fare'. In this sentence, all four words in italics come from Old Norse.

In view of all the Scandinavian loanwords and place-names, it is likely that the Vikings and the Anglo-Saxons could understand each other – the two languages must have been to some extent mutually intelligible. Wherever the Vikings settled and came into contact with another culture, they would ultimately be the ones who lost most of their identity, being assimilated into the larger population around them. For the greater part of the Viking age – roughly from 750 to 1050 – contacts, fierce or friendly, continued between Scandinavians and Anglo-Saxons. Although the Scandinavian impact on English was considerable, Norse did not

---

Some Old Norse loanwords in English

anger from *angr* 'sorrow'
bag from *baggi* 'bag, bundle'
cake from *kaka* 'flat round loaf of bread'
crook from *krókr* 'hook'
fellow from the Norse compound *félagi* meaning 'someone who puts down money',
     'a companion, a partner'
flat from *flatr* 'level surface'
law from *lagu*, plural of *lag* 'that which is laid down'
outlaw from *útlagi*, derived from *útlagr* 'outlawed, banished'
reindeer from *hreinn* 'reindeer' + Middle English *der* 'animal'

Other everyday words from Old Norse are: the verbs *get, scrape, take*; the nouns *leg, sister, skin*; the adjectives *low, odd, ugly*; and the pronouns *they, them, their*.

Some modern English words have doublets, often with different meaning, where one word comes from Old English and the other from Old Norse:

From Old English	From Old Norse
craft	*skill*
ditch	*dike, dyke*
ill	*sick*
rear	*raise*
shirt	*skirt*

Often the Old Norse word has been kept in Scotland and Northern England, such as *big* for 'build', *bairn* for 'child', *kirk* for 'church'.

---

survive much beyond the twelfth century in England. But interestingly, quite a few Norse influences first appear in texts from the centuries after the Viking influence had ended. One very common Norse loanword in English, the pronoun *they*, is an example of this time-lag.

Compared with the effects of the Norman Conquest, which was to follow, the Scandinavian influence was less spectacular and revolutionary. But, as their name implies, the Normans themselves were also 'men of the north', who had come originally from Scandinavia. This brings us to the next important epoch in the history of English, when the language came under the dominant influence of French – but French as spoken by the formerly Norse-speaking Normans.

In early tenth-century France, following a policy of appeasement, the Carolingian king Charles the Simple had given Gengu-Hrólfr, the son of a Norwegian earl, the title of Duke and extensive lands in the valley of the Seine. His name translates as 'Rolf the Walker' in English: he was allegedly a man of such enormous stature that he had to walk since no horse could carry him. The Latin scribes gave Hrólfr's name the Latinate form of *Rollo*, and called his dukedom

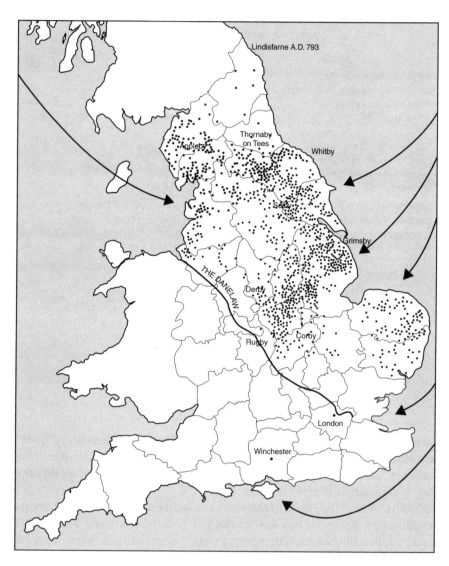

Figure 2.4   Map of the Danelaw and Scandinavian settlement-names, showing the paths of Viking incursions and settlements. The line marks the boundary between the Danelaw in the north and the Anglo-Saxon kingdoms in the south (see Figure 2.3, p. 20). Dots indicate place-names of Scandinavian origin. As a result of the Norse settlements, there are more than 1,400 place-names of Scandinavian origin in the Danelaw area alone.

Normandia, which literally means 'the land of the Norsemen', hence the English name *Normandy*.

Strangely enough, then, the Vikings were ultimately responsible for bringing not only their own language, but also the French language to England.

What was Old English like?

The English language was not born as soon as the first Angle or Saxon set foot in the British Isles. Actually, we can hardly speak of 'an English language' before the time of King Alfred in the ninth century. Even at that time, instead of a language, it would be better to think of Old English as a collection of dialects, and the origins of those dialects on the mainland of Eurasia stretch back into the mists of prehistory.

In popular history, King Alfred the Great of Wessex is a national hero who, against all odds, managed to save England from the Vikings. However, in his time, *England* did not exist as a political concept. Significantly, King Alfred himself was the author of the earliest recorded example of the word *Englisc* with reference to the English language. There was an ethnic concept *Angelcynn* 'race of the Angles', but *Englaland*, 'land of the Angles', does not appear until the turn of the millennium.

Until the ninth century there existed no official written standard but, because of the political pre-eminence of King Alfred's Wessex, the West Saxon variety became a standard form of Old English which spread to other parts of the country. We cannot tell what spoken Old English sounded like exactly, and this is true also for almost the whole history of English. Sound-recordings became available only a little over 100 years ago, so we have no first-hand information about English pronunciation in earlier times. What we believe to have been the actual pronunciation, at a certain period in the history of the language, is based on indirect sources of information, such as spellings, rhymes, puns, linguistic observations made by contemporary authors, and equivalent words in other languages.

On the other hand, we do know what written Old English looked like, because texts written in Old English have survived, even from as far back as the seventh century. Our first Old English language lesson will be The Lord's Prayer. For help and comparison we give two later English versions: one from Early Modern English and one from Modern English.

The Lord's Prayer

Old English	Word-for-word translation of the Old English
Fæder ure, þu þe eart on heofonum,	*Father our, thou that art in heavens,*
si þin nama gehalgod.	*be thy name hallowed.*
To becume þin rice.	*Come thy kingdom.*
Gewurþe ðin willa	*Be done thy will*
on eorðan swa swa on heofonum.	*on earth as in heavens.*
Urne gedæghwamlican hlaf syle us todæg.	*Our daily bread give us today.*
And forgyf us ure gyltas,	*And forgive us our offences,*

swa swa we forgyfað urum
  gyltendum.
And ne gelæd þu us on costnunge,

ac alys us of yfele soþlice.

as we forgive our offenders.

*And not lead thou us into
  temptation,*
but deliver us from evil truly.

King James Bible (1611)

Our Father which art in heaven,
Hallowed be thy name.
Thy kingdom come.
Thy will be done in earth, as it is in
  heaven.
Give us this day our daily bread.
And forgive us our debts, as we
  forgive our debtors.
And lead us not into temptation,
  but deliver us from evil.

Modern English (1989)

Our Father in heaven,
hallowed be your name.
Your kingdom come.
Your will be done,
  on earth as it is in heaven.
Give us this day our daily bread.
And forgive us our debts,
  as we also have forgiven our debtors.
And do not bring us to the time of trial,
  but rescue us from the evil one.

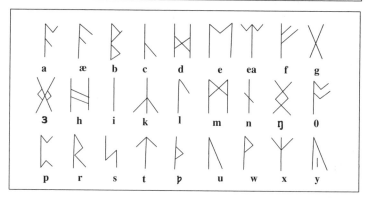

Figure 2.5   Runes
Above: A poetic inscription from the Ruthwell Cross (see Figure 7.3, p. 137)
Below: The runic alphabet
(from Dennis Freeborn, *From Old English to Standard English*, 2nd edition,
Basingstoke: Palgrave, 1998, p. 22).

For their earliest inscriptions, Germanic tribes made use of an ancient alphabet called **runes** (see p. 28). As Christianity was introduced into the Anglo-Saxon kingdoms, the Latin alphabet, which was used in Roman times, was reintroduced. The scribes had to find a way of making Latin letters represent the English sounds. The problem was that the Latin alphabet had fewer letters than Old English, which had its own distinctive speech sounds (phonemes). So, far from the ideal situation where each letter represents one speech sound, a few runic characters were pressed into service for writing Old English, such as þ 'thorn' as in *þu, þin, gewurþe*; ð 'eth' as in *ðin, eorðan*; and æ 'æsc' (ash) as in *fæder, todæg*.

Some of the words in The Lord's Prayer are identical in modern English: *on, us, and, we, of.* Others, such as *fæder, nama, becume, willa, eorðan, todæg*, are recognizable, but not words like *gewurþe, gedæghwamlican* and *soþlice*. Normally we can look up unfamiliar words in a dictionary to find out what they mean. But in an Old English text, many word forms differ from the word form listed in a dictionary. This is because Old English had an elaborate system of case endings such as *-um* in *heofonum*, which is the dative plural of the nominative singular *heofon* 'heaven'. The rich system of Old English variant forms, more similar to Modern German than Modern English, was levelled out over centuries, so that English today is extremely poor in inflections. The table gives some examples of Old English case forms (or inflections).

Examples of Old English noun inflections

The words below are the ancestors of the modern words *hound, deer, child, ox* and *foot*. But in present-day English, most of their Old English endings have disappeared.

		hund 'dog',	*dēor* 'animal',	*cild* 'child',	*oxa* 'ox',	*fōt* 'foot'
Singular	Nominative	*hund*	*dēor*	*cild*	*oxa*	*fōt*
	Accusative	*hund*	*dēor*	*cild*	*oxan*	*fōt*
	Genitive	*hundes*	*dēores*	*cildes*	*oxan*	*fōtes*
	Dative	*hunde*	*dēore*	*cilde*	*oxan*	*fōt*
Plural	Nominative	*hundas*	*dēor*	*cildru*	*oxan*	*fēt*
	Accusative	*hundas*	*dēor*	*cildru*	*oxan*	*fēt*
	Genitive	*hunda*	*dēora*	*cilda*	*oxena*	*fōta*
	Dative	*hundum*	*dēorum*	*cildrum*	*oxum*	*fōtum*

Among these inflectional forms the only noun endings to survive into Modern English are the plural of nouns with regular *s*-plural: singular *dog* ~ plural *dogs*, and the genitive singular *dog's* ~ genitive plural *dogs'*. But Modern English has kept some irregular plurals, as in *one deer ~ two deer, one child ~ many children, one ox ~ several oxen, one foot ~ two feet*.

In present-day English there is no reason to talk about the nominative, dative or accusative case, since Modern English nouns take the same form when they function as subject and object: *Dogs like children, Children like dogs*. The only exception to this is found in the pronouns *I, we, you, he, she, it, they* and *who*, which still have their distinct 'oblique' and genitive forms such as *me, my* and *them, their*.

Present-day learners of English might feel grateful for some changes in the language: while Modern English has just one form of the definite article *the*, Old English had twelve different forms, among them *se hund, sēo fot, þæt cild, þā hundas*.

Beowulf

In Old English literature there is a heroic poem known as *Beowulf,* the oldest surviving epic poem in the whole Germanic family of languages, which has captivated scholars and students alike, ever since the first printed edition was published in 1815. The author is unknown. Although the poem was probably composed in either Mercia or Northumbria, around the eighth century, it has been handed down to posterity in a later West Saxon manuscript from about the year 1000.

In vigorous language, with heavy use of metaphor, the poem tells of a young Scandinavian hero named Beowulf who, with fourteen adventurers, sails to Denmark to fight a fiendish half-human monster named Grendel that is

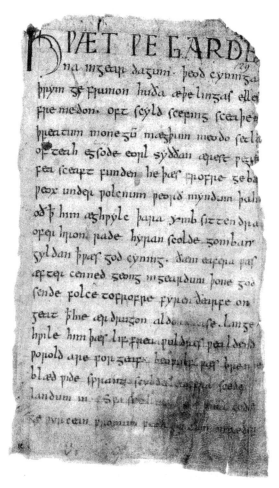

Figure 2.6   The first page of the sole surviving manuscript of *Beowulf*

ravaging the country. Fifty years later Beowulf, now king of his native land, fights a dragon that has devastated his own people. Both Beowulf and the dragon are mortally wounded in the fight. Lamenting their old king, his men push the corpse of the dragon over a cliff into the sea, and burn Beowulf's body on a funeral pyre.

We take a look at the first few lines of the poem which opens with an account of the funeral of Scyld, the mythical founder of the Danish royal family. The *Beowulf* epic consists of 3,182 lines, each line with four accents marked by alliteration and divided into two parts by a break, here indicated by a space. The text extract is given first in its Old English version, then in two Modern English translations, the first a more or less word-for-word translation by John Porter, and the second a free translation by the Irish Nobel laureate Seamus Heaney. A phonetic transcription is added to give an idea of what we believe Old English pronunciation sounded like at the time when the surviving manuscript was written (the symbols adopted by the International Phonetic Association are explained on p. 275–6).

Beowulf

HWÆT, WĒ GĀR-DEna   in gēardagum,
hwæt we: gɑ:rdɛna   in jɑ:rdawum

þēodcyninga   þrym gefrūnon,
θeədkyniŋga   θrym jəfru:nɔn

hū ðā æþelingas   ellen fremedon!
hu: θɑ: æðəliŋgas   ɛl:ən frɛmədɔn

Oft Scyld Scēfing   sceaþena þrēatum,
ɔft ʃyld ʃe:viŋ   ʃaðəna θrɛətum

monegum mǣgþum   meodosetla oftēah,
mɔnəjum mæ:jðum   meədusɛtla ɔftɛəx

egsode eorl[as],   syððan ǣrest wearð
ɛjsɔdə eərləs   syθ:an æ:rɛst wɛərθ

fēasceaft funden;   hē þæs frōfre gebād,
fɛəʃɛəft fundən   he: θæs fro:vrə jəbɑ:d

weox under wolcnum   weorðmyndum þāh,
weəks undər wɔlknum   weərθmyndum θɑ:x

oð þæt him ǣghwylc   ymbsittendra
ɔθ :æt him æ:jhwyltʃ   ymbsit:ɛndra

ofer hronrade   hȳran scolde
ɔvər hrɔnrɑ:də   hy:ran ʃɔldə

gomban gyldan;   þæt wæs gōd cyning!
gɔmban jyldan   θæt wæs go:d kyniŋg

Two translations into Modern English

What! We Spear-Danes'   in yore-days,
tribe-kings'   glory heard,
how the leaders   courage accomplished.

Often Scyld, Scef's son,   enemies' bands,
from many tribes   mead-benches seized,
terrorised earl[s],   since first he was
destitute found;   he its relief knew,
grew under skies,   in honours throve,
until to him each   of the neighbours
over whale-road   submit must,
tribute yield;   that was good king!.
                    [translated by John Porter]

So. The Spear-Danes in days gone by
and the kings who ruled them had courage and greatness.
We have heard of those princes' heroic campaigns.

There was Shield Sheafson, scourge of many tribes,
a wrecker of mead-benches, rampaging among foes.
This terror of the hall-troops had come far.
A foundling to start with, he would flourish later on
as his powers waxed and his worth was proved.
In the end each clan on the outlying coasts
beyond the whale-road had to yield to him
and begin to pay tribute. That was one good king.
                    [translated by Seamus Heaney]

3
1066 and All That

On ys for chyldern in scole, aȝenes þe vsage and manere of al oþer
nacions, buþ compelled for to leue here oune longage, and for to con-
strue here lessons and here þinges a Freynsch, and habbeþ suþ þe
Normans come furst into Engelond.

John of Trevisa, Translation of Higden's *Polychronicon*
(fourteenth century: Higden gives one of two
reasons for the decline of English)

Translation from Middle English into Modern English
One [reason] is that children in school, contrary to the usage and custom
of all other nations, are compelled to abandon their own language, and
to carry on their lessons and their affairs in French, and have done
since the Normans first came to England.

In our survey of the history of the English language, we have now come to
perhaps the most famous landmark of all. In the popular view, history is often
highly personalized: it is men and women that make history. In this case it was
Duke William of Normandy – known to the English as William the Conqueror –
who defeated the English king Harold in the fateful year 1066. This classic date
is usually remembered, though not celebrated, by the English as the beginning
of 300 years of strong French influence, changing the whole course of English history. But how far did the Norman Conquest change the course of the English
language? The wider implications of the Norman Conquest for England and
the English language are matters of debate. As *The Oxford History of Britain*
puts it:

In some respects 1066 wrought great changes; in other respects, great
changes occurred but can hardly be ascribed to the Conquest; in yet others,
the most striking feature is not change at all, but continuity.

For example, after the Conquest a number of Old Norse words – such as words now spelled *egg, get, sky, sister* and *window* – show up in written English for the first time. But does this mean that the language was changing? Or was it merely that, at this time, what had already happened to spoken Old English was now being properly recorded in writing?

For some time even before the Conquest, the relations between England and Normandy had been quite close, and a handful of French words – among them *bacun* 'bacon', *castel* 'castle' and *prisun* 'prison' – had already made their way into English. Actually, the reign of Edward the Confessor (1042–66), who had spent 25 years in Norman exile before he succeeded to the English throne, has been called 'England's Norman prelude'.

It is commonly supposed that the Norman Conquest meant the subjection of the English language to French, and that French became the dominant language of England for hundreds of years, but, in fact, England never became a French-speaking country. So why did English manage to survive? There are at least three good reasons.

First and foremost, English continued to be the spoken language of the common people. The introduction of French did not affect the peasants who tilled the land – the vast majority of the population. Also, for almost a century after the Conquest, monastic scribes kept alive the Old English standard language.

Figure 3.1   A scene from the Bayeux tapestry

The Bayeux tapestry, dating from the eleventh century, tells the story of the conquest of England by William the Conqueror and the Normans in 1066. This ribbon of cloth, 231 feet long (just over 70 metres), with figures sewn in coloured wools, is an astonishing record of history on display at Bayeux Cathedral in Normandy.

Second, the number of French native speakers was limited, probably making up no more than 5 per cent of the total population of England. Still, French was the prestige language and the most powerful positions in Church and State were filled by French-speakers.

Third, the bonds between the Normans in England and Normandy in France gradually weakened, for political reasons as well as social and cultural factors. A momentous event in Anglo-French relations was the English King John's loss of Normandy in 1204. Later, during the Hundred Years War – a series of conflicts broken intermittently by truces and peace treaties – the kings of England fought against France and finally lost all their French possessions except the port of Calais. Within three generations after the Norman invasion, the French-speaking nobility in England came to identify themselves with England, and the English language. Henry V (1413–22) promoted the spread of English and used this language in almost all his private correspondence and as a propaganda weapon against the French. In 1422 the London Company of Brewers noted: 'our most excellent King Henry hath procured the common idiom to be recommended by the exercise of writing and greater part of the Lords and Commons have begun to make their matters noted down in our mother tongue' (modern rendering).

The men who accompanied William spoke Norman French, their own local variety of the language. (The Normans had long since lost their ancestral Norse language.) This 'Anglo-Norman' lost its social status by the end of the thirteenth century, while prestigious Parisian French was being taught as a foreign language to a small minority of the population. Therefore, the French words which made their way into English after the Conquest represented two different dialects.

Loanwords borrowed before the thirteenth century often show that they came from Anglo-Norman rather than Central French. We meet spellings *ei*, *ey* alongside Central French *oi*, *oy*: compare today's English *prey* with French *proie*, English *veil* with French *voile*, English *leisure* with French *loisir*. Norman French *w* corresponded to Central French *g(u)*, which explains today's English doublets *ward/guard*, *warden/guardian*, *warranty/guarantee*. Sometimes a French word was adopted twice into English: both *gaol* and *jail* derive from Vulgar Latin *gaviola* 'little cage'. The spelling *gaol* (first recorded in 1163) is derived from Anglo-Norman *gaiole*, whereas the spelling *jail* (recorded in 1209) came from Central French *jaiole*. Today, the spelling *gaol* is an old-fashioned variant found in British English (Oscar Wilde chose to call his work *The Ballad of Reading Gaol*); but *jail* is preferred in dictionaries and is the standard spelling in North America. It has been written: 'No English spelling is more perverse than *gaol*. With its peculiar sequence of vowels, it has been misspelled as *goal* for centuries, according to the *Oxford Dictionary*.'

Middle English

In the history of English, the period from the beginning of the twelfth century until the middle or end of the fifteenth is called Middle English. This traditional term can be used so long as we remember that there was no one standard language during the Middle English period. It is in fact more appropriate to talk about 'Middle Englishes'. First, English underwent far-reaching changes over this period of 400 years. Second, after the 'golden age' of a standard written Old English around the tenth century, the language reverted to a medley of different dialects, some difficult for speakers of other dialects to understand. Above all, the English language had lost its official functions, which were taken over by French (and Latin) until the later fourteenth century.

In the linguistic transition from Old English to Middle English, two major changes are notable. Most obvious, there is an influx of French words into the vocabulary, which had previously been overwhelmingly Germanic with some Greek and Latin elements. We notice in the Trevisa passage below a number of French loanwords – *language, especially, strange, (be)cause, country* – which are still everyday English words. Also, in grammar, the inflectional system of grammatical endings is reduced and simplified. At the end of the period, very much as in today's English, the grammatical relationships of a sentence are mainly indicated by prepositions and a fixed word order.

The North and South divide in Middle English

To illustrate the North–South language divide and the English language in the late fourteenth century, here is an extract from Higden's universal history *Polychronicon*, translated by John of Trevisa from Latin into Middle English in 1387:

MIDDLE ENGLISH

Al þe longage of þe Norþhumbres, and specialych at ȝork, ys so scharp, slyttying, and frotyng, and vnschape, þat we Souþeron men may þat longage vnneþe vnderstonde. Y trowe þat þat ys because þat a buþ nyȝ to strange men and aliens, þat spekeþ strangelych, and also bycause þat þe kynges of Engelond woneþ alwey fer fram þat contray.

MODERN ENGLISH TRANSLATION

All the language of the Northumbrians, and especially at York, is so sharp, piercing, rasping and unformed that we Southerners can scarcely understand it. I believe that the reason for this is because they are near to foreigners and aliens who speak in strange ways, and also because the Kings of England always live far away from that country.

An influx of French words

Up to the middle of the thirteenth century, as far as we can tell from written records, around 900 French words came into the language. But the majority of

French loans appear during the fourteenth and fifteenth centuries so that, at the end of the Middle English period, the number of French words in English had risen to at least 10,000. There occurred a radical change in the make-up of the word stock: in the early Middle English period about 90 per cent of the vocabulary was Germanic but, at the end of the period, it was about 75 per cent.

The French borrowings were not only numerous but also covered a large number of lexical fields.

Some French loanwords in Middle English	
Administration:	*court, crown, duke, empire, minister, parliament, sir, tax*
Religion:	*baptism, cardinal, cathedral, convent, prayer, religion, virgin*
Military:	*arms, army, battle, captain, defend, enemy, sergeant, soldier*
Fashion:	*boots, button, coat, collar, diamond, dress, robe*
Precious stones:	*amethyst, diamond, emerald, pearl, ruby, sapphire, jewel*
Leisure, arts:	*art, chess, dance, literature, melody, music, paint*
Education:	*anatomy, geometry, grammar, medicine, noun, square*
The home:	*blanket, ceiling, cellar, curtain, cushion, towel*

In medieval English society the use of the French language, as well as of French loanwords, was mainly restricted to the upper classes: English remained the language of daily communication among the population at large. From fourteenth century sources, it appears that more concern was shown about the decline of French than about the maintenance of English. In 1385, John of Trevisa writes that teaching all children French

> was much in use before the first plague [that is, the Black Death of 1349], and since then has somewhat changed in all the grammar schools of England children are abandoning French, and all are construing and learning in English. [modern rendering]

French was increasingly restricted to technical uses, such as recording law cases. By the fifteenth century, it was no longer current as a spoken language in England, and anyone who needed to speak French had to learn it as a foreign language.

Often when a French word was adopted, the native English word was not abandoned: so present-day English has many **doublets**, where one word is Romance and the other Germanic. When the two words express roughly the same meaning, a choice between them usually has some stylistic effect. Generally speaking, the Romance word is more formal or abstract than the Germanic, which feels more homely and direct. A person who falls into the water has far better chances of being rescued by shouting *Help! Help!* rather than *Aid! Aid!* or *Assistance! Assistance!* And, as Simeon Potter says, 'We feel more at ease after getting a hearty welcome than after being granted a cordial reception'.

Some French-English doublets

Romance	Germanic
aid, assist	*help*
commence	*begin, start*
conceal	*hide*
desire	*wish*
encounter	*meet*
fraternal	*brotherly*
hearty	*cordial*
infant	*child*
liberty	*freedom*
marriage	*wedding*

Two-word verbs, such as *go in*, *find out* and *give in* (corresponding to *enter*, *discover* and *surrender* with Romance origin), are often taken to be typical of the Germanic stratum of Modern English. But, interestingly, this construction is found in Old Norse earlier than in English.

Law French

The greater part of the English legal vocabulary comes from the language of the conquerors. Although from 1362 English was established as the official language spoken in the courts of justice, a curious mongrel, known as *Law French* survived, and was officially abandoned only in 1731 by an Act of Parliament. Many of the following words are today familiar to audiences round the world who watch American movies or British television series focusing on legal proceedings. Mostly French in origin are:

Legal roles, such as *advocate, attorney, bailiff, coroner, defendant, judge, jury, plaintiff*

Legal actions, processes and institutions: *bail, bill, decree, evidence, fine, forfeit, jail, inquest, penalty, petition, plea, proof, punishment, ransom, sentence, suit, summons, verdict*

The names of crimes: *arson, assault, embezzlement, felony, fraud, larceny, libel, perjury, slander, treason, trespass*

French word order is preserved in *attorney general, court-martial, fee-simple, heir apparent, letters patent* – with the adjective following the noun.

The cry *Oyez! Oyez! Oyez!* has probably puzzled many people, especially if pronounced 'O yes'. Used in the past when an official or town crier called for silence, it is the Anglo-Norman form of the Old French *Oiez!* 'Hear!' Interestingly, *Oyez!* is still today the opening cry of the Marshal of the United States Supreme Court, where the phrase is sounded to bring the courtroom to order.

Who brings home the bacon?

English animal terms also show French influence – but chiefly when the animal is dead. We find these word pairs:

Animal in English	Meat in English	French
calf	*veal*	*veau*
deer	*venison*	*venaison*
ox	*beef*	*bœuf*
sheep	*mutton*	*mouton*
pig (older term: *swine*)	*pork*	*porc*

In *Ivanhoe*, Sir Walter Scott's classic novel of medieval England, Wamba the jester explains the situation as follows:

'[W]hen the brute lives, and is in the charge of a Saxon slave, she goes by the Saxon name; but becomes a Norman, and is called pork, when she is carried to the Castle-hall to feast among the nobles ...'

This is a good and familiar tale but, according to the lexicographer R.W. Burchfield, an 'enduring myth about French loanwords of the medieval period':

The culinary revolution, and the importation of French vocabulary into English society, scarcely preceded the eighteenth century, and consolidated itself in the nineteenth. The words *veal, beef, venison, pork*, and *mutton*, all of French origin, entered the English language in the early Middle Ages, and would all have been known to Chaucer. But they meant not only the flesh of a calf, of an ox, of a deer, etc., but also the animals themselves. ... The *restriction* of these French words to the sense 'flesh of an animal eaten as food' did not become general before the eighteenth century.

Many other everyday words related to food and cooking – such as *boil, cream, fruit, fry, lemon, roast, salad, sauce, sausage, soup* and *toast* – are of French origin, which suggests that French cuisine was as highly prized in medieval England, as it is today.

Grammatical endings disappear

Old English had a rather complicated system of case endings, much like that of modern German. The function of the nouns in the clause (subject, object, etc.) was indicated by case endings, such as nominative, accusative, dative. (For examples of Old English noun inflections, see p. 29.) However, the endings were later reduced or levelled, and their function was often replaced by pre-positional constructions. For example, the Old English dative noun ending *þæm lande* corresponds to Modern English *to the land, for the land*, etc.

This transition represented a major grammatical change in the structure of the language. But why did it happen in English, but not in German, for example? There is no simple explanation why the levelling of inflections took place.

Generally speaking, the natural course for any language – particularly in a bilingual environment – is change, not stability. Also, there are indications that the breakdown of the inflectional system began early and was quite advanced even before the end of the Old English period, especially in the North where the Scandinavians had settled. To put it crudely: as long as they could make themselves understood, the Vikings probably did not worry about getting all their word endings right. It may have become increasingly difficult to separate the different endings, since English normally puts the stress on the first syllable, downgrading final syllables (compare English *president* with German *Präsident* and French *président*). The final vowels *-e, -a, -u, -o* gradually coalesced into the weak neutral vowel /ə/ (called 'schwa') – a distinctive feature of Modern English – so it became more difficult, but also less important, to distinguish between word endings.

Harass or *harass?*

Even in today's English, the placement of stress on French and Latin loanwords causes uncertainty. This is because the native English habit of placing stress on the first syllable of the stem conflicts with different stress patterns found in French and Latin. A case in point is *harass* and *harassment*. In a recent poll, an American panel preferred second-syllable stress (almost nine out of ten voting for *harass*), whereas a British panel favoured first-syllable stress (almost seven out of ten voting for *harass*). According to R. W. Burchfield, 'Nothing is more likely to displease traditional RP speakers in Britain than to hear *harass* pronounced with the main stress on the second syllable'. Yet it is likely that, as a feature of the continuing transatlantic drift (p. 157), the common American pronunciation is becoming dominant also in Britain, especially among the younger generation.

Geoffrey Chaucer and William Caxton

True, the language went through radical changes after the Norman Conquest, but this does not mean that there was an overnight switch from Old English to Middle English in 1066. Naturally, transitions were gradual, from an inflectional Germanic language to a language with few grammatical inflections and a large admixture of French vocabulary. Nevertheless, by the standards of glacial slowness that usually apply to language change, the transformation of English between 1100 and 1500 was revolutionary. And changes were remarkable, not only in grammar and vocabulary but also in pronunciation and spelling (see p. 61).

The Norman Conquest forced English to play a subordinate role for the better part of 300 years. Although by the end of the fourteenth century English had superseded French everywhere except at the king's court and chancery, it was not until the early fifteenth century that the English language became the language employed in speech and writing by English folk, both high and low.

One factor that probably hastened the pace of change in Early Middle English was the loss of its official status. With French as the prestige language – the language of the court, the Church, the law courts, the administration – English reverted to being a collection of dialects. There was no standard way of writing or pronouncing the language, so scribes spelled in the way that reflected their own dialect. Often popular texts would be repeatedly copied in different parts of the country, and so a mixture of dialect traits would result. It was only when French lost its hegemony that English began to emerge from this period of 'underground' development and to enter a period of standardization.

Politically, the golden age began only in the later sixteenth century, but a literary and cultural renaissance was evident as early as the late Middle English period. Two names, above all, are associated with this: Geoffrey Chaucer, the poet, and William Caxton, the printer and translator.

In 1362 Edward III ordered that English should be used in Parliament and the courts of law, 'because the French tongue … is much unknown' (but, ironically, the original statute is written in French). In the king's service at this time was a young man by the name of Geoffrey Chaucer, who was later to be called 'the father of English literature'. While Chaucer was bilingual and, early on, was influenced by French as well as Italian literature, he wrote all his works in English.

In the 1380s Chaucer started to write his most famous work, *The Canterbury Tales*. Here we are introduced to a motley company of pilgrims, including the

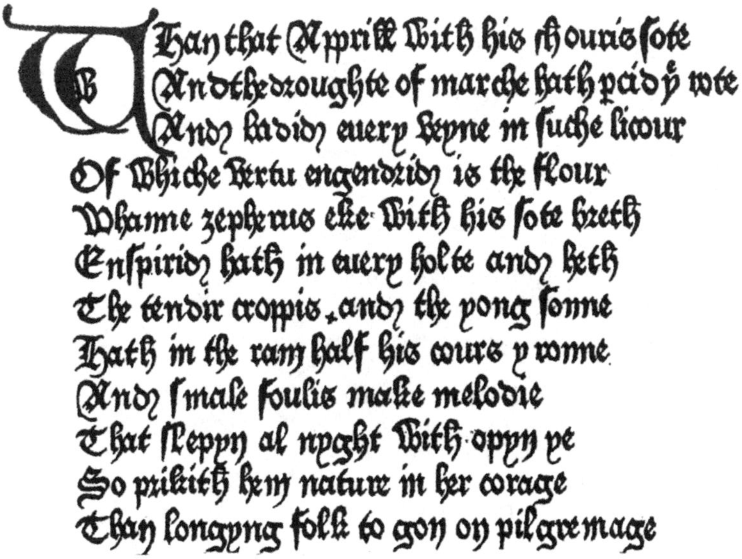

Whan that Apprill with his shouris sote
Andthedroughte of marche hath pcid yͤ rote
And badid euery veyne in suche licour
Of whiche vertu engendrid is the flour
Whanne zepherus eke with his sote breth
Enspirid hath in euery holte and heth
The tendir croppis and the yong sonne
Hath in the ram half his cours y ronne
And smale foulis make melodie
That slepyn al nyght with opyn ye
So prikith hem nature in her corage
Than longyng folk to gon on pilgremage

Figure 3.2 The opening lines of Chaucer's *Canterbury Tales*, from Caxton's early printed version (1478)

The opening lines of the Canterbury Tales

(The fifteen words of French origin are in italics)

Whan that *Aprill* with hise shoures soote
hwan ðat 'aːpril wið iz 'ʃuːrəs 'soːtə

The droghte of *March* hath *perced* to the roote,
ðə druːxt əv martʃ haθ   'peːrsəd to ðə 'roːtə

And bathed every *veyne* in swich *licour*
and 'baːðed 'evri væin in switʃ li'kuːr

Of which *vertu engendred* is the *flour;*
əv hwitʃ ver'tiu in'dʒendrəd iz ðə fluːr

Whan Zephirus eek with his sweete breeth
hwan 'zefirus eːk wið iz 'sweːtə brɛːθ

Inspired hath in euery holt and heeth
in'spiːrəd haθ in 'evri hɔlt and hɛːθ

The *tendre* croppes, and the yonge sonne
ðə 'tendrə 'krɔpəz and ðə 'juŋgə 'sunə

Hath in the Ram his halve *cours* yronne,
haθ in ðə ram iz 'halvə kuːrs i'runə

And smale foweles maken *melodye,*
and 'smaːlə 'fuːləz 'maːkən melo'diːə

That slepen al the nyght with open ye
ðat 'sleːpən ɑl ðə niçt wið 'ɔːpən 'iːə

(So priketh hem *nature* in hir *corages*);
sɔː 'prikəθ əm na'tiur in ir ku'raːdʒəz

Thanne longen folk to goon on *pilgrimages*
ðan 'lɔŋgən fɔlk to gɔːn ɔn pilgri'maːdʒəz

Modern English Version (by Nevill Coghill)

When in April the sweet showers fall
And pierce the drought of March to the root, and all
The veins are bathed in liquor of such power
As brings about the engendering of the flower,
When also Zephyrus with his sweet breath
Exhales an air in every grove and heath
Upon the tender shoots, and the young sun
His half-course in the sign of the Ram has run,
And the small fowl are making melody
That sleep away the night with open eye
(So nature pricks them and their heart engages)
Then people long to go on pilgrimages.

poet himself, on a pilgrimage from London to Canterbury Cathedral, the shrine of Saint Thomas à Becket. In Chaucer's days that was a long journey and, to pass the time, the pilgrims agree to a storytelling contest: each of the thirty or so pilgrims is to tell four tales. The work is unfinished – Chaucer completed less than a quarter of his original plan. Still, it is a classic of English literature which has inspired many later writers. This work introduces many immortal literary characters often felt to represent a microcosm of fourteenth-century English society. As an example of late Middle English, here are the opening lines of Chaucer's *Prologue to the Canterbury Tales* followed by a Modern English version. (See pp. 275–6 for explanation of the phonetic symbols which indicate how we believe it sounded when Chaucer read his lines.)

Although Middle English still varied considerably from one part of the country to another, in Chaucer's time there was beginning to emerge a standard written form of the language. By the early fifteenth century, the royal bureaucracy in the office called 'the Chancery' was using English for the king's documents and correspondence. The emerging standard was centrally based on a kind of officialese, now known as **Chancery English**. One branch of the Chancery was established in London in what is now called Chancery Lane. But the City of Westminster, where the Houses of Parliament and Westminster Abbey still stand, became the permanent home of the bureaucracy. In this period of mercantile growth, London expanded and attracted large numbers of migrants from the north and the east, especially from the East Midlands (see p. 15). As a result of this influx, the London dialect, from which the new standard English would emerge, was largely based on the East Midland dialect.

In the century following Chaucer's death, a crucial event gave an enormous impetus to the standardization of the language. This was the introduction of printing to England in 1476, when William Caxton set up his printing press in Westminster, near the royal court and Westminster Abbey. Born in Kent, he moved to the Continent where he learned the art of printing before returning to England. While still in Bruges, Caxton produced the first two books printed in English. His first book printed in England was a translation from French, *The Dictes and Sayenges of the Phylosophers* (1477). At the time of his death in 1491, Caxton had published nearly 80 printed works in English, among them Chaucer's *Canterbury Tales*.

Caxton had to make a historic decision: how to 'define the English language'. In Middle English there were numerous different spellings recorded for the same word, partly reflecting different dialectal pronunciations. For example, the word *never* was also spelled *naure, næure, ner* or *neure*. The word *might* could also be written *maht, mihte, micht, mist, michte, mithe, myhte*. Spelling in the Middle English period was a curious mixture of two systems, Old English and French, and this is one of the reasons why Modern English spelling is so inconsistent. From the

Figure 3.3   The oldest known representation of a printing press (1507)

beginning of the printing age, a trend towards a more fixed and consistent spelling is perceptible. But it was not until the later eighteenth century, 400 years later, that English had reached the stage of a fully standardized spelling.

At the spoken level there were numerous dialects, some of them hardly mutually comprehensible, as illustrated by Caxton himself in the Prologue to Virgil's *Book of Eneydos*. He tells us a story about the choice of plural form of *egg* – *egges* or *eyren*. Some merchants, probably from northern England, sailing from the Thames, stopped at a place on the Kentish coast:

And one of theym named Sheffelde, a mercer, cam in-to an hows ('house') and axed ('asked') for mete; and specyally axed after eggys. And the goode wyf answerde, that she coude ('could') speke no frenshe. And the marchaunt was angry, for he also coude speke no frensche, but wolde have hadde egges, and she understode hym not. And thenne at laste a nother sayd that he wolde have eyren. Then the gode wyf sayd that she understode hym wel. Loo, what sholde a man in thyse dayes wryte, egges or eyren?

The language we meet in Chaucer and Caxton gives a much more modern and homogeneous impression than earlier Middle English texts, and is largely intelligible to a modern reader. This point in the history of the English language, when printed books from Caxton's press are distributed throughout the country, can be conveniently used to mark the end of the Middle English period and the beginning of Modern English.

We have come to the end of our survey of the first thousand years in the history of the English language. It has been a story of three linguistic invasions:

- Beginning in the fifth century, Germanic tribes leave their homes and sail across the North Sea: on board they have the beginnings of the English language.
- Towards the end of the eighth century, Vikings begin to sail west from the Scandinavian peninsula to the Isles. They continue their 'visits' for some 300 years, ultimately building a short-lived North Sea empire but, above all, leaving permanent linguistic traces on English from their own Nordic tongues.
- In 1066, Normans invade England, eventually giving the island language a pronounced Romance flavour, as seen in the word-stock of Modern English, where Romance words actually outnumber Germanic words.

Apart from these warlike expeditions, from the Old English period and even before, the Latin language, as the language of religion and learning, made its mark on English in a more peaceful way. Latin borrowings like *cheese, copper, street* and *wine* even date from a time when the Germanic tribes were still on the Continent, before settling in Britain. This Latin influence is a continuing process throughout the history of the language. It increased during the Middle English period, when medieval Latin was the language of the Church and of learning, and has remained strong up to the present time. We take up this theme in the next chapter.

On the eve of the Modern era, English was gradually becoming a more standardized and more settled language, one that English speakers today can recognize as the precursor of their own mother tongue.

4
Modern English in the Making

When one turns to vocabulary one cannot but be impressed by the amazing hospitality of the English language. Wave after wave of words entered the language from French, Latin, and Italian ...

Robert Burchfield

So now they have made our English tongue a gallimaufry or hodgepodge of all other speeches. [*gallimaufry*, *hodgepodge* = 'ridiculous medley']

Edmund Spenser

The sixteenth century is often hailed as the golden age of the English language, though this becomes an apt description only during the Elizabethan period (Elizabeth I, 1558–1603). Yet we can see during the whole of this century that there was a growing pride and confidence in the English language. During the 200 years after William Caxton set up his printing press in London, the language continued to undergo great changes, especially changes that have social or cultural origins, rather than purely linguistic ones. This period, called **Early Modern English**, sees the forging of a modern standard English language.

A standard language is something taken for granted for present-day English. It is the variety of a language that is mainly taught in schools, that is used in published books and in public media generally. It is popularly considered to be the 'correct' form of the language. Over the centuries it has been associated with the written language. But standard English was not imposed from on high by some deity. On the contrary, it emerged slowly over a period of some three-and-a-half centuries, as result of convergence of language habits towards a variety associated with the power and prestige of England's capital. It is this convergence, this standardization, that is a major focus of attention in this chapter as well as later in Chapter 10. We should always remember, though, that the standard language is not the whole language. Often it seems to be like the visible tip of an island, most of which (a wealth of dialect variation) lies largely out of sight beneath the sea.

This chapter concentrates on the development of English in England itself, illustrated by three linguistic landmarks: the contributions of William Shakespeare, of The King James Bible and of Samuel Johnson's *Dictionary*. The development of English in North America will be in focus in Chapter 5, and of English in Wales, Scotland and Ireland in Chapter 7.

To understand linguistic developments it is often helpful to relate them to historical watersheds – cultural, social and political. In this chapter we will take a look at three important ones in the Early Modern English era: the Renaissance, the Reformation and the Restoration.

The Three 'Rs' – Renaissance, Reformation, Restoration

The dominant cultural development in Europe during the fifteenth and sixteenth centuries is usually referred to as **The Renaissance**. However, this French term itself, meaning literally 'rebirth', was not coined until the nineteenth century. For our story, the Renaissance meant three things. First, it was a period of the rediscovery and revitalization of classical learning in Greek and Latin, much of which had been preserved by Arab scholars in the Middle Ages. Second, it was a period of expansion of knowledge and flowering of art and literature, inspired partly by classical models, but also by contemporary events such as Columbus' 'discovery' of the New World. Third, it was a period of growing confidence in the modern vernacular languages of Europe, such as French, Italian and English, which were no longer automatically disdained as inferior to Latin. Contributing to all three factors was a vast increase in the use of books and the spread of education, principally through the coming of the printing press.

In England the Renaissance covers roughly the time from William Caxton to the middle of the seventeenth century. In this period no fewer than 20,000 titles were printed in English. The printers were businessmen who, naturally, wanted to sell as many books as possible. But before their books could find readers, the producers were faced with a number of problems: Should they use their native language or Latin? Which geographic variety of English should they choose for the publication of the works by English writers? Should foreign borrowings be tolerated, or should they be converted into some kind of English equivalent? How should they choose an appropriate spelling and punctuation?

Besides the Renaissance there were two other historic 'R' happenings of consequence for the English language during the Early Modern period: **The Reformation** (*c*. 1530–60) and **The Restoration** (*c*. 1660–88). In England the beginnings of the Reformation can be traced back to the late fourteenth century, but it was relaunched in the 1530s when Henry VIII, notorious for his six wives, broke from the Catholic Church, opening the way to translation of the Bible into English (see p. 58). Access to God through the English vernacular (instead of through the mediation of Church Latin) was a cornerstone of the Protestant thinking that would eventually prevail in England. This meant that English had to become a written language that could match Latin. For centuries reading and writing had largely been the preserve of the clergy, but now there was an educational drive to expand the circle of people who were able to read and write.

First sanctioned in 1549, the Book of Common Prayer, although much revised, is still an official prayer book of Anglican churches. It was compiled by Thomas Cranmer, then Archbishop of Canterbury. The aim was to produce a book in the vernacular that would be a unified and simplified equivalent of the Roman Catholic liturgical books. An example:

> Deerly beloued frendes, we are gathered together here in the syght of God, and in the face of this congregacion, to ioyne together this man and this woman in holy matrimoni; which is an honorable estate, instituted of God in paradise, in the time of mannes innocencie, signifying unto us the misticall union that is betwixte Christe and his Churche ...

It is remarkable that the text can be used, after 450 years, in today's marriage service:

> *Dearly beloved, we are gathered here in the sight of God and in the face of this congregation, to join together this man and this woman in Holy Matrimony ...*

Incidentally, Cranmer suffered a brutal death because he promoted Protestantism. The period of Early Modern English was a period of great violence, as well as a period of immensely expanding horizons. A century later, after the English Civil War, the victorious Puritans (Protestants who sought to wipe out corruption and rituals from the Church) beheaded King Charles I, and from 1649 to 1658 England was actually a kind of republic headed by Oliver Cromwell as Lord Protector. During this period, known as the Commonwealth, the Anglican Church was displaced. But the Established Church, as well as the monarchy, returned in 1660, and the period following this is known as the Restoration. To some readers this name may evoke the image of the morally lax reign of Charles II but, in its attitudes towards language, the period moved towards restraint and moderation. Texts from the late seventeenth century make a strikingly modern impression, and this period marks the emergence of a more standardized written English.

English and Latin

In the Middle English period, the English language had become accustomed to importing words from other languages. Words from French, Latin and Greek, began to infiltrate English even before the existence of a written standard and, before the end of the Middle Ages, this trickle had turned into a torrent. During the Renaissance more than 10,000 recorded new words poured into the language. Today many of these words, such as *adapt*, *benefit* and *exist*, have made their way into everyday language. But most of the Latin loanwords belong to the language of learning and science.

When Renaissance figures like Thomas More and Francis Bacon wrote in English, they often embellished their native tongue with Latinisms. More (another scholar to suffer the extreme penalty – he was executed by Henry VIII) has been credited with the coinage of *absurdity*, *contradictory*, *exaggerate*, *indifference*, *monopoly* and *paradox*. The classical languages of Latin and Greek have until recently held a strong position at prestigious English schools and universities, notably the élite universities of Oxford and Cambridge. For a student of high or humble birth, a classical education could open doors to high office.

Examples of English words from Latin and Greek

Sixteenth century

area	*circus*	*excursion*
exit	*fungus*	*genius*
index	*medium*	*orbit*
peninsula	*species*	*vacuum*

Seventeenth century

album	*apparatus*	*arena*
complex	*encyclopedia*	*focus*
formula	*lens*	*minimum*
series	*specimen*	*status*

Eighteenth century

alibi	*deficit*	*extra*
inertia	*insomnia*	*nucleus*
propaganda	*ultimatum*	*via*

Nineteenth century

aquarium	*bacillus*	*codex*
confer	*medium*	*moratorium*
opus	*referendum*	*thesaurus*

Twentieth century

alphavirus	*magnum*	*microform*
minimalist	*moron*	*multicultural*
omega-3	*onomastics*	*oracy*

The influx of Latin words was greater in English than in any other European language, with the possible exception of French. Some words previously borrowed from French were remodelled into closer resemblance with their Latin originals. In some cases this linguistic pedantry overstepped the mark, and English acquired a number 'false Latinisms', such as *advance* with the letter *d* inserted (compare French *avance*), and *debt* (compare French *dette*). Since many classical words had already been borrowed through French, there also appeared doublets – two words of the same origin but with different meanings, such as these:

Latin	English word via French	English word from Latin
corpus	*corps*	*corpse, corpus*
factum	*feat*	*fact*
historia	*story*	*history*
senior	*sir*	*senior*

By adding Latin as well as French loans to the Old English word-stock, modern English sometimes provides three words with similar meanings, though with different stylistic values:

From Old English	From French	From Latin
ask	*question*	*interrogate*
fast	*firm*	*secure*
kingly	*royal*	*regal*
rise	*mount*	*ascend*

The Elizabethan period

In 1558, when Elizabeth I came to the throne, the number of English speakers in the world is estimated to have been less than five million, practically all of them living in the British Isles. In 1953, when Elizabeth II was crowned, English was spoken by some 250 million people, and four out of five did not live in the British Isles.

Still, it was during the long reign of Elizabeth I that English took its first faltering steps towards becoming an international language. One of the Queen's favourite subjects, Sir Walter Ralegh, has gone down in history as the epitome of Renaissance man, a poet and adventurer who sponsored the first major English expeditions to the New World. He failed to establish lasting colonies, but famously popularized two American products – tobacco and the potato.

William Shakespeare, today the most famous of Elizabeth's subjects, was born in Stratford-on-Avon in 1564, six years after the Queen had come to the throne. At the age of 18 he married Ann Hathaway, and seven months later a daughter, Susanna, was born and, in 1585, the twins Hamnet and Judith. In his

Figure 4.1   The title-page of Shakespeare's *First Folio*

mid-twenties Will Shakespeare moved to London and became in time a celebrated actor and writer. In 1610 he retired to Stratford a rather well-to-do man and died there six years later.

As a writer Shakespeare was extremely productive: during a period of some twenty years (roughly from 1590 to 1610) he produced two long poems, 154 sonnets and 37 plays, and may have had a hand in others works. We know very little about his private life, more about his theatrical life – but fortunately we have his enormous literary production. It is lucky that his complete plays were published in print by two fellow actors in 1623, seven years after his death, in a volume now known as *The First Folio* (see Figure 4.1, p. 51).

The Elizabethan authorities did not take kindly to the theatrical companies. According to a document from 1574, performances were accompanied by 'frays and quarrels evil practices of incontinency [*incontinency* = 'failure to restrain sexual appetite'] in great inns, having chambers and secret places to their open stages and galleries'. When London's first playhouse was pulled down, its timbers were moved to the south bank of the Thames, where they were used to build a new playhouse, The Globe – a surprisingly large building, which could hold 3,000 people or more. Among the plays first staged there were Shakespeare's

---

A visit to Shakespeare's theatre

A Swiss tourist named Thomas Platter visited London in the autumn of 1599, the year when the Globe was built and Shakespeare's play *Julius Caesar* was performed for the first time. Here is an excerpt from his diary:

> On September 21st after lunch, about two o'clock, I and my party crossed the water, and there in the house with the thatched roof witnessed an excellent performance of the tragedy of the first Emperor Julius Caesar with a cast of some 15 people; when the play was over, they danced very marvellously and gracefully together as is their wont, two dressed as men and two as women. ...
> Thus daily at two in the afternoon, London has two, sometimes three plays running in different places, competing with each other, and those which play best obtain most spectators. The playhouses are so constructed that they play on a raised platform, so that everyone has a good view. There are different galleries and places, however, where the seating is better and more comfortable and therefore more expensive. For whoever cares to stand below only pays one English penny, but if he wishes to sit he enters by another door and pays another penny, while if he desires to sit in the most comfortable seats, which are cushioned, where he not only sees everything well, but can also be seen, then he pays yet another English penny at another door. And during the performance food and drink are carried round the audience, so that for what one cares to pay one may also have refreshment. The actors are most expensively and elaborately costumed; for it is the English usage for eminent lords or knights at their decease to bequeath and leave almost the best of their clothes to their serving men, which it is unseemly for the latter to wear, so that they offer them then for sale for a small sum to the actors.

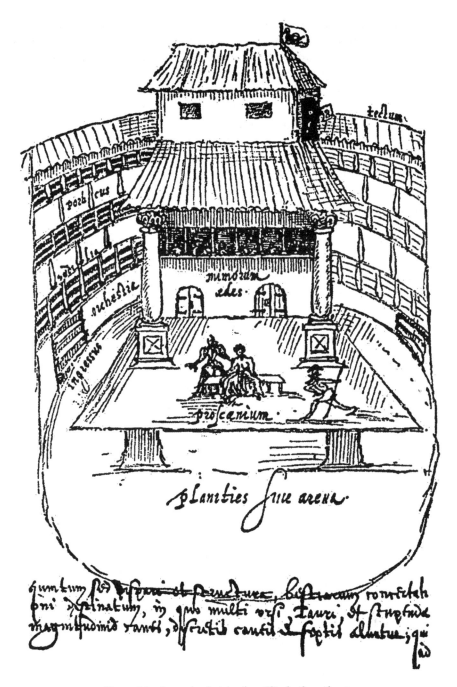

Figure 4.2 An early sketch of an Elizabethan theatre

four greatest tragedies, *Hamlet*, *Othello*, *Macbeth* and *King Lear*. In 1613 the theatre burned down during a performance of *Henry VIII* – someone had fired a canon so carelessly that the thatched roof caught fire. But The Globe was rebuilt and used until 1642 when the Puritan party closed all the theatres. Thanks to the initiative of the American actor-director Sam Wanamaker (1919–93), we can now enjoy Shakespeare's plays in the new Globe, a reconstructed copy close to the site of Shakespeare's original theatre.

Figure 4.2 (p. 53) shows the only extant drawing of the interior of an Elizabethan theatre. It was made in about 1596 by a Dutch student, Johannes de Witt, during a performance at the Swan theatre.

Shakespeare's language

Although Shakespeare's works belong to the age of Early Modern English, reading them today is not easy. The language has changed considerably in the last 400 years. While the main difficulties encountered by the modern reader are found in vocabulary, Shakespeare's grammar also differs from today's. Here are some examples.

Today, the third person present singular ending of a verb is -*s*, but Shakespeare used both -*s* and -*th* – notice the words in italics in these lines from *The Merchant of Venice*:

> The qualitie of mercie is not straind,
> It *droppeth* as the gentle raine from heauen
> Upon the place beneath: it is twice bless'd;
> It *blesseth* him that *giues* and him that *takes*

As we see here, the spelling and punctuation of the original were different from present-day usage. But it is common these days to print Shakespeare in present-day spelling, and we follow this practice in general in this book:

> The quality of mercy is not strain'd,
> It *droppeth* as the gentle rain from heaven
> Upon the place beneath: it is twice bless'd;
> It *blesseth* him that *gives* and him that *takes*

Present-day English requires a *do*-construction in negative statements, such as *I don't think so*, and interrogative sentences, such as *Do you go there often?* In Elizabethan times this *do*-construction was still competing with an older construction (familiar to speakers of other Germanic languages), so in *Macbeth* we find:

> *I think not of them* [instead of *I do not think of them*]
> *Goes the King hence to-day?* [instead of *Does the King go hence today?*]

This construction without *do* can still be found in Modern English in a jocular expression such as *How goes it?*

A common mistake by learners of English as a second language is the use of *which* instead of *who* as a relative pronoun when referring to persons. This is not acceptable in today's standard English, but was possible in the seventeenth century, as in *The Tempest*:

The mistress *which* I serve

The singular pronoun *thou* or *thee* was still in general use in Shakespeare's English, alongside the plural *you, ye*. But *you* was also used to refer to one person, as in the following lines from *Richard III*:

Clarence: Where art *thou*, keeper? Give me a cup of wine.
Second Murderer: You shall have enough wine, my lord, anon.

Here the Duke of Clarence, a nobleman, uses the familiar form *thou* to someone he takes to be a servant. But the 'servant' (who is about to murder Clarence) uses *you* in addressing his superior. The choice between *thou* and *you* in Elizabethan English has been much debated, but it was clearly a matter of tone and attitude, not hugely different from today's choice between *tu* and *vous* in French, *du* and *Sie* in German, or *ni* and *nín* in Chinese.

Thou and *thee*

In older English *you* was first used for plural and later became the neutral term of address for both singular and plural. Originally, *thou* and *thee* were used for addressing one person and were common in older translations of the Bible and in Shakespeare. *Thou* was the subject form (*I hope thou wilt*) and *thee* the object form (*I give thee my troth*). These forms still survive in the traditional usage of the Bible and the Prayer Book. So for centuries – sometimes even today – the bride in the Anglican service has taken the wedding vows with the words:

I [name] take thee [name] to my wedded husband, to have and to hold from this day forward, for better for worse, for richer for poorer, in sickness and in health, to love, cherish, and to obey, till death us do part, according to God's holy ordinance; and thereto I give thee my troth.
(Book of Common Prayer, 1662: 'The Form of Solemnization of Matrimony')

In ordinary speech, *thou* and *thee* came to express intimacy and informality, before they were all but supplanted by the unmarked form *you*. In keeping with the objectives of their Society of Friends to avoid social distinctions, the Quakers kept *thee*, a usage that is still found in special contexts today. *Thou* also survives in English dialects, particularly in the northern counties of England, where it is usually spelled *tha* and pronounced /ðə/. There it still keeps its touch of familiarity: for example in the reputed words of a Yorkshireman 'Don't thou thou me, thou thou them as thous thee'. Or, in standard English: 'Please don't use *thou* in addressing me; use *thou* to address people who use *thou* in addressing you'.

An enormous increase in vocabulary by loanwords and the creation of new words takes place between 1530 and 1660 – a unique period of expansion in the history of the language. True to the Renaissance ideal, writers felt a desire to match classical antiquity by creating a national language and literature with the aid of old words, dialect words and above all new words, mostly taken from Latin and Greek. As Richard Mulcaster patriotically put it in 1582 (where 'the English' refers to 'the English language'):

> I loue Rome, but London better, I favor Italie, but England more, I honor the Latin, but I worship the English.

Between 1590 and 1610 around 6,000 new words were being added to the lexicon every year. The peak of word-stock expansion coincides with Shakespeare's life and, in his works, it is chiefly the rich vocabulary that causes puzzlement for a modern reader. In his complete works Shakespeare used over 28,000 different words (which is a high figure compared to what other authors used), and many of them have since acquired new meanings: in Shakespeare's day, *ecstasy* carried the meaning 'madness', *fond* meant 'foolish' and *learn* was used for both 'learn' and 'teach'. Shakespeare was a great word-painter, a keen word-borrower and a subtle word-creator. Many words in current use make their first appearance in his works, such as *accommodation, assassination, countless, dislocate, laughable, premeditated, submerged*. But for some reason, other words of his did not catch on, among them *abruption, appertainments, cadent, exsufflicate, persistive, protractive, unplausive, vastidity*.

At this time, pronunciation was beginning to be standardized, but several norms must have existed side by side. We do not know for certain what Shakespeare's spoken English sounded like, but by studying spellings, rhymes, puns, contemporary linguistic textbooks and the overall development of the language, language scholars can provide a good picture of the pronunciation of Elizabethan English. Clearly, Shakespeare's pronunciation was already far removed from Chaucer's and closer to today's. One might imagine that if Shakespeare's lines were spoken by an Elizabethan actor making a guest appearance at the new Globe, they would strike a modern audience as quaint in the extreme. But in 2004 *Romeo and Juliet* was acted at the Globe by a cast trained to use a modern reconstruction of Shakespeare's pronunciation. It was the first time that Shakespeare's words had been performed in London, using Shakespeare's accent, for four centuries. The result, far from being baffling to the ear, was, according to members of the team, 'earthy', 'liberating', 'gutsy', 'a wonderful experiment'.

So what was Shakespeare's pronunciation like? The consonants were pronounced more or less as in present-day English, but the *r*-sound was pronounced in all positions, both in final position and before other consonants. *Further,* pronounced /'fɜːðə/ in present-day English (RP), Shakespeare pronounced as /'fərðər/, and *word*, which in today's RP is pronounced /wɜːd/, sounded like /wərd/. ('RP' stands for 'Received Pronunciation', that is to say present-day 'BBC pronunciation' in British English, see p. 125.) Shakespeare's pronunciation was probably closer to present-day Irish and American English. For example, he must have pronounced medial and final *rs* as a retroflex consonant, which is what we hear in today's General American English (see p. 81). Similarly, in words like *dance, after, bath* Shakespeare used the vowel /æ/, as in present-day General American, not /ɑː/ as RP. But it is present-day RP diphthongs which differ most from the language of Shakespeare:

day was pronounced /deː/ or /dɛː/
told was pronounced /toːld/
time was pronounced as /təɪm/
our was pronounced /əʊər/

The box shows the first lines of Hamlet's famous monologue 'To be, or not to be'. (For explanation of phonetic symbols, see Pronunciation, pp. 275–6.)

Hamlet, III.i

To be, or not to be – that is the question;
tə 'biː ər 'nɒt tə 'biː 'ðæt ɪz ðə 'kwestʃn

Whether 'tis nobler in the mind to suffer
'hweðər tɪz 'noːblər ɪn ðə 'məɪnd tə 'sʌfər

The slings and arrows of outrageous fortune
ðə 'slɪŋz ən 'æroʒ əv əʊt'reːdʒəs 'fɔːrtən

Or to take arms against a sea of troubles,
ɔːr tə 'teːk 'aːrmz ə'genst ə 'seː əv 'trʌblz

and by opposing end them.
ən bəɪ ə'poːzn 'end ðəm

Shakespeare's genius not only drew richly on the resources of the language, but gave it new riches. A great many of his expressions are quoted even by people who have never seen a Shakespeare play. There is an old anecdote about a visitor who, after seeing *Hamlet* for the first time, remarked that it was 'very nice, but so full of quotations'. Furthermore, Shakespeare's works have inspired modern writers and composers to re-create them, for example in the musicals *West Side Story* based on *Romeo and Juliet*, and *Kiss me Kate* based on *The Taming of the Shrew*.

Some popular Shakespeare quotations

The time is out of joint (*Hamlet*)
Though this be madness, yet there is method in't (*Hamlet*)
Something is rotten in the state of Denmark (*Hamlet*)
To hold, as 'twere, the mirror up to nature (*Hamlet*)
Misery acquaints a man with strange bed-fellows (*The Tempest*)
A horse! a horse! My kingdom for a horse! (*Richard III*)
Uneasy lies the head that wears a crown (*Henry VI, Part 2*)
At one fell swoop (*Macbeth*)
It was Greek to me (*Julius Caesar*)
The course of true love never did run smooth (*A Midsummer Night's Dream*)

The King James Bible – a milestone in the history of English

As early as the Old English period, Bible texts were available in English but, for 300 years after the Norman invasion, no new translations appeared. Then, in the 1380s, there appeared the only known biblical translations in Middle English. These were associated with the name of John Wyclif, a religious leader whose teachings – later suppressed for heresy – in many ways anticipated those of Luther's Protestant Reformation in Germany. For nearly 150 years no further translations appeared.

One of the most remarkable of the Reformation leaders was William Tyndale. Like Martin Luther, whom he visited, Tyndale held that people should be able to read the Bible in their own language. His translation of the New Testament began to be published in Cologne in 1525 and, ten years later, the first complete Bible translation followed. This Bible incorporated Tyndale's translations after he had been executed for heresy in Antwerp.

A turning-point for the nation as well as the language occurred in 1534 when Henry VIII, after divorcing one queen and marrying another, defied the Pope and made himself head of the English Church. The Church of England was now separated from the Church of Rome. In the next thirty years, five major Bible versions went to the press. The king ordered every church to keep a number of English Bible translations, and the widespread use of these and other religious texts came to exert a pervasive influence on the English language.

In 1604 King James I (the first king to unite the thrones of England and Scotland) held a conference at Hampton Court with representatives of the Established Church and the Puritans, who sought to wipe out corruption and 'popish rituals' from the Church. The Puritans were told they could either conform or be 'harried out of the land', and many disappointed Puritans did choose to emigrate after the conference (see p. 75). Yet, in one respect, the participants managed to rise above the strong religious disputes of the time. The conference laid the foundation of what Winston Churchill later extolled as 'a splendid and lasting monument to the genius of the English-speaking peoples' – the Bible translation of 1611, traditionally known in the Anglican Church as The Authorized Version. Within a generation this Bible displaced previous versions and has had an enormous impact on the English-speaking world for centuries. It was also carried to colonies in North America, where its alternative name, The King James Bible, prevails. Although written by a committee, it provided the language with a simple yet powerful and poetic mode of expression. The text was deliberately based on earlier English versions of the Bible, especially Tyndale's, and thus kept alive an earlier state of the language, including many of the old Anglo-Saxon words which ran the risk of disappearing under the Renaissance influence of classical languages. The King James Bible and Shakespeare's plays belong to the same age, yet their language

---

Bible Translations (St Matthew's Gospel 17:1–4)

Late Old English (West Saxon Gospels, ca 1000)

And æfter six daȝum nam se Hælend Petrum, and Iacobum, and Iohannem, hys broðor, and lædde hiȝ on-sundron on ænne heahne munt, and he wæs ȝehiwod beforan him. And his ansyn scean swa swa sunne; and hys reaf wæron swa hwite swa snaw. And efne! ða ætywde Moyses and Helias, mid him sprecende. Ða cwæþ Petrus to him, Drihten, god ys us to beonne. ȝyf ðu wylt, uton wyrcean her þreo eardung-stowa, ðe ane, Moyse ane, and Helie ane.

Middle English (Wyclif's version, ca 1382)

And after sexe dayes Jhesus toke Petre, and Jamys, and Joon, his brother, and ledde hem asydis in to an hiȝ hill, and was transfigured bifore hem. And his face schoon as the sunne; forsothe his clothis were maad white as snow. And lo! Moyses and Helye apperiden to hem, spekynge with hym. Sothely Petre answerynge seid to Jhesu, Lord, it is good vs to be here. ȝif thou wolt, make we here three tabernaclis; to thee oon, to Moyses oon, and oon to Helie.

Early Modern English (King James Bible, 1611)

And after six days Jesus taketh Peter, James and John his brother, and bringeth them up into an high mountain apart, and was transfigured before them: and his face did shine as the sun, and his raiment was white as the light. And, behold, there appeared unto them Moses and Elias talking with him. Then answered Peter, and said unto Jesus, Lord, it is good for us to be here: if thou wilt, let us make here three tabernacles; one for thee, and one for Moses, and one for Elias.

Present-day English (New Revised Standard Version, 1989)

Six days later, Jesus took with him Peter and James and his brother John and led them up a high mountain, by themselves. And he was transfigured before them, and his face shone like the sun, and his clothes became dazzling white. Suddenly there appeared to them Moses and Elijah talking with him. Then Peter said to Jesus, 'Lord, it is good for us to be here; if you wish, I will make three dwellings here, one for you, one for Moses, and one for Elijah'.

is in many ways very different: the Bible used a bare 8,000 words (compared to Shakespeare's 28,000) – 'God's teaching in homely English for everyman'.

To illustrate how the language has changed in the last thousand years, p. 59 shows an extract from different English translations of the Gospel according to St Matthew.

Restoration and reaction

In 1649 an extraordinary event took place in the history of England: after the execution of the king, Charles I, charged with high treason and 'other high crimes against the realm of England', the country became a republic – later, in fact, a military dictatorship. Yet, only eleven years later, monarchy was restored. The following period, from 1660 to 1688, known as the Restoration, was linguistically important because, during this period, people began to feel the need for a set of standards for the proper use of language.

A gap had already been growing between the spoken and the written word. The written language followed its own habits, which were markedly different from how most people spoke. One scholar has compared English orthography during the Elizabethan period to 'an anarchist springtime, when every man or woman set his or her own standard'. For example, Shakespeare's name is found in 16 different spellings during his lifetime, with at least six of them in Shakespeare's own hand.

Shakespeare's name

Here are five different spelling variants of William Shakespeare's signature. (Letters in brackets are difficult to decipher or appear to have been absent.)

> *Will(ia)m Shakp(er)*
> *William Shakspe(r)*
> *W(illia)m Shaksper*
> *Willi(a)m Shakspere*
> *William Shakspeare*

The usual modern spelling *William Shakespeare* is that used throughout *The First Folio* (1623) and *The Second Folio* (1632) editions of his works.

However, even in Shakespeare's time, spelling was already moving towards its own standard, and departing from the pronunciation of the spoken language. This was mainly because the pronunciation had been changing, while the spelling, because of the gradual standardization of the written language, did not keep pace with it. Even today, English spelling largely reflects the pronunciation of the language towards the end of the Middle English period. The standardization process continued over 300 years – until the end of the eighteenth century when it became possible to assert that 'one word has just one spelling'. However, even this would have been a premature claim in 1800 – as we know from today's English, where words still have variant spellings: *judgement* or *judgment, likable* or *likeable, pricy* or *pricey.*

The Great Vowel Shift

For reasons unknown, the long vowels of English have gradually changed since written norms developed. Despite this major change of spoken language, known as **the Great Vowel Shift**, which began in the fifteenth century, the spelling system has remained relatively unchanged. This table shows how English vowels have changed since Old English (OE), Middle English (ME) and Early Modern English (eModE) up to Present-day RP English (PresE). (For RP, see p. 125; for phonetic symbols, see Pronunciation, p. 275.)

	OE	ME	EMODE	PRESE
time	/iː/	/iː/	/əi/	/aɪ/
sweet	/eː/	/eː/	/iː/	/iː/
clean	/æː/	/ɛː/	/eː/	/iː/
stone	/ɑː/	/ɔː/	/oː/	/əʊ/
name	/ɑ/	/aː/	/ɛː/	/eɪ/
moon	/oː/	/oː/	/uː/	/uː/
house	/uː/	/uː/	/əu/	/aʊ/

These massive historical sound changes help to shed light on spelling in today's English. As the Great Vowel Shift affected long vowels only, short vowels in present-day English generally represent something much closer to the original pronunciation of the long vowel, giving us such contrasts as:

'long *i*'	/aɪ/	*five*	'short *i*'	/ɪ/	*fifty*
'long *e*'	/iː/	*meet*	'short *e*'	/e/	*met*
'long *a*'	/eɪ/	*sane*	'short *a*'	/æ/	*sanity*
'long *o*'	/əʊ/	*holy*	'short *o*'	/ɒ/	*holiday*
'long *u, ou*'	/aʊ/	*house*	'short *u*'	/ʌ/	*husband, hustings*

The words on the right are closely related to the words on the left, but the pronunciation of the underlined vowel is quite different, because changes that brought about differences in the length of the vowel have fed into the Great Vowel Shift. Although native speakers sometimes talk about 'long *a*' and 'short *a*', and so on, these are really inaccurate terms, as 'long *i, a, o,* and *u*' have all become diphthongs in the most widely taught accents of current English.

By the Restoration, the written English language was triumphing in learning and in literature, and no longer subservient to Latin and French. John Milton (1608–74) was the last great English poet to write in Latin as well as in his native tongue. Also, scientists like Isaac Newton and philosophers like John Locke began to use English rather than Latin, the traditional language of learning. At the same time, writers became more grammar-conscious and more critical of 'incorrect' usage. A great national language needed to be codified by rules in grammars and dictionaries.

The linguistic model was initially set by John Dryden (1631–1700), author, royal propagandist and poet laureate. He had very firm ideas about the proper form of English, and also criticized the language of Shakespeare and other Elizabethan writers. It is this period that gives birth to some of the precepts about 'good usage' and 'good grammar' which have given English speakers guilty feelings about how they use their language, and which are based on pre-scription rather than actual usage. This practice is not yet defunct, as we can see in today's newspaper columns and books on linguistic etiquette.

Dryden took a particular dislike to sentences ending with a preposition. This appears to be the prime example of grammatical constructions which, for no particular reason, are commonly condemned in popular handbooks.

'This is the sort of English up with which I will not put'

It is said that, when Winston Churchill discovered that his editor had changed all the sentences in his manuscript ending with a preposition, he indignantly returned the proofs to the editor with this marginal note: 'This is the sort of English up with which I will not put'. (The natural word order would be 'This is the sort of English I won't put up with' – and *with* is a preposition.)

Another bone of contention is the 'split infinitive'. Splitting the infinitive means placing one or more words between *to* and the verb, as in Iris Murdoch's: 'I want to really study, I want to be a scholar.' According to the usage guru H. W. Fowler, 'No other grammatical issue has so divided the nation since the split infinitive was declared to be a solecism in the course of the [nineteenth century].' Even if some people still worry about splitting infinitives, the construction is clearly current in outer space and widely familiar through reruns of the television series *Star Trek*, where the opening voice-over of every episode begins: 'To *boldly* go where no man has gone before'.

In Elizabethan England, there had hardly been a standard for written language, and people had spelled and used grammar freely according to their own tastes. Shakespeare and his contemporaries had experimented daringly with the language, yet 100 years later, during the Restoration and after, there was a strong reaction against such unbridled freedom of usage. The intelligentsia was clearly worried: what was happening to the language? Was it changing so fast that future generations would not understand without an interpreter? In the words of the poet Edmund Waller, writing in English was like writing in sand:

> Poets that lasting Marble seek,
> Must carve in Latin or in Greek;
> We write in sand ...

English gains a new domain – the language of science

For centuries, Latin had been the undisputed international language of learning and remained so, at least until the end of the seventeenth century. Nicolaus Copernicus was Polish, Galileo Galilei was Italian, Tycho Brahe was Danish, René Descartes was French, John Ray and Isaac Newton were English, and Carolus Linnaeus was Swedish, but all these scientists and scholars wrote their major works in Latin. In England, however, Newton in 1704 took a pioneering step by publishing his work *Opticks* in English only.

In England the late seventeenth and early eighteenth centuries saw the birth of modern science, associated above all with the name of Isaac Newton. He was an eminent member of the Royal Society, founded in 1660 and a model for the scientific societies or academies which would later be created in many countries. The objectives of the Royal Society were to collect and publish research findings, so that every scientist did not have to 're-invent the wheel'. But the Society was also dedicated to improving the English tongue, and formed a committee for this purpose, including John Dryden and the diarist John Evelyn. Evelyn proposed an orthographic reform, a grammar and a dictionary containing 'all the pure English words', but the plans were shelved.

Isaac Newton

Isaac Newton formulated the laws of nature which were to govern the human conception of the universe for at least 200 years. In the words of his contemporary, the poet Alexander Pope (imitating the story of creation in the Bible, 'And God said, Let there be light: and there was light', Genesis 1:3):

> Nature, and Nature's laws lay hid in night;
> God said, *Let Newton be!* and all was light.

In Dan Brown's blockbuster novel, *The Da Vinci Code*, a riddle alludes to this eulogy to Newton:

> In London lies a knight a Pope interred.
> His labor's fruit a Holy wrath incurred.

The answer to this riddle is that 'a Pope' does not refer to the head of the Roman Catholic Church but to the poet Alexander Pope. However he might appear to the world, of himself Newton said:

> I seem to have been only like a boy playing on the sea-shore, and diverting myself in now and then finding a smoother pebble, or a prettier shell than ordinary, whilst the great ocean of truth lay all undiscovered before me.

'Dictionary Johnson'

In France, the Académie Française was founded in 1635 by Cardinal Richelieu for the principal purpose of standardizing the French language. The most ardent advocate of an English Academy to match the French one was the Irish cleric Jonathan Swift (1667–1745), a great satirist (his most famous work is *Gulliver's Travels*) but also a purist in matters of language. To Swift, all linguistic change spelled corruption:

> But what I have most at Heart is, that some Method should be thought on for *ascertaining* and *fixing* our language for ever, after such Alterations are made in it as shall be thought requisite.

English had to be safeguarded. Shortened words such as *mob* from Latin *mobile vulgus* or *rep* for *reputation* or *incog* for *incognito* gave Swift the shudders. He would certainly have objected to *taxi*, *bus* and *phone*. Any abridgement of verb forms, such as *disturb'd* for *disturbed*, he considered a 'disgrace of our language', and he was horrified at contemporary vogue words like *sham* and *banter*. For Swift, the only remedy to mutilations and innovations by 'illiterate Court Fops, half-witted Poets, and University Boys' was an English Academy.

But Swift's arguments were to no avail. The idea of an English Academy was mulled over for many years but never realized. To the Anglo-Saxon mind, the notion of a body laying down the law for language perhaps felt a bit too French. In Britain or other English-speaking countries, there is still no institution corresponding to the French Academy or any other academy dedicated to 'ascertaining and fixing' the language. However, the debate made problems of language use manifest. More and more people realized the need for an authoritative dictionary.

In 1755 there appeared such a dictionary with the title *A Dictionary of the English Language*. This was the first comprehensive scholarly English dictionary and constituted an important milestone in the history of the language. The author was Samuel Johnson, whose life is extremely well documented thanks mainly to his famous biographer, James Boswell. Johnson, the son of a bookseller from Lichfield in the Midlands, was a student at Oxford but never finished his degree – it is true that he is commonly referred to as 'Dr Johnson', but this title was for an honorary doctorate conferred later. In his early years, things had looked bad: he was no success as a journalist or playwright. Yet despite setbacks and poverty, he made a name for himself in London, mostly from the brilliant conversation he engendered in the city's coffee houses. In his *Plan of a Dictionary* in 1747, Johnson says he intends to write a dictionary 'by which the pronunciation of our language may be fixed, and its attainment facilitated; by which its purity may be preserved, its use ascertained, and its duration lengthened', maintaining that 'all change is of itself evil' . However, in the preface to his dictionary, when completed, he takes an opposite view. Unlike Swift, Johnson had come to realize that languages necessarily undergo change:

> When we see men grow old and die at a certain time one after another, from century to century, we laugh at the elixir that promises to prolong life to a thousand years; and with equal justice may the lexicographer be derided, who being able to produce no example of a nation that has preserved their words and phrases from mutability, shall imagine that his dictionary can embalm his language, and secure it from corruption and decay ...

Yet Johnson's dictionary had an enormous impact and became a landmark for many generations. The spellings used in it have largely remained unchanged today. The dictionary does, however, include certain wayward definitions and examples which are often quoted, such as these:

> *Dull*   *To make dictionaries is* dull *work.*
> *Lexicographer*   A writer of dictionaries; a harmless drudge.
> *Network*   Any thing reticulated or decussated, at equal distances, with interstices between the intersections.
> *Pie*   Any crust baked with something in it.

Even his devoted biographer Boswell admitted that a few of Johnson's definitions were erroneous: 'Thus, *Windward* and *Leeward*, though directly of opposite meaning, are defined identically the same way ...' As a Scotsman, Boswell had to put up with Johnson's strong anti-Scottish prejudices, as shown in this definition of *oats*: 'A grain, which in England is generally given to horses, but in Scotland supports the people'.

The 'End of History'?

As we near the end of this chapter, we are moving away from the strictly historical view of English as an island language, towards an international perspective, where our focus will be on geography as much as on history. There are several reasons for this. One is that the essential ingredients of present-day English had already been determined by 1800. Unlike previous centuries, the nineteenth and twentieth centuries brought no new influences to compare with the profound impact of Old Norse, Norman French, Latin and Greek.

Yet English speakers and writers had grown accustomed to borrowing, and this went on further in the era of European colonial expansion. In fact English, more than other languages, seemed to give a warm welcome to new contacts with foreign languages and cultures. This selection of loanwords from languages beyond Europe testifies to extensive language contacts:

batik (Javanese)	*bazaar* (Persian	*catamaran* (Tamil)
curry (Tamil)	*hookah* (Arabic)	*jaguar* (Tupi-Guarani)
karma (Sanskrit)	*kayak* (Eskimo)	*kibbutz* (Hebrew)
lama (Tibetan)	*orang-outang* (Malay)	*safari* (Swahili)
schmalz (Yiddish)	*sushi* (Japanese)	*taboo* (Tongan)
trek (Afrikaans)	*tsunami* (Japanese)	*typhoon* (Chinese)

Such 'exotic' borrowings were simply an extension of the habit of accepting loanwords that already existed.

But, on the other hand, English has moved from being a language mainly under the influence of others to a language *which influences others*. All around the world, as we will see in Chapter 12, English is impacting on other languages. In the worldwide commerce of vocabulary, English is now primarily a creditor language, not a debtor one.

Science and the expanding English word-hoard

English vocabulary has continued to grow vastly through the last couple of centuries by use of well-established methods of word formation: for example, forming compounds and exploiting Latin and Greek formatives. One of the outstanding developments of this period has been the increase in Latin- and Greek-derived words prompted by scientific progress, and leading to unprecedented proliferation of terminology. A new lexical phenomenon – International Scientific Vocabulary – has emerged from the practice (in English and other European languages) of borrowing learned terms from classical sources. One might say Latin and Greek elements have been turned into a modern word-building kit that can expand the English lexicon indefinitely. Here are some typical results of this process:

cretaceous	*neurosis*	*parthenogenesis*	*trauma*
schizophrenia	*protoplasm*	*pterodactyl*	*psychotherapy*
polyglot	*chlorophyll*	*telepathy*	*anorexia*
nanotechnology	*monolith*	*insectivorous*	*bibliophile*

The process continues apace at the present time, even though Latin and Greek have almost disappeared from the educational curriculum. This hardly affects habits of word-formation, because classical forms like *auto-, proto-, -ology* and *-pathy* have now become living elements in the modern English language. We can even mix the elements from Latin and Greek, forming mongrel words like *television* (*tele-* 'far' from Greek, and *-vision* 'sight' from Latin) which would have horrified Johnson and the purists of an earlier age.

Our second reason for bringing our historical narrative to an end here is that the last 250 years have seen less dramatic changes in the standard language than occurred in earlier times. This is evident in spelling, which has changed very little since the early nineteenth century. Two of the major influences here have been the publication of dictionaries accepted as authoritative, such as Johnson's *Dictionary* of 1755 and Webster's *American Dictionary* of 1828, and the teaching of English reading and writing in schools. The language has not been 'fixed', but it has been **codified**.

Codification of the standard language

What does it mean to *codify* the standard language? It means to reduce it to rule: to explain how it works, where the exceptions are. This can be done **prescriptively**, by laying down the law about how people *should* use the language. It can also be done **descriptively**, by pinning down how the language is used in practice. The chief tools of codification are books such as dictionaries – specifying the vocabulary of the language – and grammars – specifying the morphological and syntactic form of a language; roughly, how words are used to form sentences. In the eighteenth century, the emphasis was on **prescription**: how to 'fix' and 'ascertain' the language (see further pp. 191–205). Nowadays, the emphasis is more on **description** (see p. 64). English is the most studied and codified language in the world, and every year the English language 'industry' ensures that more and more books are published about varied aspects of the language.

Codification leads to a great deal of argument – for example, how should we use the words *will* and *shall*? Should we end a sentence in a preposition? – but overall it leads to convergence in usage, and puts a brake on linguistic change. This shows not only in spelling, but in areas like punctuation and grammar. Similarly, in vocabulary: the word-hoard of the language continues to grow (and to lose some old-fashioned words), but its **core vocabulary** stays much to same.

A final reason for hurrying over the last two centuries at this point is that most of the rest of the book will be devoted to them. The most startling developments in English since the eighteenth century have been connected with its geographical expansion, its dispersion among ever more diverse users and uses, and the enormous variation in the language which has resulted from this. It is no longer easy to see English as a single language: according to one leading commentator, Tom McArthur (see pp. 222–7), English is now not just a *language*, but a new phenomenon – **a language complex**.

Part II

The Spread of English around the World

5
English Goes to the New World

> North America will be peopled with a hundred millions of men, all speaking the same language ... the people of one quarter of the world, will be able to associate and converse together like children of the same family.
>
> Noah Webster, *An Essay on the Necessity, Advantages and Practicality of Reforming the Mode of Spelling* (1789)

> 'Ever'body says words different,' said Ivy. 'Arkansas folks says 'em different, and Oklahoma folks says 'em different. And we seen a lady from Massachusetts, an' she said 'em differentest of all. Couldn' hardly make out what she was sayin'.'
>
> John Steinbeck, *The Grapes of Wrath*

At the end of the nineteenth century, on being asked to name the single greatest fact in modern political history, the German statesman Otto von Bismarck answered: 'The inherent and permanent fact that North America speaks English.'

We have noted a number of crucial events for the development of the English language, such as the coming of Christianity, the Scandinavian settlement, the Norman Conquest and the introduction of printing. But for the role of English today as a world language, the single most important historical factor was surely the coming of the English language to America. We cannot know exactly what was in Bismarck's mind, but we can read his remark as a prophecy about American English and its links to a foreseen military, political, economic, scientific and linguistic dominance of the United States.

When the American Revolution began, John Adams was among the first to propose American independence and, while the war was raging, he predicted that English would become the leading language in the world. In 1780 Adams, one of the Founding Fathers and a future president of the United States, wrote:

> English is destined to be in the next and succeeding centuries more generally the language of the world than Latin was in the last or French is in the present age. The reason for this is obvious, because the increasing population in America, and their universal connection and correspondence with all nations will, aided by the influence of England in the world, whether great or small, force their language into general use …

Adams was right. English was to become the voice of America worldwide. Today, it is claimed, the United States is the only superpower and the language of power is English – American English. Some Europeans still consider the United States a young nation and American English a fresh-faced, unseasoned variety of the language. Yet English has been spoken in America for 400 years, ever since the age of Shakespeare.

This chapter looks into the historical background and development of American English, while the linguistic aspects of contemporary American and British English will be compared in more detail in Chapter 8 (pp. 150–73).

English takes root in America

The English language had only just entered its modern period when it was taken overseas. Towards the end of the sixteenth century, when Shakespeare wrote his first plays and Queen Elizabeth reigned over a few million subjects, England saw herself as a naval power in the making, and this called for expansive geographical expeditions overseas. One of the initiators was the queen's court favourite Sir Walter Ralegh. In the 1580s he sponsored three expeditions to what was then called 'the New World', landing near Roanoke Island on the coast of present-day North Carolina. Arthur Barlowe, who co-captained the first voyage by Ralegh, wrote in 1584:

> The second of July … we viewed the land about us, being, whereas we first land, very sandie and low towards the waters side, but so full of grapes, as the very beating and surge of the Sea overflowed them … This Island had many goodly woodes full of Deere, Conies [rabbits], Hares, and Fowle, even in the middest of Summer in incredible abundance.

All three expeditions failed. Still, the Queen's England was buzzing with yarns and rumours about the enormous riches waiting to be grasped beyond the ocean.

Queen Elizabeth was childless and, on her death in 1603, her crown passed to the King of Scotland, James VI (in England known as James I). This change of monarchs explains why the original settlement of Ralegh's colonists was named

'Virginia' after the 'Virgin Queen' Elizabeth, while the first permanent English settlement from 1607 was named 'Jamestown'. It was here that the English language first took root, planted by a motley crew of colonists: soldiers and adventurers, well-to-do merchants, devout Puritans and deported convicts. (A Puritan was a member of a Protestant group in England opposing as unscriptural the ceremonial worship and the prelacy of the Church of England.)

Most of these settlers came from the south-west of England, from counties like Somerset, bringing with them their characteristic accent where the name of their county is heard as *zummerzet* with *s* voiced and *r* pronounced. A similar pronunciation can still be heard in certain isolated areas like Tangier Island in

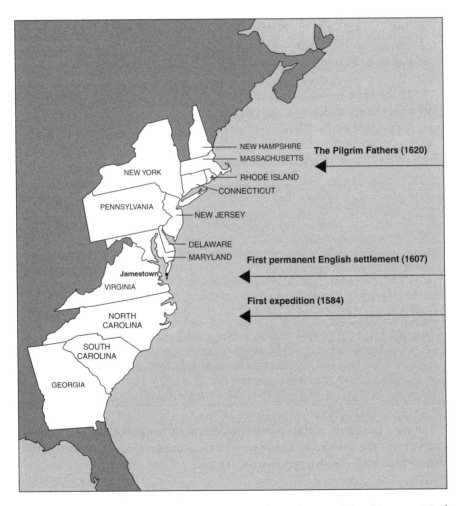

Figure 5.1   Early expeditions to America by English speakers, and the thirteen original states (with their present boundaries)

Chesapeake Bay, not far from the present federal capital, Washington, D.C. There are those who claim that this pronunciation is today as close as we can get to Shakespeare's language.

The colony was situated in a marshy area with high death rates from disease – half the settlers died in the first year. To begin with, the colony proved an extraordinarily bad investment for the owners of Virginia Company of London. Tobacco played an important role in the colony, but it impoverished the soil and made the growers dependent on the fluctuating prices of a single crop. Suspicious by nature and distrusting the colonists' loyalty, King James was not amused by the Virginia experiment. To top it all, he was a pioneer anti-smoking campaigner. As early as 1604 he wrote in *A Counterblast to Tobacco*, a polemical pamphlet:

> A custom loathsome to the eye, hateful to the nose, harmful to the brain, dangerous to the lungs, and in the black, stinking fume thereof, nearest resembling the horrible Stygian smoke of the pit that is bottomless.

In 1624 the King revoked, without ceremony, the charter of the company and placed the colony under royal control. There was no thought of making Virginia an outpost for toleration. But, as rumours kept spreading all around the British Isles of a life across the Atlantic free from religious repression and royal authority, other settlements with other loyalties were later to grow along the American coast.

Guy Fawkes, the Gunpowder Plot and Bonfire Night

Traditionally in England, on the evening of 5 November, bonfires are set alight, effigies are burned and fireworks are set off. Until recently, children could make a bit of money to buy fireworks by showing straw men called *guys*, and shouting 'A penny for the guy' to by-passers in the street.

The story behind this somewhat macabre festivity is the foiling of the attempt in 1605 by a group of conspirators to blow up the King and Parliament in retaliation for repression of Roman Catholics. One of the plotters, Guy Fawkes, was caught redhanded in the cellars of the House of Lords, tortured and executed.

The word *guy* in its modern informal sense of 'fellow, man', as in the title of Norman Mailer's novel *Tough Guys Don't Dance*, is an original American usage, now spreading throughout the English-speaking world. In many parts of the US *you guys* has become accepted as informal second-person plural (see pp. 214–15) and can be used addressing people of either sex, as in *Sorry, guys*; *See you guys later!*

During a large part of the seventeenth century throughout Europe, religious conflict was rife. James I was fully convinced of the sovereign's 'divine right to rule', which included determining the religious affairs of the nation:

> The state of monarchy is the supremest thing upon earth; for kings are not only God's lieutenants upon earth, and sit upon God's throne, but even by God himself they are called gods.

Those of James's subjects who were not members of the Church of England were denied entry to university and appointment to public service. As a result of repression, various religious groups, not only Puritans, chose to leave for foreign shores.

The Pilgrim Fathers

In American history, there is probably no year with such lustre as 1620. Every American schoolchild knows that it was in November of that year that a ship named the *Mayflower* reached land in what is now Massachusetts, with the first group of English Puritans on board. They were aiming for the colony of Virginia but caught rough weather and drifted north. William Bradford, who was to become governor as well as historian of the new settlement of Plymouth, wrote in *Of Plymouth Plantation*:

> after long beating at sea they fell with that land which is called Cape Cod; the which being made and certainly known to be it, they were not a little joyful.

It was a perilous 65-day crossing in a small ship. The colonists on board the *Mayflower* numbered 102, of whom only a minority were members of the English Separatist Church. Strictly speaking, they were not Puritans but Separatists, because they had separated from the Church of England. These first settlers, initially referred to as 'the Old Comers' and later as 'the Forefathers', did not become known as 'the Pilgrim Fathers' until two centuries after their arrival. The Separatists called themselves 'Saints', while the others on board were simply called 'Strangers'.

Before disembarking, all the men signed a document drafted by the leaders of the enterprise, promising obedience to the laws and ordinances. This *Mayflower Compact* was the first effort to establish formal self-government in the New World, and has sometimes been accorded great significance in the constitutional history of the United States. Some historians claim that this document became the basis of the Declaration of Independence. Others are more sceptical and claim that a small number of Pilgrims seized power and governed the Plymouth colony for the next 40 years. In 1629 it became part of the Massachusetts Bay colony. As 15,000 new immigrants arrived during the first 20 years, the colony proved successful. The founders never intended to create a society based on religious tolerance, but rather a 'Zion in the wilderness'. However, discontented colonists soon began to move out. Present-day neighbouring states, such as Connecticut and Rhode Island, were founded by settlers who disliked the religious and political inflexibility of Massachusetts.

Still, New England, the joint name of the colonies, was not a misnomer: practically all the early colonists hailed from England.

The slave trade

In 1619, the year before the *Mayflower* arrived in America, a Dutch ship called at Jamestown and sold some 20 black Africans to the colonists. There was a need for cheap labour on the plantations where tobacco, sugar and, later, cotton were grown. The trade grew fast, serving not only British colonies, but those of other European powers in the New World. In 1681 there were some 2,000 slaves in Virginia, but by the mid-nineteenth century, the slave population in America had risen to more than four million. This trade, in one of the vilest episodes in history, went on for almost two centuries. In the United States, slavery was finally ended in 1865 with the passage of the thirteenth Amendment to the Constitution.

  The slave trade had unforeseen consequences for the English language, as will be seen in Chapters 8 and 9 (pp. 169–72, 176–86).

The first Americanisms

The early Plymouth settlers' first winter was harsh and, without help from the native population, they would probably have starved to death. Most of them were far from cut out for a life in the wilderness. By April 1621, when the *Mayflower* set sail back to England, only 54 people were still alive. But they learned from the natives how to grow a crop whose name had previously entered their language as *maize*. In America, however, they called it *corn* – a word that may claim to be called the first Americanism, or term typical of English in America. Generally speaking, *corn* is the name applied to the most important local crop, and in England that was normally wheat or rye. To the early Americans, however, it was maize. The Pilgrims tried to grow English wheat, but without success. In the colonies, wheat would remain a luxury for the better part of two centuries.

  A few months after their arrival in America, the colonists made friends with two native Americans, Samoset and Tisquantum, who helped them to establish friendly relations with the local chief, to plant corn and, most important, to assist with communication: the surprising fact was that they could speak English. That proved a boon to the newcomers, because they would have found it tough to master the eastern tribes' language which belonged to the extremely complex language family called Algonquian (see p. 78). It is significant that they even found the name of Tisquantum so difficult that they renamed him Squanto. His life story reads, in the words of Bill Bryson, like 'an implausible picaresque novel'. In 1605 Squanto had been picked up by a seafarer and carried off to England where he worked for nine years, but was brought back to the new world in the capacity of interpreter during a mapping expedition. Squanto was then reunited with his tribe but was sold into slavery and served as a house servant in Spain before managing to get to London. Finally, he returned to his New England home with another exploratory expedition, two years before the

Pilgrims' landing. Squanto's remarkable presence at the right time was described by the leading Pilgrim, Governor William Bradford, as 'a special instrument of God'.

Some 150 years later, New England would become the hotbed of the American Revolution. One reason why 1620 is such a prominent year in American history is the nation-building influence of the descendants of these first immigrants. But there is another special reason for the bright lustre of this place and time. After the first harvest in 1621, Governor Bradford proclaimed a day of thanksgiving and prayer, shared by all the colonists and the neighbouring native population. Much later, in 1863, President Abraham Lincoln proclaimed a day of thanksgiving, and since then each president has issued a Thanksgiving Day proclamation, generally designating the fourth Thursday of November as a holiday. It has become the most important national holiday in the United States – possibly excepting Independence Day, the Fourth of July – since it embraces all Americans, irrespective of religion or ethnic background. The traditional staple of Thanksgiving dinner is turkey and, every November, some 45 million turkeys have to pay with their lives – the one day in the year when we know what some 200 million Americans are up to: they eat turkey, stuffing, cranberry sauce and pumpkin pie.

The fate of the cultures of the American indigenous population is one of the great tragedies in world history. At the time of European contact, there were perhaps as many as 240 different tribal entities in North America, and it is estimated that the indigenous population totalled some ten million. When colonists began keeping records, the native population had been drastically reduced to about one million by war, famine, forced labour and epidemics of diseases introduced through contact with Europeans.

The older English name of the American indigenous population is *Indians* (see p. 172) but today the preferred term is *Native Americans*, and we will henceforth use this name. Most tribes simply called themselves 'The People' or 'The people living here'. Many of the tribe names are distorted versions of sobriquets used by tribes for their neighbours. The outstanding characteristic of Native American languages is their diversity. According to some studies, there were more than 60 language families in North America alone, but these have now been reduced to about 35. Today, many of the Native American languages have few speakers left and are endangered or dying. Among the most important Native American language families now surviving are:

Athabaskan with 150,000 Navaho speakers in Arizona, Utah and New Mexico
Algonquian with 126,000 speakers in Montana, Canada, Michigan, Minnesota and North Dakota
Iroquoian with 22,500 speakers in Oklahoma and North Carolina
Muskogean with 9,200 speakers in Oklahoma, Mississippi and Louisiana

The Native Americans with whom the English first came into contact belonged to three language families: Iroquoian, Algonquian and Muskogean. The five original Iroquoian nations were Mohawk, Oneida, Onondaga, Cayuga and Seneca. One of the largest language families was Algonquian, including Arapaho, Cree, Cheyenne, Mohikan, Chippewa, Delaware, Shawnee, Fox and Potowatomi. Formerly inhabiting the Atlantic coastal region, members of the Algonquian family, such as the Blackfoot and Cheyenne, were later also found in the Great Plains.

Wherever the immigrants went, their newly adopted land looked very different from the English countryside, so they had to make the language fit the landscape. To describe the flora and fauna, the colonists formed compounds using familiar English elements: *mockingbird, catfish, blue jay, peanut* and *egg plant*. Words were also given new senses: in Britain the meaning of *frontier* is 'a boundary between two countries', but in America *frontier* soon came to take on the additional meaning of 'a region just beyond or at the edge of a settled area' (see p. 85).

Words adopted from Native American languages

American speakers of English adopted many loanwords from Native American languages. Here are some:

Animals
chipmunk a small, striped terrestrial squirrel
moose a large mammal with antlers
opossum a marsupial (a very early loan, first recorded in 1610)
raccoon (also *racoon*) a carnivorous mammal with a black, masklike face

Plants
pecan a deciduous tree with walnut-like edible nuts
persimmon a tree with orange-red fruits that are edible only when completely ripe
squash the fruit of Cucurbita

Cultural terms
moccasin a soft leather slipper traditionally worn by certain Native American peoples (recorded from 1612)
squaw a Native American woman (now offensive slang)
wigwam a Native American dwelling commonly having an arched or conical framework overlaid with bark, hides, or mats

---

Linguistic variety and uniformity in the United States

Historically, the settling of the United States with immigrant peoples conveniently falls into three periods corresponding to political and social events of important consequence for the English language.

First, the *Colonial Period*, from the settlement of Jamestown in 1607 to the end of colonial times. This may be put at 1790 when the last of the colonies ratified the Constitution and the first census was taken.

The *National Expansion Period* extends from 1790 to 1865 with the expansion of the original thirteen States (see Figure 5.1, p. 73) into the south and later into the Old Northwest Territory, eventually ending up at the Pacific. The latter part of this period saw a major influx of Irish, Scots and Germans, three large groups of immigrants.

During the *Third Period* – from 1865 (at the end of the American Civil War) to 1929, when the immigration laws were changed – immigration changed in both character and composition. In the first two periods the vast majority of newcomers were slaves from Africa or free immigrants from the British Isles and the countries of Northern Europe. In the third period, especially after 1890, almost three quarters of the immigrants hailed from Southern and Eastern Europe.

Despite mass immigrations during the second and third periods, it was the first period that was the most important for the development of the English language in America. The early English-speaking immigrants and their descendants remained politically and culturally dominant, while the later immigrants, although largely assimilated in a generation or two, often had to learn English as a foreign language. They generally lost their native language in a span of two or three generations. In the 1920s H. L. Mencken, journalist and author, noted: 'In cities such as Cleveland and Chicago it is a rare second-generation American of Polish, Hungarian or Croatian stock who even pretends to know his parents' native language.' The United States became in fact 'a veritable cemetery of foreign languages'.

One thing we notice, comparing the varieties of English now spoken in the United States compared with those in Britain, is that there is relatively little variation between one speaker and another, sometimes even if they live on opposite sides of the vast American continent. By contrast, Great Britain, where English has been established for 1500 years, shows noticeable differences between the speech of neighbouring counties or even neighbouring cities (as we will see in more detail in Chapter 7). To take an extreme case, one of the present authors has had the experience of taking a two-and-a-half hour train journey north from Lancaster to Glasgow, and finding the speech of his taxi-driver, a friendly conversationalist, totally incomprehensible. To take the opposite case, a native of California can speak to a native of Ohio, born and brought up 2,000 miles to the east, without either of them noticing differences of dialect or accent between them.

This difference is not difficult to explain. Over the centuries, most people in the British Isles have spent all their lives in the localities where they were born. Until the nineteenth century, there was comparatively little movement and mixing of population, even though the British Isles are small enough to fit comfortably inside the single American state of Texas. But in the United States, where the nineteenth century saw an enormous expansion and movement of the English-speaking population, a life of exploring new opportunities in new regions has been traditional and normal. By the standards of world history, the new states of the Midwest and the Far West were settled in an amazingly short period of time, aided by the speed of transportation by rail. It is no surprise that the areas of the United States that do show noticeable variation of dialect are close to the eastern seaboard, in the thirteen original states that won independence from Britain. These states were settled before the advent of modern communications, and in them are the well-known dialectal areas (see Figure 5.2, p. 81) of New England (the Northeast) and the Southern States (the 'Old South').

Throughout the seventeenth century, ships from Europe brought immigrants to the North American seaboard. Many Quakers from the Midlands and northern England settled in Pennsylvania, and the city of Philadelphia soon became the most populous community in the British colonies.

Early in the eighteenth century came a large influx of Germans, many of them from persecuted religious groups. In the main, they settled on the rich farmland between Philadelphia and the Blue Mountains, a region that later became known as 'Pennsylvania Dutch country'. Living in close-knit and rural religious communities, some of the immigrants retained their High German dialect, which generally – but mistakenly – is known as 'Pennsylvania Dutch' (*Pennsylfawnish Deitsch*). In American English, *Dutch* was applied not just to the language of Holland but also to what was felt as bewilderingly foreign – the German language – doubtless partly through the influence of the German word *Deutsch*. To linguists the dialect is known as 'Pennsylvania German'.

Beginning in 1720s, large numbers of Scots-Irish, descended from Scots who had settled in northern Ireland in the early seventeenth century, arrived in Philadelphia. In 1760 it was estimated that the city was one-third English, one-third Scots-Irish and one-third German. With the best land already in English possession, many Scots-Irish immigrants settled in the mountain valleys beyond the German belt. Their children became pioneers who carved farm-steads out of a virgin landscape in the west, and their broad Scots-Irish accent was one of the first to cross the Mississippi. In 1776, when the thirteen original states declared themselves independent, some 10 per cent of all Americans were thought to have been Scots-Irish. The first census taken in 1790 showed that the ex-colonial population of America had grown to about four million people, most of them living on the Atlantic seaboard. By 1880 the population of the United States had increased more than tenfold.

At the time of the American Revolution, the majority of English speakers in the world still lived in the British Isles. But a century later the situation had changed: the largest English-speaking population was in North America. Today, two out of three native speakers of English speak the language with an American accent.

American voices: a preview

As we have already noted, compared to the situation in the British Isles, there is far less regional variation of pronunciation in the United States. But the uniformity of American voices should not be overplayed: recent surveys of American accents have revealed a more complex picture than has been assumed as we will see later (pp. 239–41).

Pronunciation varies most along the Eastern seaboard, where the first immigrants settled, and becomes progressively more uniform as we move westwards. In the traditional division, also widely recognized by Americans in general, there are three main regional accents: **Northeastern**, **Southern** and **General American.**

The *Northeastern* accent is spoken in New England and New York State, not including New York City. A famous Eastern voice was that of President John F. Kennedy who had a so-called 'Boston Brahmin accent' (not a general Boston accent), dropping the *r* (by phoneticians called **r-dropping** or **non-rhotic accent**) in words like *vigor* /'vɪgə/, *car* /kɑ:/ and *card* /kɑ:d/. Other Americans could laugh at this trait, rendering *Park the car in Harvard Yard* as *Pahk the cah in Hahvahd yahd*. Most Americans would pronounce *r* in this position, but r-dropping after vowels is a feature the Northeast shares with much of the South.

The *Southern* accent is spoken from Virginia down to all points southwest as far as Texas. This dialect is also non-rhotic, and well-known among Americans for its slower delivery and its tendency to form diphthongs where pure vowels are found in other accents. A user of this accent is sometimes popularly described, by non-southerners, as having a 'Southern drawl'. The term especially reflects the Southern habit of lengthening

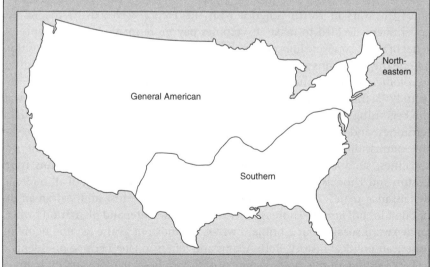

Figure 5.2   Main accent areas in the United States (compare Figure 12.2, p. 240)

vowels in stressed syllables, and turning them into diphthongs in words like *man* /mæɪn/, *lip* /lɪəp/ and *your* /joə/. Contrary to this diphthongizing tendency, however, the Southerner tends to produce a pure vowel in words like *I* and *my*, so that in popular representations these first person forms are written *Ah, ma*.

In the rest of the country there are no dramatic differences of accent, but sometimes a **Midland accent** is recognized for the east-coast region separating the Northeastern from the Southern, including Philadelphia and Pittsburgh and fanning out westward to include a large swathe of midland United States. Also some dialectologists make various other distinctions between 'north central' and 'the inland north', and so on (see further pp. 239–41). But necessarily oversimplifying at this point, we move on to our third accent.

General American is the term we can use, for convenience, for what is spoken in the rest of the country, apart from the Northeast and the South, that is to say by most Americans – although it is not a single unified accent. This pronunciation (henceforth shortened to GA) can be considered a standard variety in the sense that it is has no marked regional characteristics. In that respect it is somewhat comparable to RP in Britain, but unlike RP, it has no significant connotation of eliteness. Another term sometimes used is **Network English**, for a relatively region-neutral accent heard in broadcasting. A typical GA speaker was former president Ronald Reagan, nicknamed 'the great communicator', who started his career as a radio announcer and movie actor before going into politics. Although some people argue that GA and Network English are different, we will not attempt to distinguish between them here. Since GA is the most widespread American pronunciation it is the most useful kind of American accent to take a closer look at and to use as our 'reference accent' in this book. A list of phonetic symbols for transcribing GA, as compared with the British RP accent, is given on pp. 275–6. See also the comparison of the two accents on pp. 163–6.

The American Revolution

Since the wars in North America with the French were costly, the British government decided to make its colonies pay more for their own defence. A series of new taxes were imposed on the colonies. This aroused heated opposition among the Americans and a perception that the mother country was insensitive to colonial opinion – and spurred a growing desire for independence.

In 1775 the Second Continental Congress met in Philadelphia. That was the beginning of the American Revolution, which was more about ideas than territories and boundary disputes. George Washington was chosen to be the commanding general of the militia. Among the delegates were brilliant personalities, such as Benjamin Franklin from Philadelphia, John Adams from Boston and Thomas Jefferson from Virginia. Franklin was a jack of all trades, a Renaissance man – labels like publicist, diplomat, scientist and statesman do not do him full justice. Thomas Jefferson – lawyer, writer and plantation owner, an awkward speaker but a brilliant writer – stands out as the leading figure in American political history. Both Adams and Jefferson later became presidents.

As the split with the mother country of Britain became more and more irreconcilable, the Continental Congress adopted the Declaration of Independence in 1776. The purpose of this document was to justify proclaiming independence for the thirteen British colonies in America. Those who signed the Declaration of Independence understood the power of language to shape national consciousness. Expressions in the document like 'all men are created equal' are familiar to every American:

> We hold these truths to be self-evident, that all men are created equal, that they are endowed by their Creator with certain unalienable Rights, that among these are Life, Liberty and the pursuit of Happiness …

The Declaration was drafted by Thomas Jefferson since he, in the words of John Adams, had 'a happy talent of composition'. July the fourth, when the Congress endorsed its wording, is celebrated in the United States as the great national holiday, Independence Day.

Many Americans wanted to break with the mother country, in language as well. Some patriots proposed revenge on Great Britain by adopting French. Some even proposed Greek, but that was rejected on the grounds that 'it would be more convenient for us to keep the language as it was, and make the English speak Greek'. Most people in the young republic realized that the mother tongue could not be sent back to the mother country. But there was also a general notion that English in America should be 'improved and perfected' and given

---

Yankee

Nobody knows with certainty the origin of the word *Yankee*, but there are many interesting theories. Some believe it is derived from the Dutch *Janke*, in the seventeenth century a common nickname for *Jan* and a diminutive of *Johannes*.

James Fenimore Cooper, the American novelist, claimed that *Yankee* came from *Yengeese*, which was how Native Americans pronounced *English*.

According to another view, *Yankees* comes from *Jan Kees* – 'John Cheese' in English – a Dutch nickname for a British settler. Others agree that *John* is often rendered as *Jan* in Dutch, while *Kees* is actually short for *Cornelis* which is also a very common Dutch first name. They point to the antagonism between the landed gentry, mostly English, Irish and Scots, in the Southern states, and Dutch business people living along the Hudson River. At some point, people of primarily British extraction began referring to the Dutch as *those Jan-Kees*, hence *Yankees*.

Whatever the origin, *Yankee* is first recorded in 1765 as a name for an inhabitant of New England. The use of the term by the British to refer to Americans in general first appears in the 1780s in a letter by the famous British naval commander Horatio Nelson. More recently in countries other than the US *Yanks* or *Yankees* has been a familiar and sometimes rather disparaging term used about Americans by non-Americans.

Americans rarely use *Yankee* about themselves unless referring to a *New Englander* for a native of New England (or to the New York baseball team). In the South it is sometimes used with reference to any Northerner. An old southern joke divides the nation into three categories: Southerners, Yankees and Damyankees [i.e. Damn Yankees].

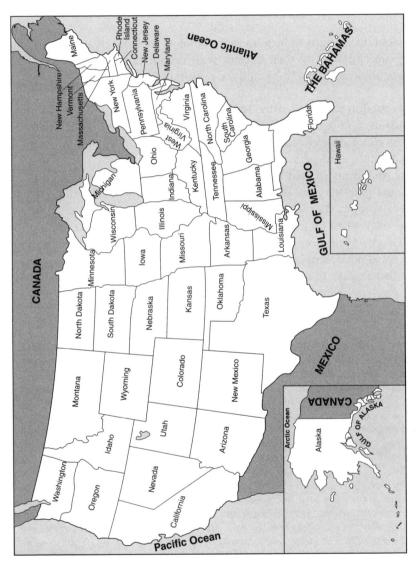

Figure 5.3 Map of the United States

its own identity. To this end John Adams (following Jonathan Swift's earlier example, see p. 64) proposed an academy: just as a constitution was necessary to prevent a government from becoming corrupt, so an academy was necessary to maintain the good health of the language. However, his proposal did not gain a hearing and, to this day, there is no academy in the United States with an official brief to regulate American English.

America, the United States, the US, the USA

The name *America* comes from Amerigo Vespucci, an Italian navigator who sailed under the Spanish flag and around 1500 explored the Atlantic coast of today's South America. *America*, or more aptly *the Americas*, actually refers to the whole of the American continent, including North America, Central America and South America.

Unofficially *American*, *Americans* refer to the people of the country we have been discussing in this chapter. Its official name is *the United States of America*, but the common terms are *the United States* (as in *the United States government*) or the abbreviation *the U.S.* (as in *a U.S. citizen*; in British texts usually written without periods: *the US*). A more informal term among Americans is *the States*, and the broad term *America* itself is sometimes used for the USA. Oddly, though, to many Americans the abbreviation *USA*, which is common in other languages in referring to the US, has a ring of nationalism (even jingoism), suggesting proud Olympic teams or commercial slogans like 'Made in the USA'.

Finally, a note on grammar: in the early days of the nation, *the United States* was treated as a plural, but now both *the United States* and *the US* take a singular verb: 'The United States *has* appointed a new Ambassador to Germany'.

The frontier moves further west

The frontier was pushing westward. After the Revolution, the government of the new nation encouraged expansion into what became known as 'the Old Northwest' – the area encompassing the present-day states of Ohio, Indiana, Illinois, Michigan, Wisconsin and part of Minnesota. Most of the people who settled in this region came from the east – Pennsylvania, New York, New Jersey and the New England states – although a large number moved north, out of Kentucky and Virginia. In 1803 'the Louisiana Purchase' from France doubled the size of the United States and opened up vast territories west of the Mississippi to pioneers, trappers and missionaries (see Figure 5.3, p. 84).

The United States rapidly pushed its frontier to the Pacific Ocean through annexation, diplomacy, technology and war. It was only a matter of time before the nation stretched from coast to coast. In 1850, when California was admitted as the 31st state of the Union, its non-indigenous population was about 150,000. But, within one year, this population grew to a quarter of a million, including the people who, in their quest for gold, had flocked from all corners of the continent.

Samuel Langhorne Clemens, alias Mark Twain (1835–1910) was the first American writer to win worldwide acclaim. He is best known for the books where he returned to the river banks of his childhood: *The Adventures of Tom Sawyer* and *The Adventures of Huckleberry Finn*. In his book *The Green Hills of Africa* Ernest Hemingway writes:

> All modern American literature comes from one book by Mark Twain called *Huckleberry Finn* ... It's the best book we've had. All American writing comes from that. There was nothing before. There has been nothing as good since.

Mark Twain's youth reads like a piece of American history. Born in 1835, he grew up in Hannibal, Missouri, on the west bank of the Mississippi river. In those days the river was the very frontier, and the government had begun to transfer the Native Americans west of the Mississippi. Twain left school at the age of 13, about the same age as the fictional Huckleberry Finn. After a few years as a compositor he returned to the river and became a licensed pilot. A roving life was, in fact, typical of nineteenth-century America.

In 1867, as the nation was nursing its wounds after the Civil War, a young livestock dealer from Chicago named Joseph McCoy struck it rich. Knowing there was a growing demand for beef in the North, he offered Texan ranchers $40 for every head of longhorn cattle driven to the new railhead in Abilene, Kansas. From Abilene the cattle were then shipped to feed the cities of the North and East. This livestock trade, full of tedium and economic exploitation, gave rise to the most romanticized period in American history. The *cowboy* attained immortality as the great hero of the West in melodramatic adventure stories known as 'dime novels'.

Spanish in America

Spanish has been spoken longer than English in what is now the United States, beginning in 1565 with the first Spanish settlement in San Agustin, Florida and later extending to areas in present-day New Mexico and California.

Early Spanish loanwords into English from the sixteenth century include *armada*, *cargo*, *mosquito*, *sombrero*. Later loans from Spanish – many of them Native American terms adopted by the Spaniards – were usually somewhat adapted when taken over by English, for example: *canoe* (compare Spanish *canoa*), *cocoa* (altered form of Spanish *cacao*, from Nahuatl), *hammock* (compare Spanish *hamaca*), *hurricane* (compare Spanish *huracán*), *potato* (compare Spanish *patata*), *tobacco* (compare Spanish *tabaco*), *tomato* (compare Spanish *tomate*).

Yet the cowboy did not ride into town from nowhere. His lineage goes back to the first European invasion of the Americas, as testified by the large number of Spanish loanwords in the lingo of western cattle raising. The first cattle in

America – six heifers and a young bull of Andalusian stock – were put ashore in 1521 in Vera Cruz, so no doubt the first American cattle hand actually spoke Spanish. He was called a *vaquero*, literally 'cow handler', later Englished to *buckaroo*. In the early nineteenth century English-speaking pioneers moving into the south and west encountered the *vaquero*, and some learned to master his skills. In time the pioneers adopted his clothes and tools, enriching the English language with *chaps* for leather leggings joined by a belt or lacing and worn over the trousers from American Spanish *chaparreras, poncho* meaning 'cape', *lasso* (also called *lariat*) from *lazo* 'loop', and *quirt* from *cuarta* 'whip'. The broad-brimmed, high-crowned cowboy hat of western movies is not named *a ten-gallon hat* for its capacity to hold liquid. It probably takes its name from Spanish *galón* 'braid' which is wrapped in rows above the brim. The cowboys learned to round up the cattle in a pen known as a *corral*. Contacts with *vaqueros* and other Spanish-speakers also gave the English language words such as these:

adobe 'a sun-dried brick' or 'a house made of adobe' (The word has a long history: it is of Egyptian origin and comes from the Coptic word for 'brick'. In Arabic it became *attob*, which via Spanish became English *adobe*. Today Adobe® is also the name of a software company.)
bronco 'rough, wild'
chaparral 'a dense impenetrable thicket of shrubs or dwarf trees'
mesa 'a broad terrace with an abrupt slope on one side'
mustang (from *mestengo* meaning 'stray animal') 'a small hardy naturalized horse of western plains directly descended from horses brought in by the Spaniards'
pueblo usually 'a Native American village of the south-western United States'
ranch (from *rancho* 'small farm') 'a large farm for raising horses, beef cattle, or sheep'
ranchero 'one who owns or works on a ranch'
rodeo 'a public performance featuring bronco riding, calf roping, and steer wrestling' from the verb *rodear* 'to surround'
stampede (from Spanish *estampida* 'explosion') was used to describe a sudden rush of cattle, but was also later applied to miners rushing westward to find gold
vigilante 'a member of a volunteer committee organized to suppress and punish crime, a self-appointed doer of justice'

The legacy of Spanish in American English recalls the earlier history of Spanish colonialization, particularly in the states of Texas, New Mexico and California. Nowadays Hispanics are the most populous minority community in the United States: American speakers of Spanish number over 10 per cent of the population, and this percentage is increasing. Recent cultural trends are reflected in food terms which have their own story to tell: *chili* 'a hot pepper of any of a group of cultivars', *tortilla* 'a thin round of unleavened cornmeal or wheat flour bread usually eaten hot with a topping or filling' and *cafeteria* 'a retail coffee shop'; *machismo* 'a strong sense of masculine pride' and *macho* 'characterized by machismo, assertively virile'.

On 24 January 1848 James Marshall, in charge of constructing a sawmill in California, shouted to his workers, 'Boys, by God I believe I have found a gold mine!' This marked the beginning the California Gold Rush. The cry of 'Gold!' spread like wildfire throughout the nation. People went crazy. Blacksmiths, masons, bakers, doctors and storekeepers alike – many of them easterners ill-suited for a life in the wilderness – all rushed to California, today called the Golden State. At that time, Gold Rush California was probably the most multicultural spot on the globe. In a letter to his wife, a doctor wrote: 'Neither the Crusades nor Alexander's expedition to India can ever equal this emigration to California.'

Even if, for most prospectors, the gold turned to sand, many words from the goldfields passed into the general vocabulary. A *pan* was a round shallow

Some milestones in the history of the United States' expansion	
1763	By the Treaty of Paris in 1763, France cedes to Great Britain all its North American possessions east of the Mississippi, with the exception of New Orleans. Antagonism grows between the colonies and the mother country.
1775–83	The American Revolution (the term preferred by American historians, but also known as The War of Independence) leads to the formation of the independent United States.
1776	The thirteen British colonies on the Atlantic seaboard declare their independence.
1783	Great Britain recognizes its former thirteen colonies as free and sovereign.
1789	The Constitution of the United States of America is ratified. George Washington becomes the first president of the first republic of the modern world.
1803	At a stroke, 'the Louisiana Purchase' doubles the size of the United States.
1819	For five million dollars, Spain agrees to cede Florida to the United States.
1830	The Indian Removal Act results in the uprooting of entire peoples from their homelands and their forced resettlement beyond the Mississippi.
1842	The pioneer wagon trains start to roll along the Oregon Trail, the overland route from Missouri to Oregon.
1846	The war with Mexico adds substantial territory to the United States, confirming Texas as part of the Union. The Northwest Boundary Dispute with Britain is settled by the Oregon Treaty.
1861–65	The American Civil War, also known as 'The War between the States', results in the defeat of the southern secessionist states, and the abolition of slavery.
1869	The rails of the Union Pacific, reaching westward, and of the Central Pacific Railroad, reaching eastward, meet up at Promontory, Utah, completing coast-to-coast communication.
1896	Utah becomes the 45th State of the Union.
1907	Oklahoma becomes the 46th State, thus completing the mosaic of states between the Atlantic and the Pacific.

container for separating gold from waste by washing, so the gold was *panned* in a river. This gave the verb *pan out* 'turn out well, be successful' as in Saul Bellow's 'If I don't pan out as an actor I can still go back to school'. *Bonanza*, a word familiar from many westerns, entered American English from Spanish where it means 'prosperity' or literally 'good weather'. It is now part of everyday speech, enlarging its meaning from 'a rich mine or pocket of ore' to any source of great wealth or prosperity. We can *stake out a claim*, an expression which goes back to the way the miner marked out his plot of land with stakes. *Strike* in the sense of 'a sudden and valuable discovery' spawned *big strike, lucky strike, strike it rich*.

New Americans

By the time the original thirteen states had won their independence, Philadelphia was the largest city in the Republic. But the opening of the Erie Canal in 1825 – the inland waterway to the Great Lakes, from Buffalo on the eastern shore of Lake Erie to Albany on the upper Hudson River, a distance of almost 400 miles – made New York the port of entry for the largest migration in history. The Erie Canal proved to be the key that unlocked an enormous series of social and economic changes in the young nation. The Canal spurred the first great westward movement of American settlers, gave access to the rich land and resources west of the Appalachians and made New York the pre-eminent commercial city in the United States. At the beginning of the nineteenth century, the Allegheny Mountains were the Western Frontier. Year after year they came: from Ireland, Scotland, Germany, Russia, Poland, Scandinavia, Italy ... No wonder the word *immigrant* itself is American, coined in 1789 – previously *emigrant* had been used for all migrants.

Despite the large number of immigrants in the third period, their influence on the English language was limited because they were largely non-English-speaking. Most of them had to learn English to survive. Many German immigrants settled in cities such as Cincinnati (Ohio), Milwaukee (Wisconsin), and St Louis (Missouri). Through German immigrants American English acquired words like *cookbook* (from *Kochbuch*), *delicatessen* (plural of *Delikatesse* 'delicacy', now shortened to *deli*) and *kindergarten* literally 'children's garden'. The typical American expression *no way* 'by no means' is said to be a translation of German *keineswegs*.

Between 1865 and 1920 more than five million Italians arrived in the United States. Three-fourths of all Italian immigrants came from regions south of Rome. Many went into the restaurant business. In *trattorie*, small family-run restaurants, they transformed Italian specialties into popular foods and beverages that have found their way into the everyday language of food, notably *pizza, spaghetti, lasagna, pasta* and *zucchini*. The first pizza in the United States, or so the story goes, was served in 1905 at G. Lombardi's on Spring Street in New York City.

Another large group of immigrants consisted of three million East European Jews, especially from Poland and Russia, who landed between 1880 and 1910. Many of the East and Central European Jews ended up on the Lower East Side of Manhattan, where English was treated almost as a foreign language. Excluded from the more established avenues of advancement, many American Jews moved into the entertainment business. Practically all the early Hollywood studios were run by a small group of poor and uneducated eastern European Jews who had arrived in the New World in the 1880s.

Some Jewish descendants still speak Yiddish, a Germanic language with Hebrew and Slavic elements that is usually written in Hebrew characters. To its speakers it is known as *mame-loshn* 'mother tongue'. Isaac Bashevis Singer, the most widely read writer in Yiddish, helped to preserve it as a literary language. The Yiddish-English – or 'yinglish' – culture which grew up in New York enriched the English language with caustic expressions, such as *Scram!* and *Get lost!* Yiddish influence is also apparent in the vernacular use of *already* as an intensifier: *Enough already! Let's eat already!* A good number of English Yiddish loanwords begin with sound combinations such as *shl-*, *shm-* and *shn-*, not found in native English words. Here are a few more words from Yiddish:

The Yiddish word legacy

bagel from *beygl* 'a ring-shaped roll with a chewy texture'
blintz from *blintse* 'a thin, rolled blini filled with cottage cheese' [a *blini* is a thin buckwheat pancake usually filled and folded]
chutzpah from *khutspe* 'effrontery'
kibitz from *kibitsen* 'to look on and offer unwanted, usually meddlesome advice to others', 'to chat, converse'
lox from *laks* 'smoked salmon'
mazuma from *mazume* 'money, cash'
meshuga or *meshugga* from *meshuge* 'crazy, senseless'
nosh from *nash* 'a snack or light meal'
schlep from *shlepn* 'move slowly or laboriously', 'clumsy or stupid person'
schlock from *shlak* 'cheap, shoddy'
shmuck from *shmok* 'a clumsy or stupid person'

English goes to Canada

In 1497, five years after Christopher Columbus discovered 'the New World' for Europeans, a Venetian mariner by the name of Giovanni Caboto – or John Cabot, as history knows him since he was sailing under an English flag – sought a westward sea route to the wealthy empires known to exist in Asia. In May 1497 he set sail from Bristol with a crew of 18 and sighted land after more than four weeks at sea. So where did they make landfall? Cabot himself was convinced that they had reached the north-east coast of Asia. Actually, their exact landing place has never been established. It may have been southern Labrador or Cape Breton Island or Newfoundland. Be that as it may, Cabot was soon followed by others and, well into the eighteenth century, hopeful explorers looked for navigable channels that might form a water route to Asia. All these explorations helped to map Canada and open up its vast natural resources to people in Europe. Europe's hatters discovered that beaver hair, when shaved and matted into a stiff felt, was the finest hat-making material available. The fur trade, destined to be the backbone of the Canadian economy for some 200 years, was born.

It is actually likely that, by the time Cabot set sail, fishermen from Bristol had already discovered the cod-rich waters off south-east Newfoundland. English, French, Spanish and Portuguese fishermen came to catch cod on the shallow, bountiful Grand Banks, often drying their catch ashore. In 1583 the English adventurer Sir Humphrey Gilbert arrived at the busy St John's harbour in Newfoundland and found it teeming with English, French, Portuguese and Spanish fishing vessels. In the Queen's name Gilbert took possession of St John's and 200 miles of the coast on either side, establishing there the first English-speaking colony in North America. So the English language has a long history in Canada. But the cod fisheries have been fished to extinction.

Cartier and Canada

In 1534 the King of France dispatched Jacques Cartier to seek a Northwest Passage to India in the region Cabot had previously explored. Sailing beyond Newfoundland, Cartier found the Gulf of Saint Lawrence where he met Iroquoians who told him of wealthy kingdoms in the north, one of them being *Canada*, as recorded by Cartier in his journal. Yet during his three voyages to the Gulf he found no such kingdoms and no Northwest Passage. A widely held belief is that Canada derives its name from the word *kanata*, which in Huron, an Iroquoian language, meant 'village' or 'community'. Today, ironically, Canada is geographically the second-largest country in the world.

When the French government saw the potential value of the fur trade, the fishing industry and other resources of northern America, it began to take a greater interest in the region, which came to be known as *New France*. In 1663, New France became a royal province, and French colonization of the Saint Lawrence area began in earnest. During the first decade of royal rule, the Crown subsidized immigration from France, but after that immigration was modest. The 10,000 settlers reported in the 1681 census were the forerunners of today's 6.7 million French-speaking Canadians.

After 1670, however, there appeared a major new player in the fur trade, when the English Crown granted a trade monopoly to the Hudson's Bay Company.

While the first English footholds in future Canada were purely commercial, the French combined the fur trade with exploration and missionary work. They began exploring the Mississippi River and, in 1682, reached as far as the Gulf of Mexico. To confirm her claims to North American territory, France needed to build permanent forts and settlements, linking the colony on the Saint Lawrence to Louisiana, newly founded at the mouth of the Mississippi. American places such as *Saint Louis* and *Baton Rouge* originated as French forts and trading posts. Even all-American *Detroit*, the automobile capital of the world and the Motown of soul music, was founded in 1701 by the French explorer Antoine Cadillac, who later gave his name to the luxury automobile. From French explorers and colonizers, North American English gave a new meaning to *prairie* (from the French word for 'meadow') which also survives in many compounds, such as *prairie chicken, prairie dog* and *prairie wolf*. Other words of French origin from this period are *levee* 'a landing place on a river, a pier', *bateau* 'a light, flat-bottomed boat', *voyageur* 'a woodsman, boatman, or guide employed by a fur company to transport goods and supplies between remote stations'.

In its heyday in the early eighteenth century, New France aspired to three-quarters of North America, including the entire Mississippi Valley and Canada (at this time comprising the area drained by the Saint Lawrence), Acadia (now the Maritime provinces) and the island of Newfoundland, shared unwillingly with the English. Still, French influence was spread very thin and the original inhabitants continued their way of life virtually unaffected by French laws or customs. The French claim was being contested by the British, who persistently tried to take over the fur trade or occupy parts of this gigantic territory. Following the defeat of France in the great colonial wars of the eighteenth century, all French North America east of the Mississippi except for New Orleans was ceded to Britain (see map p. 84).

In 1763 Canada became a British colony, and was to remain one for more than 100 years. The British victory had three results. First, it weakened the American colonies' dependence on Britain, since they no longer had to depend on the British to ward off the French; second, the British took over and expanded the Canadian fur trade; third, Britain now possessed a colony populated almost entirely by people of French descent.

The name *Acadia* was given by France to her land on the north-east coast of the continent, comprising what is now New Brunswick, Nova Scotia, Prince Edward Island, south-eastern Quebec and eastern Maine. In 1755 thousands of French-speaking settlers migrated, or were deported by the British, from Acadia to southern territories, including Louisiana, where their descendants came to be known as *Cajuns* /'keɪdʒ^ənz/, a corruption of *Acadians*. Their exodus to Louisiana is the background of a regional folk heritage including dance music and distinctive foods, such as the crayfish caught in the Bayou country – *bayou* being the name

Figure 5.4 South-eastern Canada

for a swampy, slow-moving stream in southern Louisiana. However, most of the French-speaking colonists remained in Canada, and their efforts to preserve their language and culture have been a continuing theme of Canadian history.

Loyalists' influence

At the time of the American Revolution, the English-speaking population of Canada was about 25,000. The first act of the American Continental Congress in 1775 was not to declare independence but to invade Canada. But not all American colonists supported the cause of independence: some favoured the British side during the American Revolution. They were called *Loyalists*. Of the Loyalists who chose not to stay in the United States, many left for Canada, settling first in Nova Scotia, then moving further inland. The increasingly large number of Loyalists led the British to divide the colony into Upper Canada (present-day Ontario) dominated by English-speaking colonists, and Lower Canada (present-day Quebec) which was inhabited mainly by French-speaking colonists. This division was to endure – if uneasily – until 1867, when the

Dominion of Canada came into existence. This event, known as *Confederation*, made Canada a largely self-governing state with four provinces (Nova Scotia, New Brunswick, Ontario and Quebec). Since then, six more provinces and three territories have been added. Canada achieved independence in 1931 but continues to belong to the Commonwealth of Nations, a group of sovereign states with a common allegiance to the British Crown. It was not until 1982 that Canada gained a new constitution to achieve full sovereignty. Yet Canada is a parliamentary democracy and a constitutional monarchy. The Canadians recognize the Queen as their Head of State, and the Governor-General remains the Queen's representative in Canada. Also, Queen Elizabeth's face remains on all Canadian paper currency.

Today's Canada is a multilingual and multicultural nation. According to recent statistics, 59.2 per cent speak English, 22.7 per cent speak French, 0.4 per cent

---

Canadian minorities and languages

Native people is the generally accepted term embracing all aboriginal peoples in Canada. Another accepted alternative is **First Nation**, promoted from within the indigenous community. Unlike *Native American* in the United States, however, it is not a comprehensive term for all indigenous peoples of the Americas or even of Canada. Indians divide into Status and Non-status Indians, the difference being that to be a Status Indian you must be registered with the federal government. The Indian Act defines First Nation as 'A term that came into common usage in the 1970s to replace the word "Indian" which some people found offensive. Although the term First Nation is widely used, no legal definition of it exists. Among its uses, the term "First Nations peoples" refers to "the Indian people in Canada," both Status and Non-Status.' *First Nation* has no form to denote a single individual. Officially, such a person is known as *a status Indian*.

In Canada, <u>**Inuit**</u> is the only accepted name for the people formerly known by the Algonquian word *Eskimo* – a popular but disputed etymology being 'eaters of raw meat' – which is now perceived as offensive. The singular noun is *Inuk* 'human being', thus *one Inuk, two Inuit. Inuit* is also used as an adjective: *an Inuit mechanic*. The language is called *Inuktitut*, while in technical descriptions of Canada's native languages, Inuktitut is still classified under the name *Eskimo-Aleut*.

Canada is an officially bilingual country. Today, spoken French is concentrated in Quebec, New Brunswick and eastern Ontario, while written French is ubiquitous. Canada is a member of **la Francophonie**, the community of French-speaking nations. Fewer than one in four Canadians are French-speaking, however, and over half the population speak English as a native language. The aboriginal languages are small in population, though rich in variety. The more populous minority language communities are of immigrant origin, including speakers of Chinese and of many European and South Asian languages.

Canadian English has coexisted for some 250 years with Canadian French, which is almost a century older. Bilingualism in Canada does not mean that all Canadians master both the English and French languages. What it means is that the country is officially, constitutionally and culturally bilingual.

are English-French bilinguals (but the Canadian sociolinguist J. K. Chambers finds that 'these mother-tongue figures grossly under-represent bilingualism in all guises'), and 17.5 per cent have a mother-tongue that is neither English nor French, but one of the various immigrant languages. Less than 1 per cent are native speakers of indigenous North American languages. Before the 1970s, three out of four immigrants came from the United States and Europe. But since then, most immigrants have come from Asia, increasing still further the diversity of the population. The New Canadians are encouraged to maintain their culture and language – there are more than 100 languages spoken, but half of them belong to the group of indigenous languages. The dominance of English makes the survival of indigenous languages precarious and here, as in other places around the globe, many languages are dying. A census in 1996 showed that only three of the indigenous languages (Inuktitut, Cree and Ojibway) were felt to have a large enough population to be secure from the threat of long-term extinction. From Aleut and Inuktitut, English has borrowed, among other words, *anorak* 'a hooded jacket' from *annoraaq*, *igloo* 'an Eskimo house made of wood, stone or blocks of snow or ice in the shape of a dome' from *iglu*, and *kayak* 'an Eskimo canoe' from *qajaq*.

Canadian English

British people commonly mistake English-speaking Canadians for Americans, while many Americans identify a Canadian accent as British. Yet the Canadians themselves believe that both the American and British varieties are clearly distinguishable from their own. The standard accents of English spoken in Canada and the United States are similar but not identical. Some linguists have argued that, in linguistic terms, **Canadian English** is a variety of a larger entity, **Northern American English**.

The pronunciation of English in Canada is closer to American than British English (see pp. 163–4), but the most striking thing about Canadian English is its homogeneity: 'It is certain that no Ontario Canadian, meeting another Canadian, can tell whether he comes from Manitoba, Saskatchewan, Alberta, or British Columbia – or even Ontario, unless he asks ...'; but there are exceptions: most Ontarians know Newfoundlanders from their accent. As in the case of the United States (pp. 79–80), the reasons for this are fairly obvious. One is geographical spread as a result of the role played by Ontarians in the settlement of the west. Another is that large parts of Canada became populated as late as the middle of the nineteenth century, and the longer a place has been settled, the more linguistically diverse it becomes. In the Maritime provinces of the east, where the founding population settled as early as the seventeenth century, there are much more varied accents than elsewhere in the country. This again parallels the similar situation on the eastern seaboard of the United States.

The first four items in the following list show how Canadian pronunciation resembles the general American pronunciation in the United States (see pp. 163–4):

- Like most Americans, Canadians usually pronounce *r* in words such as *heard* and *higher* and words like *dance* and *bath* have the vowel /æ/.
- Especially in casual speech, *t* is pronounced as /ᴅ/ between vowels and after /ɾ/, a feature known as 'tapping' (see p. 144). Thus, *butter* sounds like 'budder'. Such pairs as *metal* and *medal, latter* and *ladder* are therefore often pronounced the same. The city of Ottawa, the capital of Canada, sounds like 'Oddawa'. In addition, the /t/ is usually deleted after *n*, so that Toronto sounds like 'Toronna'.
- Pairs such as *cot* and *caught, awful* and *offal, caller* and *collar,* are pronounced with the same /ɑ/ vowel-sound.
- In words ending with -*ory* (*laboratory*) and -*ary* (*secretary*) most Canadians, like most Americans, pronounce the -*tory* or -*tary* part as two syllables, as in /'sekrətæri/, while in British RP English it is commonly reduced to one: /'sekrətri/.

On the other hand, the following three items show some ways in which Canadian pronunciation differs from the General American pronunciation:

- Most Canadians pronounce name of the letter *Z* as in British English, thus /zed/, not /ziː/.
- There are some words where Canadian English shows divided usage, preferring either the American or the British model (see pp. 164–6):
    missile /'mɪsəl/ or /'mɪsaɪl/
    news /nuːz/ or /njuːz/
    progress /'prɑːgrəs/ or /'prəʊgres/
    schedule /'skedjuːl/ or /'ʃedjuːl/
    tomato /tə'meɪᴅoʊ/ or /tə'mɑːtəʊ/
- A pronunciation that people think of as special to many Canadian English speakers is so-called **Canadian raising** which occurs in diphthongs before a voiceless consonant:
    /əɪ/ in *life, pipe, white* compares with RP /aɪ/
    /əʊ/ in *out, south, house* compares to RP /aʊ/

This means that *out* rhymes approximately with *boat* (if you talk British English). When a Canadian says *out and about* it may sound like *oat and a boat*! Interestingly, Canadian raising (although thought to be a more recent development) reinstates two characteristic diphthongs of Shakespearean English (see p. 61).

Center or centre?

In Canadian spelling both American and British forms are found (see p. 154–5): *center* and *centre, check* and *cheque, curb* and *kerb, tire* and *tyre.* (It should be pointed out that *check, curb* and *tire* also occur in British English, but as verbs and with a different meaning.) American spelling is more common in newspapers, while British spelling often appears in textbooks and learned journals. As J. K. Chambers puts it:

> Why do we find ourselves in this apparent state of confusion? As in so many other dilemmas, it follows from the crux of our history as British North America. Our venerable historical allegiance to Britain pulls us one way but our geographical attachment to the United States pushes us the other. ... English spelling conventions were stabilized in England just before the American Revolution and then reformed in the U.S. at a time when belligerence had cooled into disdain. The result was not exactly two traditions but a bi-modal tradition.

Wrench or spanner?

It is the same story with word choices. The Canadian English word-stock draws on both American and British varieties in cases like these:

American	British
billboard	*hoarding*
faucet	*tap*
gasoline, gas	*petrol*
sidewalk	*pavement*
wrench	*spanner*

But there is a little word *eh* (pronounced /eɪ/) that is widely considered to be a marker of Canadian speech. Its use is fairly consistent across the country, and it occurs in cases like these: *Nice day, eh?* (statement of opinion), *It goes over here, eh?* (statements of fact), *What a game, eh?* (exclamation), *Eh? What did you say?* (to mean 'pardon'). It is indicative that, as recent research suggests, new immigrants associate the use of *eh* with their developing Canadian identity, and often pick up the use of *eh* after only a few years in Canada.

* * *

In the next chapter we leave North America, to trace the expansion of English to other parts of the world. However, we will return to the United States in Chapter 8, to examine present-day American English in more detail, and to compare it with British English.

6
English Transplanted

And who, in time, knows whither we may vent
The treasure of our tongue, to what strange shores
This gain of our best glory shall be sent,
T'enrich unknowing nations with our stores?
What worlds in th' yet unformed Occident
May come refined with th' accents that are ours?

Samuel Daniel, Musophilus (1599)

By 1783 the thirteen colonies in America were lost for Britain. The English language, however, was not thrown out with the English. And, as the British Empire expanded, English spread to other continents: Australasia, Africa and Asia.

It is arguable that Australia's original inhabitants, the Australian Aborigines, have the longest continuous cultural history in the world, having begun to inhabit this vast island some 40,000–70,000 years ago. The first known Europeans to reach the continent we now call Australia were Portuguese and Dutch sailors in the sixteenth century. Initially, it was known as *Nova Hollandia* 'New Holland'; the name *Australia* is derived from Latin *terra australis incognita* 'unknown southern land'. At the time it seemed to Europeans that, logically, there must be a great Southland to balance the weight of the northern landmass of Europe and Asia, and expeditions were dispatched, among them the three voyages of James Cook, in quest of this Southland.

In 1768 Lieutenant Cook was sent on a scientific expedition to the Pacific to convey members of the Royal Society to Tahiti to observe the transit of the planet Venus across the Sun. Mission accomplished, Cook was to find the unknown southern continent, a task that took him to Australia aboard a 98-foot refitted former coal-hauling bark named the *Endeavour*. He navigated the coast of New Holland, which he claimed for Great Britain under the name of New South Wales. It was Cook and his men, including the famous botanist Joseph Banks, who later made white settlement in Australia possible.

Figure 6.1 The *Endeavour,* painted by Herb L. Kane

Australia: the First Fleet

In 1788, after an eight-month voyage from Portsmouth, eleven British ships – the First Fleet, as it is always called – with convicts, marines and civilians aboard – anchored in Botany Bay on the eastern coast of Australia. The bay had been given this name after Joseph Banks and his fellow botanist Daniel Solander had observed many new plants there. But Arthur Phillip, captain of the First Fleet and the first appointed Governor of New South Wales, found the bay an unsuitable site. He decided that the landing would be at Port Jackson (now better known as Sydney Harbour), which he found to be 'the finest harbour in the world'. The First Fleet anchored in Sydney Harbour on 26 January 1788, a date which was to become Australia Day.

Considering its consequence, the First Fleet does not seem impressive in size. The eleven ships carried just over 1,000 men and women, three-quarters of them convicts being transported to the penal colony of New South Wales to serve a seven-year term of hard labour – effectively a life sentence in view of the meagre opportunities to return. Over the next 80 years some 160,000 convicts were sent to Australia. In New South Wales transportation had ceased by 1840, but it continued to Tasmania until 1852 and to the West until 1868. Meanwhile, the immigrant population was augmented by free colonists.

The language brought to Australia was essentially late eighteenth-century English. The precise origins of the Australian accent are unknown. The older view that it was essentially Cockney no longer holds up. Most scholars agree that, from the earliest settlement, there was a range of British accents present, but that London English was a strong component. The early Australians were largely working-class townsfolk, many of them Londoners. Here is an immigrant's impression of a tavern on his first night in the new colony in 1826: 'Most had been convicts: there were a good many Englishmen and Irishmen, an odd Scotchman, and several foreigners, besides some youngish men, natives of the colony ...'

The discovery of gold in 1851 – hot on the heels of the Californian Gold Rush (see p. 88) – accelerated immigration, so that ten years later the Australian settler population had reached almost 1.2 million – a threefold increase in ten years. The gold rush also brought to an end the transportation of convicts, since the gold seemed to provide an opportunity for reward, rather than punishment. (Earlier, a royal commissioner investigating transportation had actually thought the climate was too good for the convicts, writing that 'the great charm in the Colony of New South Wales ... is the beauty of its climate'.)

Australia, Aussie, Oz

Australia is a young nation: the **Commonwealth of Australia** was formed from a combination of states only in 1901, and the Australian Capital Territory was later established for a new capital, Canberra. During the First World War *Aussie* (pronounced 'Ozzie') became an informal short form for both the noun *Australian* (as in *a dinkum Aussie* 'a real Australian') and the adjective (as in *Aussie Rules* for a code of football which originated in Australia). These days there is also an informal name for Australia: *Oz*. For obvious reasons the joking expression *Down Under*, used to refer to Australasia, is interpreted by many Australians and New Zealanders as showing a snobbish 'northern hemisphere perspective'. Although English has been spoken in Australia for more than 200 years, Australian English began to be seriously recognized as a distinct variety of English only after the Second World War.

From this time the pattern of immigration gradually changed in that Australia became increasingly populated by people of different nationalities – and they paid their own way. But the first large-scale non-British/Irish immigration did not occur until after the Second World War. Since 1967 Australia has reoriented itself from being a British bastion in the Southern hemisphere, with a staple white population made up of descendants of English, Scots, Welsh and Irish, – to becoming a multicultural immigration country attracting South and East Europeans, and in recent years many Asians.

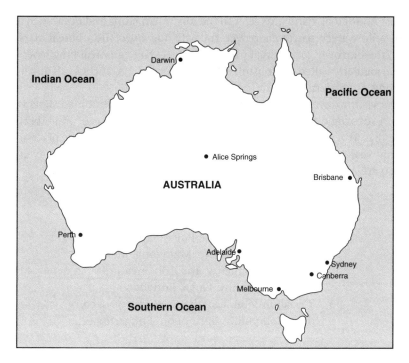

Figure 6.2 Map of Australia

Kangaroo, koala, kookaburra become English

Although Australia is a young nation, its aboriginal population has been living on this continent for many thousands of years. It has been said that 'If the history of language in Australia, currently thought in the more conservative estimates to span about 40,000 years, is reduced in imagination to a period of 24 hours, the share of English, on the same scale, is about seven minutes'. Archaeological evidence suggests that the first Aborigines migrated from Southeast Asia to Australia. Among themselves, the indigenous people do not have a uniform name but accept the term **Abo̱rigines**, derived from Latin *ab origine* meaning 'from the beginning'.

The first Aboriginal loanword in English was appropriately *kangaroo*, today's national symbol of Australia. It was recorded by the naturalist Joseph Banks in 1770, and Captain Cook referred in his diary for 4 August the same year to these strange hopping animals as 'called by the natives *Kangooroo* or *Kanguru*'. In the language that the first expedition encountered, *ganjurru* was the name for one particular species of kangaroo, not a generic name for these marsupial mammals.

Most Aboriginal loanwords refer to the Australian fauna and flora, such as the small yellow-green parrot *budgerigar*, the wild dog *dingo*, the arboreal marsupial *koala*, the burrowing marsupial *wombat*, and the large arboreal kingfisher *kookaburra*, jocularly called the 'bushman's clock' because its raucous call apparently can serve as an alarm clock in the Australian outback.

For a visitor travelling in Australia, it is fascinating to read road signs with a mixture of Anglo-Saxon names like *Liverpool* and *Newcastle* and Aboriginal names like *Wagga Wagga* and *Indooroopilly*. About a third of all the place-names on this vast continent (the size of the mainland United States, excluding Alaska) are Aboriginal, such as these in J. D. Lang's poem from 1824:

> I like the native names, as Parramatta,
> And Illawarra, and Woolloomooloo,
> Nandowra, Woogarora, Bulkomatta,
> Tomah, Toonggabbie, Mittagong, Meroo;
> Buckobble, Cumleroy, and Coolangatta,
> The Warragumby, Barga, Burradoo;
> Cookbundoon, Carrabaiga, Wingecarribee,
> The Wollondilly, Yurumbon, Bungarribbee.

The white settlement in Australia was disastrous for both the indigenous population and their languages. Today, the Aborigines number less than 400,000, many of them speaking English only. Among the surviving Australian Aboriginal languages, about 50 are in active first-language use, mostly in places remote from major population centres. It is feared that it will not be long before most of these languages die out.

Waltzing Matilda

Aboriginal languages and the Australian way of life have both added their own zestful flavouring to the English language. In 1895 the Australian folk-poet Andrew Barton Paterson, better known as 'Banjo' Paterson, wrote the popular bush ballad *Waltzing Matilda*, featuring Aboriginal loanwords like *billabong* and *coolibah*. The song has been called 'The Unofficial National Anthem':

> Once a jolly swagman camped by a billabong,
>   Under the shade of a coolibahtree,
> And he sang as he watched and waited till his billy boiled,
>   'Who'll come a-waltzing Matilda with me?
>   Waltzing Matilda, Waltzing Matilda,
>   Who'll come a-waltzing Matilda with me?'
> And he sang as he watched and waited 'til his billy boiled,
>   'Who'll come a-waltzing Matilda with me?'

Down came a jumbuck to drink at the billabong:
  Up jumped the swagman and grabbed him with glee.
And he sang as he shoved that jumbuck in his tuckerbag,
  'You'll come a-waltzing Matilda with me.
    Waltzing Matilda, Waltzing Matilda,
    You'll come a-waltzing Matilda with me.'
And he sang as he shoved that jumbuck in his tuckerbag,
  'You'll come a-waltzing Matilda with me.'

  Up rode the squatter, mounted on his thoroughbred;
    Down came the troopers, one, two, three:
'Whose's that jolly jumbuck you've got in your tuckerbag?
  You'll come a-waltzing Matilda with me!
    Waltzing Matilda, Waltzing Matilda,
    You'll come a-waltzing Matilda with me.
Whose's that jolly jumbuck you've got in your tuckerbag?
  You'll come a-waltzing Matilda with me!'

  Up jumped the swagman and sprang into the billabong;
    'You'll never catch me alive!' said he;
And his ghost may be heard as you pass by that billabong,
  'You'll come a-waltzing Matilda with me!
    Waltzing Matilda, Waltzing Matilda,
    You'll come a-waltzing Matilda with me!'
And his ghost may be heard as you pass by that billabong,
  'You'll come a-waltzing Matilda with me!'

Some Australian glosses

swagman: a vagrant worker carrying his few belongings slung in a cloth, a *swag* – a
  word which originally meant 'stolen property, loot, goods' in the Australian argot
  called *flash language* that the convicts brought with them
waltz matilda: *Matilda* was a mock-romantic word for a swag, and *to waltz matilda* was
  to hit the road with a swag on your back
billabong: a stagnant pool, backwater – in the Australian outback, a billabong generally
  retains water longer than the watercourse itself, so it may be the only water for
  miles around
coolibahtree: a eucalyptus tree that grows beside billabongs
billy: a cylindrical vessel with a wire handle for heating liquids, in which 'swaggies'
  boil water to make tea
jumbuck: a sheep
tuckerbag: a bag for carrying food (*tucker* is 'grub, food')
squatter: a major landowner in the outback – people 'squatted' on patches of land,
  grazed their animals, grew their crops and built their houses and fences. As authority arrived, it generally accepted the claims of whoever was in apparent possession
  of the land
trooper: a cavalry soldier, or perhaps a mounted militiaman or policeman

Australian English

Considering its geographical spread Australian English is remarkably uniform – compare the situation in North America (pp. 79, 95). 'From Perth to Sydney', says the phonetician John Wells, 'is over 3000 kilometres, yet their accents are virtually indistinguishable'. Australia is, after all, the sixth largest country in the world, and the English language has had little more than 200 years to spread into all regions of the country. Generally speaking, variations of accent are socially or ethnically rather than geographically determined. Some vowel sounds resemble those found in Cockney or 'London vernacular' (see pp. 128–30). It is generally assumed that these derive ultimately from the language brought to Australia by the early immigrants, since many of them came from the southeast of England. The characteristic sound of Australian speech is found especially in its vowels. Here are a few differences between 'broader' Australian English and standardized British pronunciation (RP, see pp. 125–8):

- In words such as *say* and *Australia* the diphthong is a wider sound pronounced close to /aɪ/ where RP has /eɪ/. This pronunciation lies behind the jocular form *Strine* for 'Australian English', so the puzzling book-title *Let Stalk Strine* translates into *Let's Talk Australian*.
- In words such as *now*, where RP has /aʊ/, the diphthong approximates to /æʊ/ or even /ɛə/.
- In words such as *father*, where RP has /ˈfɑːðə/, Australians say /ˈfaːðə/.
- RP-vowels /iː/ and /uː/ are often pronounced as diphthongs, so that *see* and *do* resemble /səɪ/ and /dəʊ/.
- Some vowels are pronounced with the tongue higher than in RP, so that *ham* sounds rather like /hɛm/, and *pen* sounds rather like /pɪn/.
- In words like *happy*, the final -*y* is pronounced /i/ in RP, but has a more salient pronunciation in Australian English – more like a long vowel: /ˈhɛpiː/.
- The most common vowel in English, the unstressed schwa vowel /ə/, is more generally used than in RP. For example, *chatted* in RP is pronounced with a 'short *i* vowel': /ˈtʃætɪd/, whereas in Australian English it is pronounced with a schwa: /ˈtʃætəd/ – so that *chatted* and *chattered* sound alike. John Wells relates how an Australian newsreader while working in the UK got into trouble for reporting that 'the Queen chattered to factory workers' – he intended to use the verb 'chatted'!

The vocabulary of Australian English tends to be colloquial and informal, much like the stereotypical 'Aussie'. The language is full of imaginative, colourful and fun expressions, such as these:

> *bald as a bandicoot* 'completely bald' (a *bandicoot* is a rat-like species of marsupial)
> *dinkum*, also *dinky, dinky-di* 'genuine, right', as in *a dinkum Aussie* 'a real Australian'

full as a goog 'dead drunk' (*goog* means 'egg')
hoon (also *yobbo*) 'loutish youth'
ocker 'the archetypal uncultivated Australian man'
prang 'minor car accident'
sanger or *sanga* 'sandwich'
sheila 'girl', as in *a beaut sheila* 'an attractive girl'

Typical of colloquial Australian English are shortened words (like *beaut* for *beautiful*), including words ending in the suffix *-o* or *-y/-ie* like *arvo* (for *afternoon*) and *tinnie* (for a can of beer). The Australian settlers came upon flora and fauna so completely alien to their previous experience that the words in their language had to be given new meanings, and new words had to be coined or borrowed from native languages. There are now over 10,000 English words and phrases with an Australian origin or meaning. Some examples of Australianisms that can be found in an Australian English dictionary, such as *The Macquarie Dictionary* or the *Australian Oxford Dictionary*, include:

barbie, also spelled *bar-b-q*, *BBQ* 'barbecue'
bush 'uncultivated expanse of land remote from settlement', as in *bush nurse, bush breakfast, bush house, bushman, bushranger*
esky (but called *chillybin* in New Zealand) 'portable icebox'
footpath corresponding to *pavement* in the UK and *sidewalk* in the US
g'day /gəˈdaɪ/ ('good day') an expression used at a greeting or a parting during the day
lay-by 'buying an article on time payment' corresponding to US *instalment*, UK *hire-purchase*. (In the UK *a lay-by* is an area beside a highway where vehicles can pull off the road and park, called *a rest area* in Australia)
outback 'remote, sparsely inhabited Australian hinterland', as in *the Great Outback*
walkabout (as in *go walkabout*) is, according to *The Macquarie Dictionary*, 'a period of wandering as a nomad, often as undertaken by Aborigines who feel the need to leave the place where they are in contact with white society, and return for spiritual replenishment to their traditional way of life'
weekender 'a holiday cottage'

New Zealand – Aotearoa

From Australia we head due south-east towards **New Zealand**, 'a country with 70 million sheep, three million of which think they are people', according to a humorous cliché. It takes its name from the Dutch province Zeeland. Since New Zealand is officially bilingual, it is also known as **Aotearoa**. This translates as 'land of the long white cloud', which is a native Maori name for these islands. The Maori population had been living here for at least 600 years before the arrival of settlers from the northern hemisphere.

In 1769, before arriving in Australia, James Cook navigated the rocky coast of these islands. He claimed New Zealand for the British Crown and was the first to use Maori words in written English, some of them (like *pah* 'a fortified village') later becoming part of general vocabulary for New Zealanders. However, the English language did not gain a foothold in New Zealand until the middle of the nineteenth century, when British immigration began in earnest after the signing of the Treaty of Waitangi in 1840 between Maori tribal leaders and the British Crown. Unlike Australia, New Zealand was never a penal colony. In the early days, especially from 1840 until the end of the 1850s, most settlers came from higher social strata or from rural areas in the home country. A Scottish element in the settlement is evident from place-names like Ben Nevis, Invercargill and Dunedin (the Gaelic name for Edinburgh). After 1861, when gold had been discovered in New Zealand, there was also a great influx of Australians. In the 1870s the population doubled, due to a development policy of assisted immigration from Britain, with nearly all the new settlers coming from southern England. However, by 1890 the English language in New Zealand was beginning to crystallize into a distinguishable variety, though very close to Australian English.

When the Europeans arrived in New Zealand they encountered Maori, a Polynesian language radically different from English, spoken by the native Maori population. In the North Island especially, many place-names are of Maori origin, for example Hokitika, Rotorua, Taranaki, Te Anau, Timaru, Wanganui. At the beginning of the twentieth century, the English-speaking population had increased to three-quarters of a million, while the Maori population was in decline, in part through exposure to unfamiliar diseases which accompanied European settlement. This appalling situation was however checked, and today about 5 per cent of the 3.4 million New Zealanders can converse in Maori. Since 1987 the Maori language has had official status alongside English, as is reflected in official names such as Victoria University of Wellington with this letter-head:

VICTORIA UNIVERSITY OF WELLINGTON
Te Whare Wānanga o te Ūpoko o te Ika a Māui

Words borrowed from Maori for local trees, flowers and animals or referring to traditional indigenous culture are regularly used in New Zealand English. Pronunciations and spellings are modified to match Maori pronunciation. The native Maori language does not have separate plural forms, and the word *Maori* is itself a case in point: thus *one Maori, many Maori.*

Pakeha is the Maori term for the white settlers. While few *pakeha* speak Maori, a considerable number of Maori words have entered the New Zealand English vocabulary. About six words in every 1,000 words of New Zealand English are of

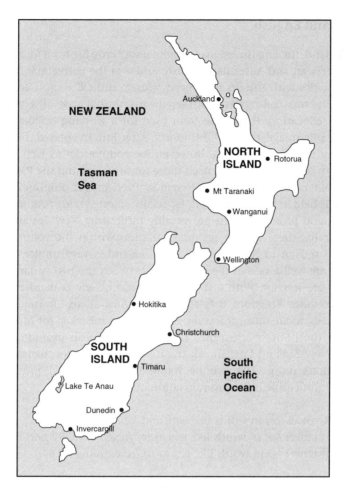

Figure 6.3   Map of New Zealand

Maori origin. Most refer to flora, fauna and place-names, but an increasing number also derive from Maori cultural and social concepts. There are trees called *kauri*, *totara*, *rimu*, birds called *kiwi*, *tui*, *moa* and fish called *tarakihi*, *moki*. Other Maori borrowings commonly used in New Zealand are *koha* 'gift, present' and *taonga* 'object of value, property, treasure'. *Kia ora* is a Maori greeting, often used for *hello* when answering the phone. *Kiwi* is a universally familiar Maori word applied to any of the three species of flightless nocturnal birds peculiar to New Zealand. The brown kiwi became the national symbol of New Zealand, like the kangaroo of Australia. The word is used not only for the bird but also for the kiwi fruit and, familiarly, for the New Zealanders themselves (*Is your husband a Kiwi?*). It applies even to their dollar currency (*Last week the Kiwi went up*) and to their variety of English (*Take a crash course in Kiwi*).

New Zealand English

In New Zealand, the English language comes under crossfire from four directions: British, American and Australian English, and also the native Maori language. Historically, ties with Britain have been strong, and *OE* – short for 'overseas experience' – was commonly considered an essential part of a young New Zealander's education. It was the term used for a working holiday, almost a mandatory pilgrimage, to the Old Country. After Britain entered the European Community in the early 1970s, however, for commercial as well as cultural reasons New Zealand reoriented itself more towards Asia and the Pacific.

Among older New Zealanders, RP (standardized British pronunciation – see pp. 125–8) is held in high esteem but, especially among young people, American vocabulary and pronunciations are steadily infiltrating New Zealand English. As in Australia, there is little regional variation within the country. Even if the English spoken in Australia and New Zealand is very similar, most New Zealanders are well aware of the differences between the two variants (though Australians are less so). With a sigh of resignation, New Zealanders often say that, in the United Kingdom, they are taken for Australians – in much the same way as Canadians are more or less resigned to being mistaken for Americans.

Many of the noticeable features of Australian English pronunciation also belong to New Zealand English. All the items in the list for Australian vowel pronunciations on p. 104 can be found in New Zealand pronunciation. Particularly noticeable is the pronunciation of:

the RP back vowel /ɑː/ in words like *bath* and *father* as /aː/
the RP front vowel /æ/ in words like *pan* as /e/ (resembling RP *pen*)
the RP front vowel /e/ in words like *pen* as /ɪ/ (resembling RP *pin*)

Illustrating the second of these, the story is told of an American whose phone call to a New Zealand friend was answered by the friend's daughter:

> When he asked to speak to her father he thought she replied 'He's dead'. After his momentary shock he realized that she was saying 'Here's Dad'.

The third pronunciation feature, /pɪn/ for *pen*, leads to joky tales of a New Zealander asking for *an igg for brickfast*, and the like.

There are three more specific characteristics we can mention for New Zealand pronunciation:

- Short *i*-sounds (as in *pin*) resemble the neutral schwa sound /ə/ of /pən/, as if it were spelled 'pun'. For the British meal *fish and chips*, an old joke says that people in Australia eat *feesh and cheeps* (with something like a close /i/ vowel) and in New Zealand *fush and chups* (with /ə/). This vowel shift, combined the three listed above, suggests that a kind of **chain shift** (see pp. 240–1) has affected a number of short vowels in New Zealand English. (A partial analogy is the Great Vowel Shift which affected long vowels in Middle English and Early Modern English – p. 240.) To some extent, the same combined vowel shift has affected the other Southern Hemisphere varieties of Australian and South African English. A rough picture can be given as follows:

'SOUTHERN HEMISPHERE CHAIN SHIFT'

/æ/ → /e/ → /ɪ/ → /ə/ (or /i/)

'pat' → 'pet' → 'pit' → something like 'put' or 'peat'

Here, the /ə/ option is NZE, and the /i/ option AustE. 'Put' and 'peat' are extremely rough approximations: the *ea* in 'peat' is meant to be pronounced as short vowel.

- The diphthong in words like *air*, *chair* and *hair* is closer and sounds like /ɪə/ rather than RP /eə/. So, pairs such as *air* and *ear*, *bear* and *beer*, *chair* and *cheer*, *hair* and *here*, *rarely* and *really*, often sound alike.
- Like Australians, most New Zealanders generally do not pronounce /r/ after vowels in words such as *hard* and *speaker*. But in the originally Scottish settlements of the South Island, some speakers retain a Scots trilled *r* (see p. 143), known as the 'Southland burr'.

In New Zealand English, declarative utterances sometimes have a rising instead of a falling intonation. This 'High Rising Terminal', which is also found in Australian English and some varieties of American English, is most common among young people and women. To those unfamiliar with this trait, it can sound as if a speaker is asking a question instead of making a statement, as in

Nick: *What are you doing now?*
Sue: *I'm working at the university.*

As for spelling, New Zealanders use British spellings in words such as *colour* and *labour*, while Australians vary between *color* and *colour*, *labor* and *labour*. The official spelling of one of the leading political parties is the *Labor Party* in Australia, but the *Labour Party* in both New Zealand and Britain.

In terms of vocabulary, New Zealand English stands its ground against Australian English, even if the differences should not be overstated. There are a number of Australasianisms which are found in both varieties, for example:

backblocks 'remote, sparsely inhabited inland country'
beaut 'fine, superior': 'She's a real beaut'.

cocky 'a farmer'
crook 'unpleasant' (*a crook job*), 'sick' (*go crook*), 'cease to function' (*The fridge has gone crook*)
Rafferty's rules 'no rules at all': 'Out here it's always been Rafferty's rules. Make 'em up as you go along.'
skite 'boast, brag': 'People reckon you're skiting.'

The endings *-ie* and *-o* typical of Australian English are popular here, too. Since sailing is a big sport in New Zealand, there are many *boaties* (sailing enthusiasts), as well as *posties* 'post(wo)men' and *truckies* 'truck-drivers'. Typical colloquialisms in *-o* are: *arvo* 'afternoon', *compo* 'compensation', *smoko* 'a break from work' (with or without a smoke). When New Zealanders, like Australians, make fun of the British – a good-humoured pastime called *pommie-bashing* – they talk, for example, about *English sunbathing*, i.e. sunbathing fully dressed. (*Pommie*, often derogatory according to *The Dictionary of New Zealand English*, is a term for a 'Briton'.)

Lexicographers have identified several thousand words and phrases in New Zealand English, which are either of New Zealand origin or have taken on particular meanings in New Zealand. Some examples:

bach /bætʃ/ 'a week-end cottage', often by the sea
big bickies 'big money': 'That costs big bickies'
glide time corresponding to British *flexitime* and American *flextime*: 'irregular working hours that suit the employee'
judder bar 'a speed bump in the road, to stop speeding'
nappy valley 'a suburb where young couples with children are predominant householders', an ironic play on *Happy Valley* (*nappy* is a baby's *napkin*, called *diaper* in the US)
section 'a piece of land for building a house'; in Australia it is also a *block*
tramping 'hiking, taking extended walks for pleasure or exercise', corresponding to *bushwalking* in Australia

Further examples are included in *The Dictionary of New Zealand English* or *The New Zealand Oxford Dictionary*.

Australian and New Zealand English, as we have seen, have many traits in common, which distinguish them from the English of North America. These similarities are also shared, to a considerable extent, by the native speaker's English of South Africa, to which we turn in the next section.

English in Africa – the Inner Circle

The history of the English language in Africa begins with early colonial jostlings for power among the European maritime powers on the West African

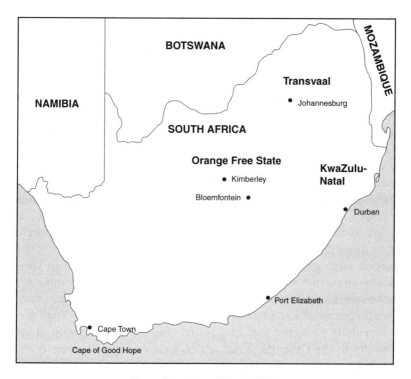

Figure 6.4 Map of South Africa

coast – Portuguese, Dutch, French and British were the chief nationalities involved. From this grew the slave trade, shipping African slaves to the New World colonies of these same nations. The British share of this iniquitous trade grew with the country's growth in maritime and commercial power, reaching its apex in the later eighteenth century. Millions of slaves were transported in the most barbaric conditions in British vessels across the Atlantic, up to the abolition of the slave trade in 1807. Curiously, the first consequences of relations between the English language and black Africa are most in evidence across the Atlantic, in the development of creoles (composite languages, see pp. 176–9) with English vocabulary, for example in Jamaica and in the Gullah t111ongue of the Atlantic seaboard of mainland America. A similar development of pidgin and creole languages based on English took place on the coast of West Africa. We will return to pidgins and creoles in Chapter 9.

The situation was different in South Africa, where the circumstances encouraged settlement of white English-speakers in larger numbers, and a variety of native-speaker English developed and spread in a similar way to the Englishes of Australia and New Zealand. This is the topic we turn to now.

English comes to South Africa

In 1652 the Dutch East India Company set up a permanent trading post at the Cape of Good Hope and brought the Dutch language to the southern tip of Africa. The English language in South Africa had its early beginnings some 150 years later when Britain bought the Cape from the Dutch, but it truly began to take root from 1820 with the first organized immigration of British settlers in the Eastern Cape, the majority of them coming from rural south-east England. These early British settlers came from the lower social echelons and faced grim conditions in the Cape, which hastened the 'bonding process', and the linguistic assimilation alongside it. They were not able to go back 'home' and renew contacts, or remind themselves of their original accents. In 1822 the governor, Lord Charles Somerset, made English the only official language of the Cape and tried to anglicize the Afrikaners, as the descendants of the Dutch and French Huguenot settlers were called, by importing British schoolmasters and missionaries.

A second large group of English-speaking immigrants arrived in the mid-1800s and settled in Natal, beyond the borders of the Cape. They differed from the first major group of British settlers in social and regional origins: they represented higher social strata and came more often from northern English counties, particularly Yorkshire and Lancashire. Unlike the first group of settlers from Britain to the Cape, the Natal settlers were occasionally able to go back 'home' and renew contacts. Also, they maintained their accents, which were considered more prestigious, and were successful in 'creating a corner of Victorian England on alien soil'.

This pattern of settlement is still evident in the varieties of speech distinguished today. A distinction can be made between Cape English, Natal English and General South African English variables. The first two of these might be likened to the North-eastern and Southern accents of the United States (pp. 81–2), simply because they reflect early English-speaker settlement areas. The third, like General American, is less regionally specific.

An interesting subvariety of South African English is sometimes referred to as 'South African Indian English'. In the 1860s British settlers in Natal began importing Indian labourers to work on their plantations. For communication among themselves the early immigrants used an Indian language (Bhojpuri or Tamil) and sometimes the pidgin Fanagalo – a mixture of Zulu, English and some Afrikaans. However, while working as a lawyer in South Africa, the young Mahatma Gandhi observed in 1909 that educated young Indians began using English 'even when it is not necessary to do so'.

The discovery of valuable minerals in the 1870s led to drastic changes both economically and socially, speeding up immigration from Britain. In the last quarter of the century more than 400,000 immigrants, mainly from Britain, arrived in South Africa. English became the dominant language in the mining communities.

The Dutch spoken by the early settlers in the seventeenth century eventually evolved into a distinct language – **Afrikaans**. From 1899 to 1902 the grimly fought Boer War raged between Great Britain and the two Afrikaner (Boer) republics: the South African Republic (Transvaal) and the Orange Free State. Against the might of the British Empire at its height, the Boers eventually lost the war and their independence, but they retained their language and culture. In 1910, when Britain unexpectedly granted South Africa independent dominion status, the Act of Union laid down that 'Both the English and the Dutch languages shall be the official languages of the Union'. After the First World War, South Africa was dominated politically by the Afrikaners, whose history made them generally ill-disposed to everything British, including the English language. Despite this there was a dual language policy, with Afrikaans alongside English. Huge efforts were made to build up Afrikaans, and massive resources were ploughed into improving the status of the language. Realizing that it was valuable to maintain constitutional links with Britain, South Africans kept their membership of the British Commonwealth of Nations until 1961, when the dominion became a republic.

From 1948 until 1994, South Africa was racially segregated under a pernicious system known as *apartheid*, Afrikaans for 'separateness'. In the early 1990s, negotiations began between the governing Nationalist Party and the formerly illegal ANC (African National Congress). In April 1994 the first free elections were held. The ANC won the election and Nelson Mandela, an international symbol of resistance to apartheid during his long years of imprisonment, became the first black President of the Republic of South Africa.

Nelson Mandela

In his autobiography *Long Walk to Freedom*, Nelson Mandela recalls his first day of school:

> *On the first day of school my teacher, Miss Mdingane, gave each of us an English name and said that thenceforth that was the name we would answer to in school. This was the custom among Africans in those days and was undoubtedly due to the British bias of our education. The education I received was a British education, in which British ideas, British culture and British institutions were automatically assumed to be superior. There was no such thing as African culture … That day, Miss Mdingane told me that my new name was Nelson. Why she bestowed this particular name upon me I have no idea. Perhaps it had something to do with the great British sea captain Lord Nelson, but that would only be a guess.*

The name given to Mandela at birth was Rolihlahla. In Xhosa, Rolihlahla literally means 'pulling the branch of a tree', but its colloquial meaning more accurately would be 'troublemaker' – all according to Mandela himself.

With the birth of the new Republic the linguistic situation also changed. There are now eleven official languages. According to the constitution of 1995,

'Afrikaans, English, isiNdebele, Sesotho saLebowa, Sesotho, siSwati, Xitsonga, Setswana, TshiVenda, isiXhosa and isiZulu shall be the official South African languages at national level'. No language is singled out for special status, although in practice English is institutionally entrenched and widely used as a lingua franca.

Among all the countries where English is spoken as a major first language, the situation of English in South Africa is unique. English is only in fifth place in terms of the population of native speakers: it is the language of a minority within a white minority, while the majority (three-quarters) of South African citizens are black. Although English is the home language of less than 10 per cent of the population, it is dominant in government at higher levels, business, technology, higher education and the media. Most South Africans speak a language of the Bantu family of languages, but it has been estimated that one out of two South Africans know some English. Afrikaans is the mother tongue or second language for several million people in Southern Africa.

There are different reasons for the success story of English in South Africa. One reason is that there has been a positive shift among Afrikaners in their attitude towards English. Another reason for the support of English is the fact that using it avoids the potential divisiveness of using any particular African language. Ethnicity and linguistic identity are strongly linked, so that a politician using Xhosa would lose Zulu support – English can be resorted to as a 'neutral' option. Furthermore, to the linguistically diverse black majority, Afrikaans has been perceived as the language of oppression. Yet the popularity of English among black Africans is hardly based on enthusiastic feelings for the language or for the culture it represents. Rather, it is based on a wish to succeed, to give their children an education and a linguistic platform on which to realize their dreams of a better future. It is ironic that here, as in so many other countries, the colonial language, English, tends to stand somehow for liberation and a window on the world.

Some words of South African (Afrikaner) origin have contributed to the international English vocabulary, for example *trek* originally 'a journey by ox wagon' but now also used for any arduous journey, *veld* 'a grassland, usually with scattered shrubs or trees', *spoor* 'a track, trail, scent', *springbok* 'a swift and graceful southern African gazelle', *blesbok* 'a South African antelope', *bushbuk* 'a small African striped antelope'.

Here are some features of the native-speaker English pronunciation as encountered in South Africa (RP is used as a reference accent, see pp. 125–8):

- As in Australia and New Zealand, the vowel of *pan* is raised to something approaching RP *pen*, and the vowel of *pen* is raised further, to something approaching *pin*, so that *rack* may sound like *wreck* and *beg* like *big*.
- The short-i vowel /ɪ/ is pronounced in a similar way to Australian English for some words (*fish and chips* with /i/, see pp. 108–9), and in a similar way to

New Zealand English for others (*lip, bit, slim* with a schwa-like pronunciation – /ləp/, /bət/, /sləm/). This phenomenon, known as the 'KIT split', depends on the neighbouring consonants. In general terms, /i/ occurs with the consonants /k/, /g/ and /ŋ/, and usually before /ʃ/. In most other cases, the /ə/-like variant is used.

- As in North American English, the *t* in a word like *matter* is pronounced as a voiced consonant, sounding like *madder* (see pp. 96, 164).
- Also like Australian and New Zealand English (and 'modern' RP), South African English is modifying the pronunciation of the long *u*-vowel /u:/ so that it resembles the French pronunciation of *u*, or the German pronunciation of *ü*, in words like *Sue, rude*.
- Some long vowels and diphthongs have also undergone special development in South African English. The /ɑ:/ vowel of *bath* or *car* is pronounced far back in the mouth, sometimes approximating to /ɒ:/ The diphthongs of words like *fine* and *phone* have almost become simple long vowels: for broad South African speech these sounds can be shown symbolically as /fɑ:n/ and /fʌ:n/.

Considering the country's varied mixture of races, native languages and patterns of settlement, it is not surprising that South African English shows greater variation than Australian and New Zealand English. Bantu, Afrikaner, and Indian speech have all had an impact. Yet, there is a common ground shared by the native-speaking South African, Australian and New Zealand varieties. The most likely explanation of this common ground is the influence of South-eastern British English of the nineteenth century.

English in Africa – the Outer Circle

South Africa is a country where English of the Inner Circle and the Outer Circle (in the sense of Kachru, see p. 2) meet in one country. We have given some attention to the native-speaker variety of South Africa, and now we turn to the non-native speaker varieties of the indigenous black peoples, here and elsewhere in Africa. But first, some history.

At the end of the eighteenth century, the Cape Colony was the only permanent European settlement in Africa. The full-scale colonization of Africa began only in the late nineteenth century with traders, explorers and missionaries fanning out to 'open Africa to trade and civilization'. The European Great Powers squabbled over African colonial dainties. By 1914, at the beginning of the First World War, only Ethiopia and Liberia remained independent, self-governing territories on the empire-builders' maps of Africa.

After the Second World War, the European colonial powers were physically and psychologically weakened. One after another, African colonies won their independence. In 1957 the Gold Coast became the Republic of Ghana, the first nation in sub-Saharan Africa to win independence; while, for Zimbabwe (formerly Southern Rhodesia), the colonial era dragged on to 1980. Although English is an official language in both countries, there are few other points of similarity between them. In fact, these two states illustrate how complicated it is to talk about **African English** as a cover term.

African English, referring to the English language in former British colonies, can be subdivided into three categories outside South Africa:

- **West African English** in Gambia, Ghana, Cameroon, Nigeria, Sierra Leone
- **East African English** in Kenya, Tanzania, Uganda and possibly Somalia and Sudan
- **Southern African English** in Botswana, Lesotho, Malawi, Namibia, Swaziland, Zambia, Zimbabwe

'African English' is a convenient but simplistic term. It can refer to all forms of English, including pidgins and creoles, used in West Africa since the establishment of trading posts in the seventeenth century. But it may also refer to the forms of English spoken and written by educated black Africans in territories formerly administered by the British. In this second sense, African English dates from the early nineteenth century.

Unsurprisingly, the English spoken in Africa is far from uniform. In a nation like Nigeria, it can differ on a scale running from the 'top dialect' or **acrolect** found, for example, in national newspapers and broadcasting, to the 'bottom dialects' or **basilects** – local varieties (including pidgins and creoles, see pp. 176–7), some of which an English-speaking visitor may find incomprehensible. The greater part of everyday usage probably belongs to a spectrum of **mesolects** – or middle dialects – on a scale extending from the popular varieties to the standard.

Yet there is a kind of family resemblance between African varieties, just as there is between the 'southern hemisphere' Englishes discussed earlier in this chapter. This shows particularly in pronunciation. The English of native speakers is termed a **stress-timed** language, in which there is a big difference, in length and prominence, between stressed and unstressed syllables. In this sentence, the underlined syllables are more prominent than the others: *To-MOR-row is SAT-ur-day*. On the other hand, African English pronunciation tends to be **syllable-timed** (like the native Bantu languages of Africa, and also, incidentally, languages as remote as French and Japanese). This means that each syllable tends to have an equal value, as is suggested by this rendering: TO-MOR-ROW-IS-SAT-UR-DAY (see creoles, pp. 177–8).

The pronunciation of vowels tends to be different from Standard English, and the most frequent vowel of native speaker English – schwa /ə/ – is avoided. The number of vowels in native African languages is smaller than the vowels of native-speaker English, and this is probably why African English tends to merge together a number of vowels and pronounce them alike. For example /waka/ for *worker*, and /development/ for *development*. According to David Crystal, the syllable-timing style of pronunciation is likely to have increasing influence around the world, because of the likely future demographic predominance of Outer Circle speakers of English over Inner Circle speakers (see p. 236).

English in South Asia

The geographical region of South Asia accounts for more than a fifth of the world's population. Most of this population live in the three nations of India, Pakistan and Bangladesh, which formerly made up 'Greater India' under British rule. By the time of independence in 1947, India had a population of 350 million, but today the population exceeds a billion. Some estimates have suggested that, by the year 2050, India's population will be the largest in the world, surpassing that of the People's Republic of China, and that the population of Pakistan will be the third largest in the world, surpassing that of the United States.

In this populous region, the English language plays a very important role. It is reasonable to talk about **South Asian English** as long as we remember that, like 'African English', this is far from a uniform variety.

Throughout South Asia there are competing claims of regional languages, as well as controversies over the role of English. In India, Hindi is the national language and the main language of 30 per cent of the people, but there are 14 other official languages in different regions. (Ten of these languages, including Hindi, are Indo-European languages, remotely related to English.) English itself enjoys associate status and is the most important language for political and commercial purposes. In Pakistan, the constitution recognizes Urdu as the official language, while 'the English language may be used for official purposes until arrangements are made for its replacement by Urdu'. Formed as an independent state in 1971, Bangladesh has a population largely consisting of Bengali speakers. Nevertheless, English is a compulsory school language and a popular optional subject at university level.

In India, publications in English have an immense influence: home-grown newspapers written in English are available in any average-sized city, and of the seven daily papers which have been in existence for over 100 years, four are written in English. India publishes more books in English than in any other language, and is the third largest English book-producing country in the world after the US and the UK.

'The jewel in the crown'

At the beginning of the sixteenth century, the Portuguese gained control of the trade arteries between the Mediterranean and India. Some one hundred years later British, Dutch and, later, also French trading companies entered the race for the Far Eastern markets. The British East India Company, originally a small company of adventurous and enterprising merchants, secured a foothold at the trading post in Surat, later also in Madras (now known as Chennai), acquired Bombay (now Mumbai) from Portugal, and established Calcutta (now Kolkata) as a trading centre. The British relied primarily on military power, on commercial clout, but also on successful alliances with native princes. The Company became so powerful and its staff so self-indulgent that, in 1773, the British government had to get directly involved, and made the East India Company its semi-official agency.

Eventually the British, directly or indirectly, controlled virtually the whole Indian subcontinent. In 1858, after a widespread uprising known as the Sepoy (or Indian) Mutiny, the administration of India was transferred from the East India Company to the British Crown. The days of Company rule were over.

The colonial government, known familiarly as *the British Raj*, paved the way for the leading role of English as a second language. In 1835 the historian and statesman Thomas Macaulay proposed the creation of 'a class of persons Indian in blood and colour, but English in taste, in opinion, in morals and in intellect'. His suggestion led to dramatic consequences. Civil servants were recruited from the English-speaking universities in Bombay, Calcutta and Madras. While all senior posts were reserved for the British, an influential Indian middle class helped to extend the power of British institutions. English was the medium of education, an official language of state and a vehicle of national unity. Incidentally, it enabled the Indian National Congress, later the Congress Party, to grow into a pan-Indian mass movement for independence, finally achieved in 1947.

When a language is transported to new cultures, as in South Asia, it undergoes striking changes. As in many other countries in the postcolonial era, the newly formed nations of the Indian subcontinent began with an ambivalent or negative attitude to the English language, as an instrument of former colonial control. The spiritual founder of independent India, Mahatma Gandhi, had deplored the dominant influence of English, saying that 'real education is impossible through a foreign medium'. Leaders understandably gave pride of place to the indigenous languages of the subcontinent, such as Hindi, which has more native speakers than English. However, as the decades have passed, the influence of English has increased rather than declined. At the same time, English has become more 'indigenized'. As Salman Rushdie puts it:

> We can't simply use the language in the way the British did: it needs remaking for our own purposes. ... the British Indian writer simply does not have the option of rejecting English, anyway. His children, her children, will grow up speaking it, probably as a first language; and in the forging of a British Indian

identity the English language is of central importance. It must, in spite of everything, be embraced.

Rushdie is only one of many writers who have made Indian English literature famous throughout the world. Such writers – G. V. Desani, Vikram Seth and Arundhati Roy, for example – have grappled with the complexity of the post-colonial experience, and found that 'indigenized' English, with all its imperial baggage, nevertheless gives them a voice to express cross-currents of a multi-cultural society seeking its own identity. Moreover, English gives them a world audience, including especially other postcolonial societies (for example, in the Caribbean and in South Africa) who share much of their experience.

Conversely, words from the South Asian cultural sphere have also invaded and enriched English. During the colonial period lasting some 300 years, over 900 words entered English from Indian languages, such as *bungalow, cheetah, dinghy, guru, mogul, nirvana, pundit, thug, yoga*. Three interesting early examples are *brahmin, juggernaut* and *jungle*.

In traditional Hindu society a *brahmin* is a member of the highest of the four major castes. In American English it is now a term for a member of a cultural and social elite, especially a descendant of old New England families: *a Boston Brahmin*. Oliver Wendell Holmes, himself a member of the Harvard medical faculty, called New England's Brahmin caste 'the harmless, inoffensive, untitled Aristocracy'.

In Hindi *Jagannātha* is a form of the Hindu deity Krishna. His worshippers at centres in Orissa and Bengal were reputed to throw themselves under the wheels of a huge wagon on which the figure of Krishna was drawn in an annual procession. In Britain *juggernaut* is a rather uncomplimentary term for a very large lorry or truck that carries goods over long distances (corresponding to *semi* in the US). The word is also used metaphorically about something large and powerful that destroys everything it meets, as in *the juggernaut of war*.

To a reader of Rudyard Kipling's *The Jungle Book*, the word *jungle* has an exotic ring to it. But in Hindi *jangal* meant 'wasteland, uncultivated area', quite the opposite of lush vegetation. When it was taken over in Anglo-Indian it was gradually extended to an 'area of thick tangled trees'. In modern English the word is also used metaphorically for a world of ruthless competition or disorder, as in *corporate jungle, concrete jungle*.

English in Southeast Asia

Southeast Asia may be defined as the area of Asia south of China and east of the Indian subcontinent, and including the nations of Malaysia and Singapore. In 1786 the British established a bridgehead on Penang Island in the Strait of Malacca, and five years later the Malay Peninsula was taken over from the

Dutch. In 1819 Sir Thomas Stamford Raffles ('Raffles' is now best known as the name of a splendid Singapore hotel) acquired Singapore for the East India Company and founded a settlement there on the site of a fishing village. In 1826 Singapore became the governmental centre of 'the Straits Settlements', which also comprised Malaya and adjacent islands. Together with Singapore, Sabah and Sarawak, Malaya became the Federation of Malaysia in 1963, though two years later Singapore left the federation.

Early on, English became a school language in Britain's possessions in Southeast Asia, even if only a fraction of the population were able to attend school. Among those who received a British education, English became the natural language of contact. With the exception of the Philippines, which came under direct American influence, the English spoken in Southeast Asia had its origin in British English, though it is now heavily influenced by American English (see Figure 8.1, p. 151). Some estimates suggest that 350 million Southeast Asians speak English, but such a figure of course has to be treated with caution. Whatever the case, English is an important language in the region. It is not possible to talk about 'Southeast Asian English' as a specific variety. Local English varieties are developing, adopting new words, such as *agak-agak* 'estimate, guess' in Malaysia, *mug* 'cram, study hard' in Singapore. Here we will deal only with three countries where English today has some official or semi-official status: Singapore, Malaysia and the Philippines.

Today the island nation of Singapore is a multilingual society with four official languages: Mandarin Chinese, English, Malay and Tamil. English is the language of instruction in schools and an important language in government administration, the law courts, education and business. Many Singaporeans shift easily between Standard English and the popular variety familiarly known as **Singlish**, but the political leaders of Singapore stress that Singaporeans should speak internationally accepted English to avoid finding themselves in a 'cultural backwater'.

The official situation is very different in Malaysia, where Bahasa Malaysia (or Malay) became the official language after independence in 1957. Yet English, while considered a foreign language, is a compulsory school subject and a prestige lingua franca.

Among the main English-speaking countries in Southeast Asia, the Philippines has by far the largest population, with some 70 million people. After the Spanish-American War of 1898, a strong American presence emerged in the Philippines. This brief but crucial conflict gave the United States control of the remaining Spanish empire, including the Philippines, Guam and Puerto Rico, and turned the United States into an international power for the first time. During the Second World War the Philippines was occupied by Japan but became independent in 1946. Both English and Tagalog (locally called Pilipino) are now official languages. English is used in administration, the law courts, the armed forces and the police. In the media, Tagalog is widely used, but English still dominates.

After a disreputable colonial episode known as 'the Opium War', in 1842 Britain acquired from China the island of Hong Kong, and later also part of the mainland, Kowloon Peninsula. Later, China leased the adjoining New Territories to Britain for 99 years. On 1 July 1997 the whole colony of Hong Kong was returned to Chinese sovereignty.

In spite of 150 years of British rule, English has always played a secondary role in Hong Kong. The Cantonese dialect of Chinese is the first language of more than 98 per cent of the population and, with Hong Kong as a through-port between China and the world, Mandarin Chinese (or Putonghua, to use the Chinese name) is becoming increasingly important as the standard language of the People's Republic of China. After the transfer of power there has been uncertainty about the future role of English. Reports have claimed 'Hong Kong is unlearning English' and tourists have voiced growing frustration at not being understood. An educated guess, though, is that the English language will continue to be important in Hong Kong's role as an international centre of trade, business and finance.

By contrast, a boom is reported for the English language in Mainland China, especially in Shanghai. In the world's most populous country, there is surprisingly good competence in the English language among young people, as more and more parents, keen for their children to achieve, want their children to have exposure to this international language. It is a familiar, global pattern: English is seen as a window on the world.

New Englishes

The term **New Englishes** has been in use for about 20 years to describe the varieties of English emerging, typically in Outer Circle countries like India, Pakistan, Kenya, Nigeria, the Philippines, Fiji, Malaysia and Singapore. The use of this term invites controversy. It seems to claim that the English language is becoming plural: that instead of one standard international English extending all over the world, English is fragmenting into competing and possibly mutually incomprehensible 'languages'.

What has happened is actually more subtle. In the decades since independence, such countries have, for various reasons, maintained the educational, administrative and political functions of English. But the British or other mother-tongue speakers of the language no longer hold sway. As a result, regional varieties of the language, sharing some characteristics with the local languages, tend to develop their own prestige values, and some kind of standardization – or convergence of local varieties – begins to take place. At this stage there is a fear that the speakers of the regional variety, however well educated in their own regional English, will no longer be able to use English for purposes of international communication.

Broadly, there are three main levels of English to consider. At the 'top level', the international standard (whether coloured by American or British English) is retained for leading newspapers and for other public media, as well as for 'official' purposes. This international English is also typically regarded as the ultimate aim of English language education. At the middle level, there is a regional, 'standardizing' variety, which is used as a general lingua franca within the region, for example, between speakers of different languages in India. At the 'bottom' level, there are local varieties which mix English more strongly with characteristics of native languages. These 'vernacular Englishes' are valued for their role in maintaining local identities and allegiances, but are scarcely intelligible to the rest of the world. In a city like Singapore, the contrast is enormous between the clean, efficient, unemotive design of the international airport and the hotels, and the homely, pungent, lively atmosphere of the local markets. The difference between Singaporean international English and the vernacular 'Singlish' of the food halls is very much like this.

Taking Singlish as an example of vernacular English, we note that the pronunciation is quite remote from those of BBC English or General American: for example, the RP diphthongs /eɪ/ and /əʊ/ in *say* and *know* are frequently replaced by the pure vowels /e/ and /o/. Consonants at the end of syllables are often elided. The vocabulary of Singlish contains a large admixture of words from languages like Malay and Chinese (Cantonese and Hokkien dialects): for example, *jalan* 'to walk or stroll'; *agak-agak* 'to guess or approximate'; *kachau* 'to annoy or tease'. Very characteristic are short words at the end of an utterance, like *lah*, which add a particular emotive force to what precedes. In grammar, Singlish shows features that are found again and again in 'nativized' English outside the Inner Circle. The verb *be* can be omitted, as in *The teacher so strict!* The subject of a sentence can be omitted when it is clear from context: *Eat already?* And verbs often have no *-s* ending to signal the singular: *She eat meat.*

Another characteristic of New Englishes is their speakers' tendency to practise what linguists call **code-switching** – changing from one language to another in the same utterance – for example, switching from English to Malay and vice versa. The following comes from the spoken English of Malaysia, very close to that of Singapore:

Chandra: Lee Lian, you were saying you wanted to go shopping, nak perga tak? [Malay: 'Want to go, not?']
Lee Lian: Okay, okay, at about twelve, can or not?
Chandra: Can lah, no problem one! My case going to be adjourned anyway.
Lee Lian: What you looking for? Furniture or kitchenwares? You were saying, that day, you wanted to beli some barang-barang [Malay: 'buy … things'].

Chandra: Yes lah! Might as well go window-shopping a bit at least. No chance to ronda [Malay: 'hang around'] otherwise. My husband, he got no patience one!

Lee Lian: You mean you actually think husbands got all that patience ah? No chance man! Yes or not?

Chandra: Betul juga [Malay: 'True also']. No chance at all! But if anything to do with their stuff – golf or snooker or whatever, then dia pun boleh sabar one [Malay: 'he too can be patient'].

Here we find two women lawyers in Kuala Lumpur talking in a mixture of standard English, the local vernacular English, and Malay. The oddity of this is that one of the women is Chinese and the other Tamil – neither would speak English or Malay as a native language. Their dialogue is a veritable pot pourri of dialect and code-switching. It reminds us that much of the world, particularly in the Outer Circle, is multilingual, and that one of the uses of the New Englishes is to provide a neutral lingua franca between people whose mother tongues are different.

The New Englishes show English adapting to new cultures, societies and linguistic environments. The emerging varieties are in a state of flux and variation, but are beginning to be codified – for example, there is a dictionary of Singaporean and Malaysian English, the *Times-Chambers Essential English Dictionary* produced by a partnership including the National University of Singapore. But the New Englishes are caught in a magnetic field, attracted, on the one hand, towards the international pole – the need, as David Crystal says, 'to promote **intelligibility**' – and, on the other hand, towards the indigenous pole – the need to 'promote **identity**'. It is difficult to say which of these poles of attraction will prove stronger.

7
English Varieties
in the British Isles

> Within the British Isles, now as in the past, the English language exists
> and persists in an uncountable number of forms. Only one form – that
> taught to foreigners – is 'standard'.
>
> Robert Burchfield, *The English Language* (1985)

> Diversity among the regional dialects of England, particularly pronun-
> ciation, is greater than in any other part of the world where English is
> spoken as a native language.
>
> Celia M. Millward, *A Biography of the*
> *English Language* (1989)

Unlike spelling, which has been more or less standardized for the last two
centuries, pronunciation varies immensely among the hundreds of millions
of people who speak English as their first language. In Great Britain, pronunciation reflects both regional and social factors. There are, of course, different
geographical varieties: South-Western ('West Country') English, Northern
English, Scottish English, and so forth. But what is traditionally characteristic
of Britain, especially of England, is that many people are particularly conscious of accent as a class marker – a sensitivity to pronunciation which is
unparalleled in the English-speaking world, perhaps in the whole world.
Although no one English accent has official status, there are some widespread
attitudes to different accents, which may be of interest to learners of English
as a foreign language. In England, research has shown that RP (the 'BBC
accent', associated with southern England) has a high rating as being pleasing,
articulate and prestigious. In comparison, Northern accents (for example) are
rated poorly for these qualities, especially urban accents. But this is only
one side of the picture: for warmth and friendliness, the North does better
than RP.

RP (Received Pronunciation)

In the nineteenth century a particular English accent became the predominant prestige accent among the ruling classes of Britain and even of the British Empire. It was a class accent rather than a regional accent, fostered at élite schools such as Eton and Harrow. It is a paradox that such schools, despite their exclusiveness, were known as 'public schools'. (Nowadays 'independent schools' is a more popular term.) This accent became entrenched at the élite universities of Oxford and Cambridge ('Oxbridge') and in the upper ranks of English society wherever they might live.

The technical term now used is **Received Pronunciation** (in the sense of 'accepted pronunciation'), or RP for short; but there have also been more popular labels such as an **Oxbridge accent**, or **BBC English**. Although it is spoken by only a small and declining proportion of the British population, RP is an important point of reference when discussing different varieties of pronunciation in the English-speaking world. Because it is widely described and used in dictionaries and other books on English, we treat it in this book as a **reference accent**, one that can be used as a basis for comparisons with other accents. Our other reference accent is General American (GA, see pp. 81–2).

Salient features of the RP accent

The symbols used for describing the GA (General American) and RP (Received Pronunciation) accents are explained at the end of the book (pp. 275–6). Here we will simply point out one or two of the salient features of RP. As we see here, most differences of English accent are in the pronunciation of vowels.

- Unlike GA and Scottish and Irish accents, RP has no *r*-sound following a vowel (this is called **r-dropping**): *car* is pronounced /kɑː/, and *work* is pronounced /wɜːk/.
- RP has a set of diphthongs which end in the 'obscure' vowel schwa /ə/, where rhotic accents have an *r*-sound following a simple vowel. For example *here* is pronounced /hɪə/, *where* /weə/, and *pure* /pjʊə/.
- In RP the long back vowel /ɑː/ is used in words like *dance* and *glass*, whereas in Northern English accents a shorter and 'fronter' vowel is used: /a/. In the same words, GA uses /æ/ – compare RP /glɑːs/ with GA /glæs/.
- In words like *bus, cup, run* the more open vowel /ʌ/ in RP contrasts with the closer vowel /ʊ/ in northern English – compare /kʌp/ with /kʊp/ 'cup'.
- In RP the 'short o' vowel in *not, dog* is pronounced /ɒ/, whereas in GA it is pronounced /ɔː/ or /ɑː/: compare *boss* /bɒs/ with /bɔːs, bɑːs/.
- In RP the 'long o' vowel in *note, so, both* is pronounced as a diphthong beginning with schwa: /əʊ/. In many other accents, this vowel is pronounced with rounded lips as /oː/ or /oʊ/. Compare, for example, RP /nəʊ/ *no* with Scottish English /noː/.

Although we have been focusing on RP, the above features are actually found fairly generally across southern England.

RP acquired special importance as a model of pronunciation in many countries where English is taught as a second or foreign language. A distinguished English linguist actually defined RP as 'the kind of English that foreigners want to learn'. It is an accent which is both acceptable and comprehensible in large parts of the English-speaking world. However, the British linguist John Sinclair claims that

> RP is not a very useful model of pronunciation. It has some very complex sound combinations, particularly diphthongs, and it is not very closely related to the spelling system. Unlike other varieties, RP speakers make much the same noise saying *poor, paw, pour* and *pore*, and do not distinguish between *ion* and *iron*. So it is not the linguistic features of RP that give it such an appeal, but its social status and, above all, its availability in the classroom.

As a minority accent, it may seem that RP has acquired a status out of all proportion to its use, but language is not quota-based in democratic elections. According to the phonetician David Abercrombie, 'RP is a privileged accent: your social life, or your career, or both, may be affected by whether you possess it or not'. And Melvyn Bragg writes: 'We are, each one of us, all talking advertisements for our history. Accent is the snake and the ladder in the upstairs downstairs of social ambition. Accent is the con man's first resource.' (Con man = confidence trickster.)

RP as a form of pronunciation was historically rooted in the British class system but its status was enhanced by broadcasting. When the BBC started broadcasting in the 1920s, the news readers, dressed in dinner jackets invisible to their listeners, were recommended to use RP. This explains why this accent is also known as **BBC English**. One reason why the pioneers in British broadcasting favoured this accent was that it was thought to be the language form that would be most widely understood and accepted. Their problem, for the spoken language, was parallel to the dilemma of William Caxton (see pp. 43–5), the printer and translator who 450 years earlier had to choose a form of written English that would be most widely understood and accepted.

But Abercrombie's assessment above, although it dates only from the 1980s, now seems antiquated. In recent years, strict BBC guidelines have been relaxed, and different regional dialects can now be heard among regular broadcasters on radio and television. Also outside broadcasting, attitudes have changed. When asked whether RP would be a sensible model for learners of English, the well-known linguist M. A. K. Halliday said: 'I don't get too hung up on RP because the British don't use it now very much. I talk a kind of an international English which is not strictly RP in many ways, but it's good enough'. We can broadly distinguish three types of standardized accent:

- **General RP** is a mainstream variety, often used as a teaching model. It is used in many dictionaries and is also the variety that we represent in RP transcriptions in this book (see pp. 275–6).
- **Refined RP** used to be mainly associated with upper-class families and certain professions such as officers in the navy. It is increasingly declining and often regarded as affected. It can be heard in old British movies, where *off* is pronounced with a long vowel /ɔːf/ ('awf') instead of a short vowel /ɒf/, and where *powerless* sounds like /ˈpɑːlɪs/ instead of /ˈpaʊələs/.
- **Near-RP** can be described as basically RP except for a slight mixture of regional or individual characteristics.

The pyramid of standardization

How pronunciation varies in England has been idealized as a triangle-shaped or pyramid-shaped diagram showing regional variation along the horizontal axis and social stratification along the vertical axis. Here we show the diagram as a two-dimensional triangle, although it is better to think of it as a three-dimensional pyramid. At the apex of the pyramid is RP – a **region-neutral** accent which, in theory, does not vary from one part of the country to another, and is spoken by the 'upper crust' – people of education, wealth and influence. In the square area at the bottom of the pyramid there is maximum variation – that is, less advantaged, less educated speakers show the 'broadest' regional accents, so that there are the greatest differences of pronunciation between one geographical location and another. The line running along the base of the pyramid is meant to show the broad-ranging pattern of variation at the bottom of the pyramid, whereas the point at the top of the pyramid is meant to show a lack of variation from one region to another among speakers of the 'accentless' RP. This diagram, although no longer as realistic as it was, is still a useful starting point.

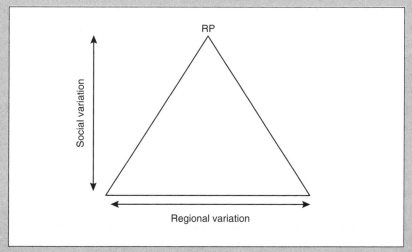

Figure 7.1 The pyramid of standardization

But we should not think of accents as confined by clear-cut boundaries, in either social or geographical terms. Actually there is a **continuum** or **scale** leading from RP towards increasingly 'broad' versions of regional accents, as already suggested by the pyramid diagram. Depending on how generously it is interpreted, near-RP can be extended to cover a growing percentage of today's population.

The diagram is also less rigid and unchanging than it looks. People can alter their position in the pyramid, for example, by acquiring a more prestigious accent. And it is worth noting that many speakers are inclined to *accommodate* their accents, perhaps unconsciously, to different social groups. So a bank clerk from Birmingham or Bristol, working in London, might well adapt to the prevailing accent of the workplace. This might entail a move towards RP, or towards a version of Estuary English (see p. 130).

To call RP 'the British accent' is actually inappropriate: a minority accent even in England, it is exceptional in other parts of the UK. RP fails to count as a 'standard British pronunciation', partly because of its élite associations and partly because of its alien 'Englishness' for the many of the inhabitants of Scotland, Wales and Northern Ireland.

In the rest of this chapter we take a look at some regional varieties in the British Isles: Cockney, 'Estuary English', Welsh English, Northern English, West Country English, Scottish English and Irish English. The emphasis will be on the most obvious indicators of regional variation, which are in general features of pronunciation, although other features – such as grammar – cannot be ignored.

Cockney

The word *cockney* has two meanings: a working-class Londoner and the variety of English spoken by 'cockneys'. *Cockney* is an old word derived from *cokeney*, which in the fourteenth century meant 'cock's egg', and was used as a nickname for a malformed egg. Later it came to be applied by country people to townsfolk, apparently because people in cities were considered ignorant of real country life and its customs. By the early seventeenth century the term was restricted to Londoners: 'Londiners, and all within the sound of Bow Bell, are in reproach called Cocknies'. To have been born within the sound of Bow Bells (the bells of St Mary-le-Bow in the City) is the traditional test of cockneydom. But in modern times this church is at some distance from the working-class heartland of London's East End, and the term 'cockney' is reasonably used to refer broadly to a traditional working-class London accent. (These days many young people's speech in the East End reflects non-cockney influences from immigrant communities – see pp. 237–9.)

Internationally, the cockney dialect is perhaps best known from the musical *My Fair Lady* by Lerner and Loewe, adapted from George Bernard Shaw's play

Pygmalion (1913), in which he poked fun at the way English speech reflected the notorious English class consciousness: 'It is impossible for an Englishman to open his mouth without making some other Englishman despise him,' says Professor Henry Higgins. In the play, Higgins is an expert in phonetics: 'You can spot an Irishman or a Yorkshireman by his brogue. I can place any man within six miles. I can place him within two miles in London. Sometimes within two streets.' To win a bet, Higgins undertakes the task of turning the flower-girl Eliza Doolittle into a lady who can move in high society without being taken for a cockney. She is drilled with jingles, such as *The rain in Spain stays mainly in the plain*, where she begins by pronouncing the vowel spelled *ai* as the cockney /aɪ/: '*The rhine in spine sties minely in the pline*', then changes miraculously to the elegant /eɪ/ in Higgins's RP.

Another typical cockney feature is **aitch-dropping**, that is, dropping initial /h/ so that *hammer* becomes /ˈæmə/, and words like these sound the same: *hedge* and *edge, heat* and *eat, hall* and *all* – but Eliza in *My Fair Lady* did eventually learn to get all her aitches right in the test jingle *In Hertford, Hereford and Hampshire, hurricanes hardly happen*. It is not uncommon for Americans to believe that this aitch-dropping is a general English feature. As Mark Twain put it: 'Some of the commonest English words are not in use with us – such as *'ousemaid, 'ospital, 'otel, 'istorian*'. Aitch-dropping prevails in working-class accents in most of England, but is unknown in North America, which suggests that it caught on in England after the American colonies were founded.

In cockney *th* sounds are often replaced, so that *think* becomes 'fink' and *thirty thousand* 'firty fahsn' with /f/ instead of /θ/, and *bother* may be pronounced as 'bovver' with /v/ instead of /ð/.

The 'catch in the throat' technically known as a **glottal stop** /ʔ/ is another of the hallmarks of cockney, but is nowadays found in many British varieties, especially among younger speakers. It is produced by bringing the vocal chords tightly together, blocking off the air-stream, then releasing them suddenly. In cockney it occurs, for example, instead of /t/ between vowels, as in *better* and *vital*, making these words sound like *beʔer* and *viʔal*. The glottal stop has been spreading also to other usages, such as replacing /t/ at the end of a word (*clean it out, mate* can sound something like *clean iʔ, ahʔ, miʔe*).

After a vowel, /l/ has become a vowel. Thus at the end of syllables, a vowel sound /o/ or /u/ is often heard instead of /l/: *well* will be pronounced /weu/ and *field* /fɪu/. A syllabic /l/ is rendered as a vowel in words like *bubble, middle* and *pickle*. Thus *people* is pronounced /ˈpiːpo/ or, with the glottal stop, /ˈpiːʔo/.

On radio and television cockney usage is often linked to **rhyming slang**. This form of slang consists of word play where the intended word is replaced by a phrase that rhymes with it, as in *trouble and strife* for 'wife', *bees and honey* for 'money', *cobblers' awls* for 'balls', *Bristol City* for 'titty'. Then the rhyming slang phrase is shortened, so that the rhyme disappears: for example, *take a butcher's*, cockney slang for 'take a look', is based on the rhyming slang *butcher's hook*. By a similar process, *Bristols* means 'breasts' (slang *titties*) and *cobblers* means 'nonsense' (slang *balls*).

Estuary English

John Wells, Britain's leading expert on English pronunciation, defines **Estuary English** on his website as follows:

> Estuary English is a name given to the form(s) of English widely spoken in and around London and, more generally, in the southeast of England – along the River Thames and its estuary.

On the same website, he writes:

> Estuary English is a new name. But it is not a new phenomenon. It is the continuation of a trend that has been going on for 500 years or more – the tendency for features of popular London speech to spread out geographically (to other parts of the country) and socially (to higher social classes). The erosion of the English class system and the greater social mobility in Britain today means that this trend is more clearly noticeable than was once the case.

The term Estuary English (EE for short) became a buzzword in the 1980s and 1990s, and excited plenty of controversy. This 'lingo' was condemned by some, including a British Education Minister, as a bastard 'cocknified' English that was infecting the speech of the country – even, allegedly, that of the Queen's youngest son, the Earl of Wessex. The name itself is a misnomer: it suggests that EE is located in the Thames estuary – downriver from London – whereas in fact it can better be seen as a more general spreading of features of popular London speech outside the metropolis – to the south-east generally and even beyond. It is influenced 'from below' by cockney, as well as 'from above' by RP. But there are some features that it does not take over from cockney, no doubt because they are stigmatized – for example, *h*-dropping and the broad vowel of /mæ:f/ for *mouth*. The /f/ and /v/ for *th*-sounds, although stigmatized – are also catching on in EE.

Wells mentions four features of (cockney) pronunciation as characteristic of EE. The first two have been already mentioned:

- Turning /l/ after a vowel (or the so-called syllabic /l/ of *people*) into /u/ or /o/, for example /mi:u/ for *meal*.
- Using the glottal stop instead of /t/ especially between vowels and at the end of words, as in *waʔer* for *water*, and *Gaʔwick airporʔ* for *Gatwick airport*.

- Pronouncing the final *y* after a consonant (as in *pity*) with a longish vowel sound rather like /i:/ (as if spelled *pittee*). In traditional RP this is a short vowel /i/ as in /'pɪti/.
- Pronouncing the beginning of words like *tune* as if spelled *choon*, and the beginning of words like *duke* as if spelled *juke*. This process, known as affrication, can also take place in the middle of a word before /u:/, as in *reduce* pronounced like *rejuce*.

People who disapprove of Estuary English often make satirical (and phonetically dubious) remarks: that 'How about you?' in EE sounds like *Abbar choo?* and 'around the corner' like *ran a coe na*. With its widening social and geographical spread, Estuary English is arguably a new accent undergoing standardization – a new RP. But this is hardly something that lies around the corner (*ran a coe na*),

Figure 7.2 Map of England and Wales

and is strenuously disputed by leading sociolinguist Peter Trudgill: 'It will never, in my view, become anything more than a regional accent, albeit the accent of a rather large region.' There is little doubt, however, that the emergence of EE, however ill-defined it may be, is a sign of the changing times which have seen a levelling of the old social class distinctions enshrined in the RP 'pyramid' diagram (Figure 7.1, p. 128).

Those who have been taught English as a foreign language by a teacher speaking RP might be excused for believing that everyone in England speaks that way. But in fact spoken English in the British Isles has always been far from uniform. For example, populations in areas of northern, south-western and eastern England speak forms of English which most non-Brits will find quaintly unfamiliar. We have no space to discuss all these regional varieties, but will briefly focus on (a) the North and (b) the West Country, areas that are relatively remote from the London metropolis, and no doubt for that reason preserve distinctive older features of the spoken language.

The North

Nearly a half of the population of England speaks with some kind of **Northern accent**: people in Great Britain have no problem recognizing someone from 'up North', although southerners will be vaguer in detecting different more specific northern varieties. In fact, in this sense 'northern' might more accurately be glossed 'Midland or Northern England' (see the map on p. 131). It includes not only the northernmost parts of the country, but also great industrial cities like Manchester, Liverpool, Leeds and Newcastle, and large parts of the Midlands. In terms of accent, even Birmingham is in some respects a 'northern' city. Characteristic features of northern accents are these:

- /ʊ/ (not RP /ʌ/) in words such as *love, bus, blood*. So the vowels in *put* and *putt, stood* and *stud* are pronounced the same.
- /a/ (not RP /ɑː/) in words such as *aunt, bath, laugh, past*. Thus *ant* and *aunt* are pronounced alike. *Taskmaster* contains two examples of the same vowel /a/ – /ˈtaskˌmastə/ – whereas in RP it is /ˈtɑːskˌmɑːstə/.
- /a/ (instead of RP /æ/) in words such as *ham, mad, sad*.

In the 'true North', for example in Lancashire and Yorkshire, there is a strong tendency to use pure long vowels instead of the diphthongs of RP: for example *don't know* using the pure vowel /oː/, and *the rain in Spain* using the pure vowel /eː/ or /ɛː/.

In all these differences of vowel sound, northern English actually represents an older variety of English than RP: the distinction between /æ/ and /ɑː/, for example, emerged in the South of England in the eighteenth century, and the

North has not caught up with it. This, however, is unlikely to worry most northerners, as northern regions tend to foster pride in local speech, and many a northerner will want to be audibly identifiable as a Yorkshireman, a 'Scouser' (from Liverpool) or a 'Geordie' (from Tyneside), as the case may be. (Our choice of masculine 'man' here reflects a well-known sociolinguistic finding that generally men show a greater attachment to the local accent, whereas women lean more towards prestige forms.)

Nevertheless, there can be social pressures here, as elsewhere, to adopt a pronunciation which moves some way up the social ladder towards RP. For example, a Manchester or Leeds professional who doesn't want to sound *too* northern may settle on a compromise vowel for *bus* – something like /bəs/ – between the northern /bʊs/ and the southern /bʌs/.

If northern English is conservative in pronunciation, it can also be conservative in grammar – for example, in Yorkshire we can still hear Shakespeare's familiar second-person pronoun *thou/thee* (see p. 55). But another well-known Yorkshire feature – the reduction of the definite article *the* so that only a single consonant remains, if that – was never used by southerners. This feature is rendered in writing as *t'*, as in *Put t'dish in t'oven*, but its pronunciation varies according to what follows. In this example, the first *t'* would probably be pronounced as a glottal stop /ʔ/ and the second as a /t/.

The West Country

The dialect of the south-western counties of England such as Devon and Somerset is often called **West Country** (see the map on p. 131) – although that term might also apply to counties like Gloucestershire, on the South Wales border. The most striking feature of the West Country accent is its preservation of the /r/ sound after a vowel, as in /baːrn/ for *barn* (compare /baːn/ in RP) and /nɜːrs/ for *nurse* (compare /nɜːs/ in RP). This /r/ was general to English, even in London, in Shakespeare's day (see pp. 56–7), and was subsequently lost – but not before it had been exported by early colonists to America, where it famously still survives and flourishes (see p. 81). In the most widely used American pronunciation, as in the West Country, the /r/ is formed not by a trill or tap of the tip of the tongue, as commonly in Scotland (see p. 143), but by a bunching of the tongue towards the back of the mouth, a so-called **retroflex r**, which yields a heavy 'burr' sound often affecting the preceding vowel. To this extent, a transcription such as /baːrn/ or /nɜːrs/ is misleading, as the /a:/ and the /r/ occur together (or at least are overlapping sounds), rather than in succession. The /r/ following a vowel, although enshrined in English spelling, has been on the retreat in England for centuries. It is still found in various enclave areas in the West and the North, but is preserved most strongly in the West Country.

Another old and declining feature of West Country pronunciation is the use of a voiced consonant, especially /z/, where the corresponding voiceless consonant /s/ is standard. The West Country county of Somerset in this way is sometimes rendered as *Zummerzet* – a pronunciation that is nowadays, however, used more in joke than in authentic speech.

Grammatically, the traditional dialects of the West Country have some strange features, particularly in the use of pronouns and verbs: *Give it to he, not they – her don't need it.* This shows a curious reversal of the normal use of pronouns in standard English (*Give it to him, not them – she doesn't need it.*) As for verbs, a characteristic feature of the Somerset dialect is the use of the single verb form *be* instead of the different forms *am, is, are* in standard English, and a similar use of the negative form *ben't: I be, you be, she be, they be, I ben't, she ben't*, and so on. These features are now declining and being mixed with standard forms, like so many survivals of dialect grammar and vocabulary.

Vernacular grammar

But here let's notice a more general point. There is a whole range of flourishing non-standard grammatical features which are spread across dialect areas and are even found outside Britain, in the United States and in other Inner-Circle English-speaking countries. We can call these phenomena collectively **vernacular grammar** – the grammar of the popular, untaught variety of a language often found in colloquial speech. Its main features are:

- *Ain't* as a general negative form of the verb *be* or *have* in the present tense: *I ain't, you ain't, she ain't*, and so on.
- The *-s* form of the verb, used where an *-s* does not occur in standard English: *I says no*; *Whatever they wants they gets.*
- The opposite pattern: the form without *-s* used where an *-s* form is standard; for example *were* instead of *was*, and *don't* instead of *doesn't*: *It were a bloody mess; She don't have no manners.*
- The so-called 'double negative', as in the previous example, where two or more negative words are used to express a single negative idea: *I **ain't** done **nothing*** meaning 'I haven't done anything'.
- With some common verbs, the past tense form is used instead of the past participle form, and vice versa: *You done it last year. Well she's broke 'er leg.*
- Use of oblique pronouns like *me, them*, in subject position where *I, they*, etc. would occur in standard English: *Me and Jody had a contest.*
- *What* used to introduce a relative clause or comparative clause: *She's got the book what I had last week; It's harder than what you think.*
- *Them* used instead of *those: Did you post all them letters on Monday?*

These features of vernacular grammar are looked down on as uneducated, but are surprisingly resilient and widespread in popular speech in England and elsewhere.

English in Wales

Both English and Welsh are spoken in Wales. **Welsh** (*Cymraeg* in Welsh) is a Celtic language (see Figure 7.2, p. 131; pp. 14–15) and spoken by more than one-fifth of the Welsh population of 2.8 million. Unlike other Celtic-speaking areas, in Wales the indigenous tongue is not languishing under the threat of extinction, even if English remains the predominant language. Both Welsh and English are by law on an equal footing in Welsh government administration. Road signs are bilingual, and there is a television channel broadcasting in Welsh. It is hard to resist the external pressure to learn and use English, but also there is a strong impulse to strengthen national identity through the Welsh language.

Recorded literature in Welsh goes back even beyond Old English literature, to the sixth century. After the Anglo-Saxon invasions (see pp. 17–19), Wales remained a stronghold of the British people who had been displaced from the territory of the English, and who spoke the British or Old Welsh tongue. The English language began to encroach on Welsh when, from the end of the eleventh century, Norman barons started to take over the region under the sovereignty of the Norman kings of England. In a sense, Wales became England's first colony and, from the early fourteenth century, was ruled from England as a principality. In 1301 King Edward I conferred on his heir, who was born in Wales, the title of 'Prince of Wales', and since then it has become tradition for the first-born son of a British monarch to be given this title. By the Acts of Union of 1535 and 1543 Wales was incorporated with England, and this promoted the use of English for official and educational purposes. Although English is today the native language for the majority of the Welsh, this is quite a recent phenomenon. It was only in the second half of the nineteenth century that the linguistic scales tipped in favour of English. This was partly as a result of compulsory education in English, and partly because the opening of the Welsh coalfields meant a large influx of English speakers into South Wales. In a sense, the United States has been an English-speaking country for longer than Wales. Recently there are signs that the Welsh language is making a come-back: the 2001 census showed an increase in the percentage of Welsh speakers (from 19 to 21 per cent) for the first time for almost a century.

Although the average Welsh speaker of English is readily understood by other British speakers of English, there are one or two grammatical features of the Welsh dialect which sound rather 'unEnglish', and may be due to the influence of Welsh language as a Celtic **substratum**. (A 'substratum' is a linguistic term denoting a native language which affects another more dominant language that encroaches on its territory.) We meet invariant interrogative forms such as *isn't it? is it?* and *yes?*: *You're leaving, is it?* The tag question, here corresponding to *are you?*, is used independently of the verb form in the previous phrase, like French *n'est-ce pas?* or German *nicht wahr?* We also find some cases of unusual word-order, such as *Very interested, I for was* and *Intended for Plas Newydd, this lot is*, where the verb is placed at the end, and the predicative part in front. Exclamations can be introduced by *there*: *There's young she looks!* corresponding to *How young she looks!*

Still, it's not grammar but pronunciation that is most noticeable in Welsh English. For example, the final /i/ vowel found in RP is lengthened to /i:/, as in /'vali:/ for *valley*. This word, in its plural form /'vali:z/ *valleys*, has a special relevance to the Welsh, as it refers to the mining valleys of South Wales, where a good proportion of the population lives. The Welsh are well-known for their love of singing, and perhaps it is no coincidence that when they speak it is with a 'sing-song' intonation, where the voice often rises from a stressed syllable to an unstressed syllable. For example, in

Lóvely dáy, ísn't it?

the voice rises from *Love* to *-ly*, and from *is* to *n't*, falling again on *it*. This lilting melody is particularly strong in the valleys. One non-English sound you will often hear in Welsh English – although it's actually a sound of the Welsh language – is the 'voiceless *l*' (/ɬ/ in phonetics) that is spelled *ll* and occurs in many Welsh place-names – *Llangollen*, *Llanelli* and *Llandudno*, for example. The English have a poor record of speaking Welsh names, and often pronounce the *ll* as if it were spelled *thl* or *kl*: 'Thlangothlen', 'Klanethli'.

English in Scotland

The English language has a long and proud pedigree in Scotland. Some 1,400 years ago, long before Scotland or England was a state, the northern Old English dialect known as **Northumbrian** filtered into the region that today makes up the Lowlands of Scotland (see map, p. 139). Its earliest known form has survived in the runic inscriptions carved on a seventh- or eighth-century church cross, called the Ruthwell Cross, not far from the English border in south-west Scotland.

These fragments of the poem *The Dream of the Rood* represent in fact one of the earliest texts in any form of English. The words here are spoken by the cross on which Christ was crucified (the original text is transcribed from the runic inscription; to check what the runes look like, see Figure 2.5, p. 28):

ORIGINAL TEXT	MODERN ENGLISH TRANSLATION
ondgeredæ hinæ god almeʒtig	Girded him then God Almighty
þa he walde on galgu gistiga	when he wished to ascend the gallows
modig fore allæ menn …	brave before all men….
ahof ic riicnae kyniŋc	I held aloft the powerful king,
heafunæs hlafard hælda ic ni dorstæ	The Lord of Heaven, I dared not bend.

Figure 7.3   An engraving of the four sides of the Ruthwell Cross

At this time the peoples in the region now known as Scotland were a diverse mixture of Celts and Angles, but two factors in particular promoted a cohesive process. One was the advent of Christianity, which came from Ireland to the island of Iona and then to the Anglian kingdom of Northumbria. Another was the impact of Scandinavian attacks. Faced with the Viking peril, from the end of the eighth century on (see p. 22), the rival peoples were compelled to unite forces. Nevertheless, the Vikings settled and left their mark on the English language in Scotland – what now has become **Scots**. Even today some traditional Scots words seem curiously familiar to a Scandinavian visitor (Swedish words in brackets):

bairn (barn) 'child', *big* (bygga) 'build', *blae* (blå) 'blue', *brig* (brygga) 'bridge', *flit* (flytta) 'move house', *gate* (gata) 'road, street', *gowk* (gök) 'cuckoo', *ken* (kunna) 'know', *kirk* (kyrka) 'church', *kist* (kista) 'chest'

In early medieval Scotland there was in fact a profusion of languages. The Celtic language **Gaelic** (pronounced /'geɪlɪk/ or /'gælɪk/) was the most widespread language, yet English has adopted only a few words of Gaelic origin – here are some of them:

> *bog* from BOGACH
> *cairn* (as in *Cairn terrier*) from CARN
> *crag* from CREAGH
> *glen* from GLEANN
> *loch* (as in *Loch Ness*) where *loch* is pronounced /lɒx/ (with the final sound in German *ach*)
> *plaid* (pronounced /plæd/) from PLAIDE
> *slogan* from Scots *slogorne* 'battle cry', ultimately from SLUAGH-GHAIRM (where SLUAGH means 'host' and GAIRM 'shout').

The variety of Northern Old English that later became Scots was used in the Lowlands (the area bounded by England to the south and the Highlands to the north – see Figure 7.4, p. 139). The language of the Northern Isles was **Norn**, a Norse language established by the Viking settlement. Apart from Gaelic, another Celtic language closely allied to Welsh, **Cumbric**, was spoken in the south-west. Then, after the Norman invasion of England in 1066, Scotland came under Anglo-Norman influence: Norman French became the language of the nobility and Latin became the academic, ecclesiastical and legal language. Later, Scots – the Scottish descendant of Old English – became the majority language and the language of courts and kings. By the fifteenth century Scots had acquired a rich literature, and a new set of loanwords from French.

Why do French words never spoken by the English crop up in Scots? Anglo-Norman barons had been given land in both England and Scotland, which led to repeated conflicts when the English king laid claim to the Scottish Crown. Scotland responded by forming an alliance with France, known in history as the **Auld Alliance** ('the old alliance'), which made a lasting impression on the language. Among the French words borrowed into Scots are *douce* 'sweet' from DOUX / DOUCE; and *fash* 'bother' (from se fâcher), as in the expression *Dinna fash yersel!* 'Don't worry!' Even the supremely Scottish word *tartan* appears to come from TIRETAINE, an Old French word for a kind of cloth.

Robert Bruce, the latest of eight generations of Norman barons, led the Scottish forces to victory over the English in the famous Battle of Bannockburn in 1314, and England soon recognized Scotland as an independent kingdom. During the sixteenth century, there was an increase in Southern English influence. After centuries of border warfare, in 1603 a union was formed between

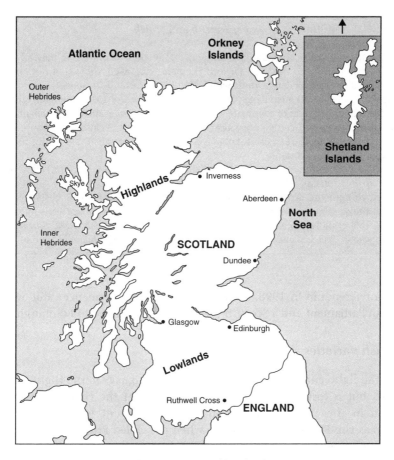

Figure 7.4 Map of Scotland

the two countries when King James VI of Scotland moved from Edinburgh to London to become James I and king of both countries. In his own words:

> What God hath conioyned then, let no man separate. I am the Husband, and all the whole Isle is my lawfull Wife.

King James himself was no mean linguist. His native tongue was Lowland Scots, and it is said that he never lost a strong Scottish accent. But he could also use standard southern English – **Southron** as the Scots said – and to this variety he adapted his own writing. The court's move south led to a loss of cultural and linguistic autonomy in Scotland. Worse, in 1707 the Scottish Parliament literally voted itself out of existence when Scotland became part of the United Kingdom of Great Britain. Since then, Scotland has been governed from Westminster in London, although it has its own legal and educational system.

> ### *Scots, Scottish* and *Scotch*
>
> Among themselves, Scots may have differences, but there is one thing they all agree on: they do not like to be called *English*. They are *Scots*, even *British*, but not *English*. There are a few other related words which should be treated with sensitivity.
>
> **Scots** (in the plural) means the people of Scotland: *the Scots*. The singular *a Scot* can be used for either a man or a woman, in addition to *a Scotsman* and *a Scotswoman*. *Scots* is also an adjective: *a Scots family, Scots law, the Scots Guards*. As a singular noun, *Scots*, as we have just seen, refers to a language (or variety of English, according to your viewpoint) used in Scotland.
>
> But the most common adjective is **Scottish**, as in *Scottish dancing, Scottish universities, the Scottish Highlands, a Scottish accent*.
>
> Even though the Scots are called **Scotch** in many parts of the English-speaking world, they prefer the form *Scots*. On the other hand, *Scotch* is used for some well-established combinations such as *Scotch terrier, Scotch eggs, Scotch tweed, Scotch wool, Scotch whisky. Scotch* is also used as a noun in the sense 'whisky made in Scotland'.

After a referendum in 1998, a limited degree of independence came when a Scottish Parliament and a Scottish Executive were restored to Edinburgh.

Scottish varieties

Until the eighteenth century the predominant language in the Highlands was **Gaelic**, but it lost ground following the defeat of the Highlanders by the English in the 1745 Rebellion. This traumatic event in Scottish history, known as **the Forty-Five**, took place when the exiled Prince Charles Edward Stuart ('Bonnie Prince Charlie') landed in Scotland to reinstate the Catholic heirs of the Stuart dynasty, ousted from Britain 60 years before. But within a year, the Prince, leading the clansmen, was defeated in the disastrous Battle of Culloden. The Highlanders were in for hard times: the native dress was forbidden, and the native language, Scottish Gaelic, was suppressed or discouraged.

Today English is spoken in the whole of Scotland, but Gaelic is heard in the homes of the north-west, above all in the Western Isles (the Hebrides), and is mastered by some 80,000 of Scotland's five million inhabitants. The Scots who are not Gaelic speakers (the vast majority) can be said to speak two languages – Scots and English – or one language – Scots English – according to your viewpoint. We will try to explain this riddle below.

Scots, spoken in parts of the Lowlands, is sometimes known as **Broad Scots** or (remembering its literary heritage of over 600 years) **the Guid** /gyd/ **Scots Tongue** 'the good Scots tongue'. The term **Lallans** refers particularly to the variety of Scots revived through a twentieth-century literary renaissance.

Opinions differ as to whether Scots should be regarded as a variety of English or an independent language, rather as Danish and Swedish are closely related but still considered distinct languages. Supporting the independent language theory is the recent decision of the European Bureau of Lesser Used Languages (an agency of the European Union) to recognize Scots as a language. But in any case, it is important to remember that Scots is not a Gaelic language or even descended from Gaelic, but has its roots in the Northumbrian dialect of Old English.

For an outsider, Scots can be hard to understand. A lot of the vowel sounds, and their spellings, are different from English – for example, *hoos* 'house', *hame* 'home', *tak* 'take', *auld* 'old'. (The Great Vowel Shift [see p. 61] which refashioned the vowel system of English English did not take place to the same extent in Scots.) There are also divergences of grammar and vocabulary.

With the loss of Scottish independence in the seventeenth and eighteenth centuries, the ancestral Scots tongue lost status, being regarded by leaders of opinion as a barbarous dialect. But it made a glorious come-back in a literary revival personified in Scotland's national poet, Robert Burns. In the twentieth century, another great poet, Hugh MacDiarmid, was the leading spirit of a further revival of literary Scots (or Lallans) known as the Scottish Renaissance.

In the Scottish Parliament, the normal working language is English, but people are allowed to address the Parliament in Scots. The Parliament's website also contains pages in Scots, and the following extract, with its translation into standard English, will illustrate the difference between the two tongues:

Scots

Walcome til the Scottish Pairlament wabsite

The Scottish Pairlament is here for tae represent aw Scotland's folk.
We want tae mak siccar that as mony folk as can is able tae find oot aboot whit the Scottish Pairlament dis and whit wey it warks. We hae producit information anent the Pairlament in a reenge o different leids tae help ye tae find oot mair.

English

Welcome to the Scottish Parliament website

The Scottish Parliament is here to represent all Scotland's people.
We want to make sure that as many people as possible are able to find out about what the Scottish Parliament does and in what way it works. We have produced information about the Parliament in a range of different languages to help you to find out more.

Given the chequered history of languages in Scotland, it is not surprising that the present linguistic situation is complex. Although Scots is often regarded as a separate language from English, there is actually a continuum of variation linking 'broad' Scots with **Scottish (standard) English**, which we will abbreviate ScotE. This can be described as standard English with a Scottish flavour, and can be typified as the language of the middle class. This variety is the result of long-lasting political, economic and linguistic intercommunication with England. In terms of lexis and grammar, present-day Scottish English varies rather little from English found in other parts of the Inner Circle, but it is usually easy to identify a Scottish accent and intonation.

Although the standard 'regionless' British pronunciation – RP – is spoken by a few Scots, this prestige accent has not enjoyed the same respect in Scotland as it has in England. By contrast, a Scottish accent is socially recognized as 'good English' even in Southern England, which cannot be said for many Northern English accents, such as *Scouse* in Liverpool or *Geordie* in Newcastle.

In Scotland, there seem to be *r*-sounds burring everywhere. Many visitors from abroad find it comfortable to hear *morning paper* sound more or less as it is spelled, /ˈmɔrnɪŋ ˈpeːpər/, with clearly audible *r*'s. But it is above all the ScotE vowels which differ from RP. In RP we have the same vowel in *nurse* /nɜːs/, *bird*

Figure 7.5   Robert Burns

Auld Lang Syne

On 25 January Scots all over the world gather to eat, drink, recite and sing. The most prominent dish on the Burns Night supper table is haggis, made from heart, lungs and liver chopped up with suet, oatmeal, onions and seasonings, and boiled in a sheep's stomach. It takes some Scotch whisky to wash down the meal, and the most important toast is to *The Immortal Memory*. This unofficial Scottish holiday is celebrated in memory of the poet Robert Burns, born on 25 January 1759. A Burns Night ends with the company singing *Auld Lang Syne* (which is Scots for 'old long since', that is to say, 'the good old days'):

> Should auld acquaintance be forgot,
> And never be brought to mind?
> Should auld acquaintance be forgot,
> And auld lang syne!
>
> For auld lang syne, my dear,
> For auld lang syne,
> We'll tak a cup o' kindness yet,
> For auld lang syne.

Burns never claimed authorship of the poem. In a letter he wrote: 'It is the old song of the olden times, which has never been in print. I took it down from an old man's singing.' It is the best-known contribution of Scots to World English.

The singing of *Auld Lang Syne* traditionally ushers in the New Year in Scotland; then after midnight it is customary to visit friends, bringing a symbolic gift.

Robert Burns was born in a cottage near Ayr on the west coast of southern Scotland. An avid reader as a child, he was encouraged by his father, a struggling tenant farmer of little education. Looking for money to emigrate, he published his first collection of poetry, *Poems Chiefly in the Scottish Dialect*, in 1786. It was an immediate and overwhelming success. Burns is considered the greatest poetic voice of Scotland. His lyrics, written in Scots and infused with lively irreverent humour, celebrate love, patriotism and rustic life. After a number of amorous adventures, Burns settled in the town of Dumfries where he lived until his early death in 1796, first as a farmer and later as an officer in the excise. His last home, like his birthplace, is now a museum.

/bɜːd/ and *heard* /hɜːd/, but in ScotE they are pronounced *bird* /bəːrd/, *heard* /hɛːrd/, *word* /wʌrd/.

In general, ScotE strikingly preserves pure vowels, even when they are followed by /r/. For example, *here* and *cord* are pronounced /hir/ and /kord/. The pure /o/ is also used for words like *go*, instead of the diphthong /əʊ/ of RP. As a consequence, ScotE has considerably fewer diphthongs than other accents including RP, American and Australian accents. The Scots make no systematic difference between short and long vowels: *pull* and *coat, foot* and *boot* all have a shortish vowel.

This *r*-sound, by the way, is usually quite different from the *r* of American or West Country English. In ScotE it is stereotypically a **trilled or tapped** *r* pronounced with the tip of the tongue, as contrasted with the back-of-the-tongue **retroflex** *r*. However, nowadays a variety of *r*-sounds, including the retroflex *r*, are current in Scotland, and the trilled *r* is not the most common.

In RP the pairs *witch* and *which, weather* and *whether* are all pronounced with initial /w/. In Scottish English the *wh*-spelling is respected and words like *which* and *whether* are pronounced with initial /hw/, as in General American (p. 164).

Turning now to vocabulary: the Scots use some words which are rarely heard south of the border:

aye for 'yes'	*burn* for 'stream, brook'
dram for 'drink'	*dreich* for 'dull'
haar for 'mist'	*bonny* for 'pretty, beautiful'
outwith for 'outside, apart from'	*wee* for 'little'

There are also words which are shared with northern dialects of English, but are thought of as typically Scottish: *ken* 'know', *kirk* 'church', *lass* or *lassie* 'girl', *lad* or *laddie* 'boy'.

Grammar also shares some features with northern English: for example, a preference for using a contracted verb + *not*, rather than a verb + *n't*: for example, *I'll not do it* rather than *I won't do it*. The dislike of *n't* is also noticed in questions spelled out as *Are you no coming?* instead of *Aren't you coming?* ScotE also has a form of negation with the shortened negative form *nae*, as in *I cannae* ('can't') *help it, You dinnae* ('don't') *have to go*.

One of the most characteristic grammatical features is the double modal verb construction, for example combining *might* + *can*, as in *I might could go* ('I might be able to go'). This is found in some parts of the Lowlands, and also in some southern areas of the United States – thanks to the Scots-Irish settlements in Appalachia and further south.

English in Ireland

Every year on 17 March in cities all over the English-speaking world, a rather obscure fifth-century British bishop is commemorated. Why? Because the descendants of the people he worked among have dispersed all over the English-speaking world. He is known in history as Saint Patrick, the patron saint of Ireland, who came from Great Britain and converted the island to Christianity. In the United States alone, where **Saint Patrick's Day** is celebrated with much gusto and pageantry, more than 40 million Americans claim Irish descent, making Irish Americans (by this reckoning) the third largest ethnic group in the country. In the early 1800s Ireland was the most densely populated country in Europe but, half a century later, one of the least. At the time of the disastrous Irish famine 1846–51, large numbers of Irish left their homeland,

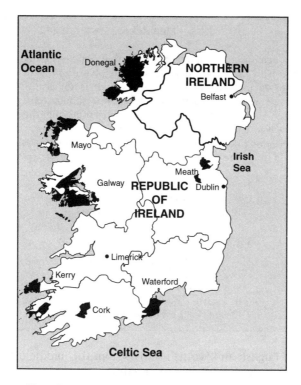

Figure 7.6   Map of Ireland (Gaeltacht areas in black)

voluntarily or by necessity, many of them bound for Australia, Newfoundland and America. By 1855 one-third of New York's population was Irish-born.

There are two official languages spoken in Ireland, **Irish** and **English**, differing enormously in background and spread. The indigenous language was Irish, a Celtic language closely related to Scottish Gaelic (which was indeed originally exported from Ireland into Scotland). Sometimes called **Irish Gaelic** or **Gaelic**, it has become a potent national symbol.

The earliest known contacts with speakers of a Germanic language were with the Vikings. They colonized the Irish seaboard and founded the cities of Dublin, Cork, Waterford and Limerick, which became important trading stations with an Irish-Scandinavian population. In spite of the long Viking presence in Ireland, lasting from the ninth to the early eleventh century, Old Norse had little direct impact on the development of Irish English.

The twelfth century saw an invasion of Ireland by Anglo-Norman adventurers – French speakers in the main. The earliest recorded use of English in Ireland dates from the mid-thirteenth century.

During the following 300 years English was spoken only in the eastern coastal area around Dublin. The English spoken in Ireland today has its roots in a

---

Limerick

Limerick is a borough of southwest Ireland on the Shannon River estuary, but the word also stands for a light humorous, nonsensical, often bawdy piece of verse. The link between Limerick the place and limerick the verse form is not clear.

A limerick is not necessarily bawdy, but in its most popular form it involves the sexes in ribald situations. It consists of five lines with a rollicking triple metre and the rhyme scheme *aabba*. The first line typically begins with *There was ...* and ends with the name of a place or a person. Here are two quite decent samples (with underlining showing the position of stressed syllables, and so helping to indicate the rhythm):

> There <u>was</u> a young <u>la</u>dy of <u>Wilts</u>
> Who <u>walked</u> up to <u>Scot</u>land on <u>stilts</u>.
>   When they <u>said</u>, 'Oh, how <u>shock</u>ing
>   To <u>show</u> so much <u>stock</u>ing!'
> She <u>an</u>swered, 'Well, <u>how</u> about <u>kilts</u>?'

> There <u>was</u> a young <u>la</u>dy named <u>Bright</u>
> Who could <u>tra</u>vel much <u>fas</u>ter than <u>light</u>.
>   She <u>star</u>ted one <u>day</u>
>   In a <u>re</u>lative <u>way</u>
> And came <u>back</u> on the <u>pre</u>vious <u>night</u>.

---

second wave of English and Scottish settlers from the middle of the sixteenth century on, but Irish was still the predominant language and an important symbol of Irish identity. The colonists kept their language and their Protestant religion, in a country where the majority has remained staunchly Catholic to this day. Generally speaking, those who settled in the south came from western and southern England, while those who settled in the north came from the Lowlands of Scotland. To this day, there are strong similarities between the English of south-western Scotland and that of northern Ireland.

In the seventeenth century, Ireland suffered a chequered history of colonization, rebellion, military conquest and subjugation. In the eighteenth century, power was in the hands of an Anglo-Irish Protestant governing class, while Catholics were deprived of land, political power, and religious freedom.

In 1801 Ireland became a part of the United Kingdom, and in 1833 Catholics were at long last granted toleration and political rights. At that time, about half of the population was English-speaking. Particularly as a result of the disastrous Great Famine of 1845–50, millions of Irish emigrated, especially to the United States, in the nineteenth and early twentieth centuries. During this period the use of the Irish language was in catastrophic decline. But when southern Ireland became virtually independent of Great Britain in 1921, Irish became an official language, together with English, and a compulsory school subject. Despite powerful governmental and public support, however, Irish has continued to lose ground to English. Today, while bilingualism is widespread, native speakers of Irish form a small minority, mainly limited to the **Gaeltacht** /'gerᵊltæxt/, the Irish-speaking districts in the west.

Total independence was achieved in 1949 with the proclamation of the Republic of Ireland. But part of the island, **Northern Ireland** (also known as the Six Counties or Ulster) remains within the UK, which is hence known in full as 'the United Kingdom of Great Britain and Northern Ireland' (see p. 16). In this part of Ireland, the Irish English dialect is distinctively different, and is noticeably similar to the nearby Lowland Scots of south-west Scotland, from which many of its Protestant settlers originally came. Indeed, as with Scots in Lowland Scotland, the 'dialectal variety' called **Ulster Scots** has been given European recognition as an independent language, sometimes known as **Ullans**. Like most things in Northern Ireland, this involves both politics and religion. The Catholic and Republican community of Northern Ireland (wanting

---

Literary Ireland

It is remarkable that the three 'Celtic countries' of Wales, Scotland and Ireland, with venerable literatures in their own Celtic languages, have enormously enriched the culture of English-speaking peoples through their contributions to literature in English. Ireland has an outstanding literary tradition, using the imported English language as its own, with a long line of authors well known throughout the world – among them are four Nobel laureates. Here is a sample:

Jonathan Swift (1667–1745), known for his bitingly satirical works, including *Gulliver's Travels* and *A Modest Proposal*.

Oscar Wilde (1854–1900), renowned as a wit in London literary circles. He achieved recognition with the novel *The Picture of Dorian Gray* and the brilliant dialogue of his plays, such as *The Importance of Being Earnest*.

George Bernard Shaw (1856–1950), playwright, essayist and critic, today perhaps best known for his play *Pygmalion* (see p. 129). He won the 1925 Nobel Prize for literature.

John Millington Synge (1871–1909) whose plays based on Irish rural life, and written in a lyrical style modelled on rural dialect, include *The Playboy of the Western World*.

William Butler Yeats (1865–1939) whose poetry, inspired by Ireland's landscape and Celtic traditions, ranges from early love lyrics to the complex symbolic works of his later years. He won the 1923 Nobel Prize for literature.

James Joyce (1882–1941) whose extraordinary literary innovations have had a profound influence on modern fiction with works such as *Ulysses* and *Finnegans Wake*.

Samuel Beckett (1906–89), whose novels include *Murphy* and *Malone Dies*. Beckett is known to a wider audience for his absurdist plays, such as *Waiting for Godot*. He won the 1969 Nobel Prize for literature.

Seamus /'ʃeɪməs/ Heaney (born 1939), whose poetry is typified by dense, earthy imagery and concern for the political crises of his homeland. His works include *Death of a Naturalist*, *Field Work* and a translation of *Beowulf* into modern English (see pp. 31–2). He won the Nobel Prize for literature in 1995.

to become part of a united island of Ireland) has espoused the rights of speakers of Irish Gaelic. Correspondingly, the Protestant and Loyalist community (wanting Northern Ireland to remain part of the UK) has espoused the rights of speakers of Ulster Scots. But the vast majority of the Irish, whether in the Republic or in Northern Ireland, use English for everyday purposes.

Linguists employ different terms to describe the English language as used in Ireland: **Anglo-Irish** is the old name associated with English colonization. **Hiberno-English** has often been used in linguistic scholarship (*Hiberno* being derived from *Hibernia*, the Roman name for Ireland). We will use a more neutral term, **Irish English**, which also fits into the pattern set by *American English, Indian English, Scottish English* and so on.

The Republic of Ireland is officially bilingual. Here is a short extract in English and Irish from the home page of the Parliament of Ireland:

> Following the Anglo-Irish Treaty of December 1921 – when Britain recognised Ireland's independence as the Irish Free State, with jurisdiction over twenty-six of the country's thirty-two counties – the third Dáil was elected in June 1922.
>
> I ndiaidh Chonradh Angla-Éireannach Mhí na Nollag 1921 – nuair a d'aithin an Bhreatain neamhspleáchas na hÉireann mar Shaorstát Éireann a mbeadh sé chontae is fiche de dhá chontae is tríocha na tíre faoina dhlínse – toghadh an tríú Dáil i Meitheamh 1922.

Some Irish (Gaelic) words are regularly used in newspapers in English, such as *Dail* or *Dáil* (/dɔɪl/ or in Irish /dɑ:lʲ/) 'the Irish parliament', *Taoiseach* /ˈtiːʃəx/ 'Prime Minister' and *Garda* /ˈgardə/ 'the Irish police force' or 'an Irish police officer'; police officers in the plural are *gardai* /ˈgardiː/.

In Irish English, as in other varieties in the British Isles, there is a continuum of usage. It runs from the standard variety, which differs little (apart from the flavour of the Irish accent) from other standard varieties around the world, to the vernacular forms which often reflect an Irish (Gaelic) substratum (on 'substratum', see p. 135).

Here are some grammatical traits of Irish English, which you might meet in reading authors such as Joyce and Synge, and which can be traced to influences from the Irish language:

- The usage *after* + *ing*-form of the verb corresponds to a perfect tense elsewhere in the English-speaking world: for example, *I'm after breaking a shoelace* 'I've just broken a shoelace'. *She is after telling me all about it* 'She has told me all about it'.
- The so-called cleft construction, with initial *it*, is common: *It is looking for new jobs a lot of them are* 'A lot of them are looking for new jobs'.

- As Irish has no words for *yes* and *no*, a positive or negative answer is expressed more fully: *Is that yours? – It is not. Are you ready? – I am.*

As for pronunciation, we will content ourselves with mentioning two features of the Irish accent. The vowels tend to be pure vowels (such as /e:/ in *face* and /o:/ in *go*), and this trend is strengthened, as in ScotE, by pronouncing an /r/ after a vowel, as in *start* /start/ and *nurse* /nʌrs/. However, like the American or West Country *r*, this Irish *r* is pronounced as a retroflex consonant, which sometimes gives the impression that Irish and Americans have similar accents. Furthermore, in Irish English /t/ often corresponds to RP /θ/ and /d/ to RP /ð/ so that *thin* and *tin*, as well as *though* and *dough*, may sound alike.

The northern Irish accent can be strikingly distinctive, one of its most memorable features being a rise of intonation at the end of utterances, so that statements sound like questions to the outsider. There is a report of the actress Shirley MacLaine's reaction to a man from Northern Ireland, who confused her by 'asking questions all the time'. However, this intonation pattern is not quite the same as the declarative 'High Rising Terminal' heard among younger speakers in Australia and New Zealand (see p. 109). It is a rise after which the voice stays at the top of its pitch range, on what has been called a 'Northern Irish plateau'.

8
American and British English

The official language of the State of Illinois shall be known hereafter as the American language, and not as the English language.

Act of Legislature of Illinois (1923)

Whose English language is it, anyway? From the tone of the new 'BBC News and Current Affairs Stylebook and Editorial Guide', you'd think the Brits invented it. With unmistakable disdain, the broadcastocrats in London call what we speak 'American'.

William Safire, in the column 'Language',
The New York Times

After surveying the English of the British Isles in Chapter 7, in this chapter we take a further, closer look at today's American English and its background, especially as it compares and contrasts with British English. (We will use the abbreviation AmE and BrE for these two 'reference varieties' in this chapter.) We make no apology for devoting further space to these two regional varieties, particularly AmE. First, between them, they represent a large proportion of all native speakers of English (83 per cent). Second, they have historically been the origin of the whole gamut of world-wide English. Figure 8.1 shows the global provenance of English, branching out from the two rootstocks of BrE and AmE.

This map explains in a nutshell where the various 'Englishes' of the world came from, but also to some extent how things are at the present day – for example, Australian English still shows itself as a variety more closely related to BrE than to AmE. A third reason for focusing on these two regional varieties is that, throughout the twentieth century, BrE and AmE provided the chief native-speaker models which non-native-speaking teachers of English aimed to instil. (Whether they will continue to dominate the twenty-first century in the same way as they did the twentieth is unclear. We will return to this on pp. 233–7.) But, of course, since 1900 the balance of power has shifted markedly from BrE to AmE. Now, there is no doubt not only that AmE is the most

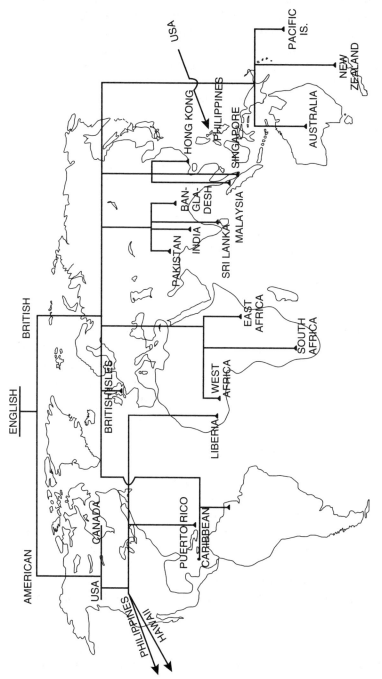

Figure 8.1 The spread of English in the world

populous native-speaker variety (with four times as many native speakers as BrE), but that it looms larger than BrE as a target-variety to be learned and imitated throughout the world. This comment applies to its influence on English both as a foreign language and as a second language and native language. World English is influenced by AmE not only through educational channels, but through other channels of communication, such as TV networks, movies, the internet and popular culture disseminated through the new digital media. On this popular level, American culture and the American version of the English language seem to be all-powerful. For example, although (as we have seen) Australian English is descended from British rather than American English, the trend in the past thirty years has been for Australian English to move somewhat towards AmE, as well as to develop its own language resources independent of both AmE and BrE. This trend of borrowing from AmE is no surprise, as the same trend is happening in BrE (see pp. 157–9). But it seems that Australians are a little ahead of the British in using American terms like *truck*, *elevator* and *freeway*, although they stick to BrE words like *petrol*, *boot* (of a car) and *tap* (AmE *faucet*). Similarly, the American word *gotten* (inherited, of course, originally from the British) is making some headway in Australian English, although it has made few inroads so far into BrE.

While in our historical Part I we tended to mention BrE before AmE, being chronologically the earlier development, now we cannot but acknowledge the superior influence of AmE. When we come to list differences between AmE and BrE, we will place AmE first, on the left. Later we will come back to the influence of AmE on the English of other nations, in particular its influence on BrE, but now let's turn to the issue of differences between these two major regional varieties, which we call 'reference varieties'.

'Divided by a common language'?

Someone – and nobody seems to be sure if was George Bernard Shaw, Winston Churchill or Oscar Wilde – described the United States and Britain as 'two nations divided by a common language'. This saying is very popular, partly because it is witty and paradoxical, and partly because it has a ring of truth. Every Briton who travels to the United States, and every American who travels to Britain, is sure to come home with stories of being astonished by strange usages or being laughed at for their own strange usages, because of the differences between American and British English. This kind of thing is often played up for humorous purposes. Bill Bryson says:

> Sometimes these differences in meaning take on a kind of bewildering circularity. A tramp in Britain is a bum in America, while a bum in Britain is a fanny in America, while a fanny is Britain is – well, we've covered that. ...

In common speech, some 4,000 words are used differently in one country from the other. That's a very large number indeed. Some are well known on both sides of the Atlantic – *lift/elevator, dustbin/garbage can, biscuit/cookie* – but many hundreds of others are still liable to befuddle the hapless traveller.

He then presents a list of corresponding words in AmE and BrE, and challenges the reader to cover up the left-hand column and think of the American equivalent for each British word. Here is a shortened and re-ordered version of that list:

List A		**List B**	
AMERICAN	BRITISH	AMERICAN	BRITISH
yard	garden	*boxscore*	baseball game summary
trunk (of a car)	boot	*cabana*	beach hut
VCR	video recorder	*cheesecloth*	muslin
zucchini	courgettes	*crosswalk*	pedestrian crossing
duplex	semi-detached house	*downspout*	drainpipe
station wagon	estate car	*goldbricker*	skiver
realtor	estate agent	*ground round*	best mince
pacifier	baby's dummy	*teeter-totter*	see-saw

List A on the left is different from List B on the right. On the left are words which are listed in order of their frequency of occurring in a large database (or corpus) of American English conversation (approximately 400 hours of continuous talk recorded and transcribed). Quite a few speakers of British English will be familiar with the American meanings of the everyday words in List A. On the right, though, are words that do not occur at all in that vast body of 400 hours' conversation. These are not exactly in the first rank of words of common speech that British visitors need to master in the United States. Nearly half of the items in Bryson's list are in this category of rarely occurring words.

Contrary to the impression often given (and reinforced by amusing accounts like Bryson's), the differences between AmE and BrE vocabulary are rarely so great as to cause serious misunderstanding. The 4,000 differences Bryson mentions sound a lot, but this needs to be placed against the enormous size of English vocabulary (there are over 600,000 different words in the latest version of the *Oxford English Dictionary*, many of them, admittedly, obsolete). In fact, the travellers' tales of misunderstandings would not be so noticeable and amusing unless, as a rule, Americans and Britons found themselves able to understand one another. Another point to make is that very often the lists of equivalent items are misleading. Sometimes listed AmE/BrE pairs are not true translations of one another: for example, *cookies* and *biscuits* are somewhat different commodities. In Britain biscuits are small flat thin pieces of pastry, as in *chocolate biscuits*, eaten as a snack; in the US biscuits are little breakfast breads and part of a meal, not a snack. An American reader says: 'The only biscuits that

I could think of that are eaten as snacks are dog biscuits – doggies love them but I wouldn't dare eat one myself!'

'Two nations divided by a common language' – let's trace the history of this idea. Is it really true that AmE and BrE are so different? And if so, why don't we consider them different languages? There was a time, shortly after the Declaration of Independence, when the patriotic founders of the American nation looked ahead with confident relish to the time when AmE and BrE would diverge and so become different languages. This hope was cherished by the great dictionary-maker Noah Webster, who published his *American Spelling Book* in 1783, the year of independence, and whose name still lives on in the Webster dictionaries: the premier lexicographic dynasty of the United States. But as time went on he changed his views and recognized that the English language was in the New World to stay. This he implicitly admitted in the title of his greatest work, published in 1828: *An American Dictionary of the English Language* – America's answer to Samuel Johnson's *Dictionary of the English Language* (see pp. 64–5) – which was enormously influential not only in spelling but in pronunciation.

Webster, 'the schoolmaster of the Republic', devoted his life to giving American English an identity of its own. The reforms he promoted led to one of the most conspicuous areas of divergence between AmE and BrE – differences of spelling. Webster's spelling proposals were widely adopted in the United States and produced such variants as *labor* (AmE) vs. *labour* (BrE) familiar to today's international student of English. Most of these changes were undeniable improvements. But the reforms when adopted were more timid than Webster had intended: today, the vast majority of English words are still spelled the same in AmE and BrE.

Some differences in spelling between American and British English

- In words of more than one syllable ending in *-our* in BrE, AmE omits the *u*:

AME	BRE
behavior	*behaviour*
color	*colour*
favor	*favour*
humor	*humour*
labor	*labour*

There are exceptions, such as *glamour* in AmE, *tenor* in BrE.

- In words like *theater*, *-er* in AmE is often equivalent to *-re* in BrE:

AME	BRE
center	*centre*
kilometer	*kilometre*
liter	*litre*
theater	*theatre*

The spelling *theatre* also occurs in AmE where it's said to have 'snob appeal'.

- Some words spelled *-ense* in AmE have *-ence* in BrE:

AME	BRE
defense	*defence*
license (noun)	*licence* (noun)

- In verbs like *travel* (ending with an unstressed syllable vowel + consonant) the British double the final consonant before -*ing* and -*ed*:

AmE	Mainly BrE
cancel: *canceling, canceled*	*cancelling, cancelled*
travel: *traveling, traveled*	*travelling, travelled*
program: *programing, programed*	*programming, programmed*

In BrE the spelling of *program*, except in the computing sense, is *programme*. Notice also: *traveler* (AmE) vs. *traveller* (BrE)

- Nouns ending in -*ogue* in BrE are shortened to -*og* in AmE:

AmE	BrE
catalog	*catalogue*
dialog	*dialogue*

- In words from Latin and Greek, BrE keeps the spellings -*œ*- and -*æ*-; but sometimes the AmE spellings with -*e*- are found in BrE too:

AmE	BrE
ameba	*amœba*
maneuver	*manœuvre*
encyclopedia	*encyclopædia, encyclopedia*
medieval	*mediæval, medieval*

- Verbs with the suffix -*ize* in AmE are often spelled -*ise* in BrE, although -*ize* occurs in Britain too:

AmE	BrE
baptize	*baptise, baptize*
criticize	*criticise, criticize*
sympathize	*sympathise, sympathize*
regularize	*regularise, regularize*

Hundreds of verbs follow this pattern. But some verbs are always spelled -*ise*, in both AmE and BrE: *advertise, advise, arise, comprise, compromise, disguise, despise, devise, disguise, exercise, improvise, revise, rise, supervise, surprise.*

- There are some spelling differences that are unique to particular words, for example:

AmE	BrE
ax, axe	*axe*
check (in a bank)	*cheque*
draft (a current of cold air)	*draught*
gage	*gauge*
gray, grey	*grey*
curb (by the side of a road)	*kerb*
mold	*mould*
plow, plough	*plough*
pajamas	*pyjamas*
skeptical	*sceptical*
story (in buildings)	*storey*
tire (around wheels)	*tyre*
woolen	*woollen, woolen*

From a present-day standpoint, there is no doubt that in spelling, as in other respects, AmE and BrE belong to the same language. They are varieties, it is true, but the differences should not be allowed to obscure their close similarity on many levels.

One way to start thinking about this is to note that the 'standardization pyramid' diagram we used to illustrate variation in the UK (Figure 7.1, p. 128) can also be applied, although on a rather different scale, to the differences between regional and social dialect on a global level. At this stage, we are focusing specifically on AmE and BrE. But let's think principally about AmE.

At the top of the pyramid, we have something close to **an international standard of written English**. One of this book's authors had the experience of reading a lengthy book by an American author, and only realising around page 400 that the book was written by an American rather than a British writer. It is true that American spellings could not be detected, because the book was produced by a British publisher, but through hundreds of pages there was no detectable sign in vocabulary or grammar that the book was written in American English. (The book was a biography of the British novelist Anthony Trollope, which easily led to the wrong supposition that the book was by a Briton.) At last there occurred the tell-tale word *envision* (an American variant corresponding to the British *envisage*). This example is not an isolated instance: on the level of serious academic or informative writing, we feel justified in talking of an **international standard English** or **world standard English**, sometimes abbreviated WSE. In science, for example, an international standard for printed English (leaving aside the spelling and the style conventions laid down by particular journals) is taken for granted. Its spoken analogue also exists to a lesser degree – for example, in TV broadcasts by CNN, where the accent of the newsreader may be the only clue that points to a particular part of the English-speaking world.

But as we move down the pyramid of standardization – to less standardized and locally variable varieties – of course the differences begin to show. Big steps down the pyramid are taken when we move from published printed communication to public spoken communication (for example, in cinema and radio) and from there to private chat, in conversational settings. Here we begin to meet noticeable differences between AmE and BrE, not only in pronunciation and spelling but in vocabulary and grammar. Then, a further move to the dialectal base of the pyramid will bring us to what sociolinguists call the 'basilect', where we meet, for example, vernacular and dialectal grammar (pp. 134, 169). The pyramid has roughly the same shape and function, whether we are thinking of World English (p. 226), English of the Inner Circle (p. 2), English in the United States and the UK, or English within each of these countries, or any other single country. Where unintelligibility sets in between American and British speakers, towards the lower end of the pyramid, is also where there will be problems of comprehension if we consider differences among American speakers or among British speakers within a single country.

In retrospect, then, the question 'What are the differences between American and British English?' is rather too simplistic. What we find is a large spectrum of variation, and the gap of the Atlantic Ocean – often jokingly called 'the pond' in these days of globalization – is not the only factor (although a major factor) in determining that variation.

Looking at the top part of the pyramid, if we study the main standardized varieties of AmE and BrE, we come to the conclusion that:

- in **grammar** they are very similar;
- in **spelling** they are very similar (in spite of those changes Webster promoted);
- in **vocabulary** they are different in some areas, but strikingly the same in core vocabulary;
- in **pronunciation** they are clearly different, but generally mutually intelligible.

We take a look at each of these topics in the later part of this chapter.

Americanisms and Americanization

A further factor we have to bear in mind is the continuing **transatlantic drift** by which AmE habits are imported into the UK and into other English-speaking countries. The lists of differences between American and British vocabulary published from time to time have suffered from chronic obsolescence: they have begun to go out of date almost as soon as they have been compiled. The most famous writer on this topic was H. L. Mencken, journalist and iconoclast, whose book entitled *The American Language* went through several editions and supplements between 1919 and 1948. The list of American-British differences he published in 1936 included *bakery, bank account, hardware* (for British *ironmongery*), *raincoat, living-room* and many more. But these are now totally normal words to use in relevant senses in the UK.

The reason is simple: the British have been so busy borrowing linguistically from the Americans that what was originally felt to be an Americanism has become thoroughly at home in Britain. This happened over and over again in the nineteenth and (especially) twentieth centuries, but after its adoption, naturally enough, a word's American aura was soon lost: it was no longer felt to be a foreign import. According to Mencken:

> When I became interested in the subject (... in 1910), the American form of the English language was plainly departing from the parent stem, and it seemed likely that the differences between American and English would go

on increasing. ... But since 1923 the pull of American has become so powerful that it has begun to drag English with it, and in consequence some of the differences once visible have tended to disappear.

Yet Mencken, as we see here, kept up the pious fiction of Webster, that 'American' was, or would become, a different language from 'English', and continued to use the title *The American Language* for the later editions of his book.

The word *Americanism* has its own story to tell. It originated in the United States, and its first user, John Witherspoon, defined it in 1781 as a 'use of phrases or terms, or a construction of sentences ... different from the use of the same terms or phrases, or the construction of similar sentences in Great-Britain'. Witherspoon, a Scot who embraced the colonial cause, was even so a critic of Americanisms. The first *Dictionary of Americanisms*, by the American John Pickering, published in 1816, portrayed them as provincialisms that Americans should purge from their usage, in order to conform to the 'English standard' of the old mother country. This attitude was not unusual in the early decades of the United States. But from the middle of the nineteenth century things began to change: not only did Americans grow bolder in asserting and justifying their right to bring innovations into the language, but the British began to borrow more and more from the Americans.

This did not mean that the term *Americanism* lost its negative connotations. On the contrary, in Britain *Americanism* was almost a synonym for 'barbarism' among commentators – a hostile attitude that has persisted among many up to the present day, although with decreasing influence. The irony, of course, is that once an Americanism has become successfully established in British usage, it becomes 'British' and the negative attitude disappears. Numerous linguistic imports have undergone this sea change: *dutiable, lengthy, bunkum* and *blizzard* were early examples; later in the nineteenth century arguments raged over *advocate, placate* and *antagonize*. (Some new usages of British origin, like *talented* and *scientist*, were apparently mistakenly denounced as Americanisms.)

In the twentieth century we have seen the American variant *radio* gradually displace *wireless*, and American *commuter* become accepted in place of the long-winded *season ticket holder*. Numerous popular words and phrases have been taken over from AmE: *bawl out, bonehead, (big) bucks, dumbbell, go-getter, jerk* and the like. Among usages to recently cross the Atlantic have been *movie, guys* (= 'people'), *I guess* (= 'my opinion is') and *cool* (= 'superb, relaxed, fashionable') – four familiar items which are 'classic' Americanisms, but are nevertheless slipping more and more securely into British usage. One of the odd consequences of this transatlantic drift is that the British make use of American idioms whose literal meaning they are unlikely to know such as the *three strikes and you're out* (referring to a strict law enforcement policy) and *in the right ball park, a ball park figure* (referring to an approximation). These come from baseball, a sport that has never caught on in Britain. But it is difficult to keep up with these changes: the continuous and instantaneous flow of communication across the Atlantic, as elsewhere in the world, means that new usages coming from the US can become almost immediately assimilated. During the disputed presidential election of 2000, *hanging chads*, resulting from defects in voting machines, suddenly became common currency in the British media, as well as in the international media of CNN and the like. A similar story could be told of *WMD* as an abbreviation for 'weapons of mass destruction' in the aftermath of the Iraq war.

The notion of 'Americanism' itself is a moving target, and it is no longer practical to try to list Americanisms as in a glossary. Perhaps, indeed, the concept of 'Americanism' has had its day, and is giving way to the concept of 'Americanization' – the ongoing and often unnoticed influence of the New World on the Old. But, of course, in this, Britain is no different from other countries in importing linguistic cargo from America. There may be exceptions to the trend; there may even be occasional borrowings from BrE in AmE, such as an increasing use of *shop* to mean a small store. But at this point in history, Americanization appears to be a global, and not just a transatlantic, phenomenon.

Persistent transatlantic differences of vocabulary

Yet not all features of American English become features of British English. A challenging question is: why do some American-British differences persist indefinitely, without the British usage giving way to the American usage? For example, there appears to be little temptation for the British to adopt an American accent. Some small changes can be observed (for example, the tendency for the word *princess* to be stressed on the first syllable (*princess*) rather than on the second (*princess*). Perhaps overall people's pronunciation of their native language is too intimately bound up with who they are: to change one's accent is to change one's identity.

Borrowing of words from AmE has always been patchy. On the lexical level, many persistent differences between AmE and BrE seem to be located in particular areas of the vocabulary, such as *transportation* (AmE) (*transport* in BrE). Different terms referring to aspects of the *railroad* (AmE) (*railway* in BrE) system are well known:

AmE	BrE
engineer	*driver*
conductor	*guard*
freight	*goods*
one-way ticket	*single ticket*
round-trip ticket	*return ticket*

Similarly, terms referring to cars and road travel are frequently different:

AmE	BrE
divided highway	*dual carriageway*
gas, gasoline	*petrol*
gearshift	*gear lever*
hood	*bonnet*
license plate	*numberplate*
muffler	*silencer*
overpass	*flyover*
truck	*lorry*
trunk	*boot*
windshield	*windscreen*

(Some of the American terms here, though, are now competing in BrE with the British equivalent: *lorry* and *goods* are fighting for survival against *truck* and *freight*.) Part of the explanation for such differences is that rail and car travel originate from a period when the United States and Britain were comparatively isolated from one another, both physically and culturally: the later nineteenth century and the early twentieth century. After the American achievement of independence in 1783 and the subsequent estrangement of the countries, movements of people and communications across the Atlantic were relatively infrequent. In 1889 the British author Rudyard Kipling claimed:

> The American I have heard up to the present is a tongue as distinct from English as Patagonian.

No doubt Kipling was indulging in a degree of humorous exaggeration. But it is difficult to realize now that the vast majority of the inhabitants of Great Britain up to the early 1900s had never met an American, and would not have even recognized an American accent. From the early twentieth century, with the coming of the *movies* (BrE *films*, a term which is also widely used in Hollywood), and the *radio* (BrE *wireless* is now dated) plus the intervention of the United States in the First World War, this situation changed dramatically. Further technological advances, such as air travel and television, led to an explosive increase in Anglo-American communication. But by that time, the language of rail and road transport had become well established and the differences institutionalized. The same period, incidentally, also saw the emergence of the *elevator/lift*, the *phonograph/gramophone*, the *subway/underground*, all three named differently in AmE and BrE.

From the mid-twentieth century onwards, however, separate terms introduced through technological advances and inventions seem to be less frequent, although it is noticeable that when the British started to build large multi-lane highways like the German *Autobahn*, they created the term *motorway*, instead of borrowing one of the existing American terms such as *expressway*. Technological terms on both sides of the Atlantic seem to be converging on an American standard, for example, in the prolific terminology of the computing and electronics industry. Yet a recent interesting exception is the term *cellular phone* or *cell phone* (AmE) which contrasts with the British *mobile phone*, popularly truncated to *mobile*.

Apart from everyday popular technology, the US and the UK also stick to substantially different vocabularies for education: even the word *school* is interpreted differently, to include tertiary education in the United States, but only elementary and secondary (high school) education in the UK. The American education system blossomed in the nineteenth century under German rather than British influence. Now, though, British education is increasingly adopting American terminology: for example, in using *graduate students* alongside *post-graduate students*, and *semester* or *trimester* alongside *term*.

Finally, many of the persistent differences between American and British usage seem to belong to the domestic arena, or at least to things that relate to the family or local life, rather than to the international sphere. These are stay-at-home words that tend not to travel much through modern communications: an example is AmE *faucet* vs. BrE *tap*.

The *Harry Potter* books by J. K. Rowling have been best-sellers on both sides of the Atlantic, but it is significant that for the American edition of the book, some changes were introduced to make these British books more intelligible to a young American readership. A listing on the webpages of the Department of Translation Studies, University of Tampere, Finland gives 203 changes in all (presumably this is an exhaustive list) made in the 'translation' of the British editions of the first four *Harry Potter* books. Here is a selection of the changes made:

BRITISH EDITION	AMERICAN EDITION	
a lot	a bunch	
at weekends	on weekends	
barking	off his rocker	[also BrE]*
beetroot	beet	
bins	trash-cans	
biscuits	cookies	
Bit rich coming from you	You should talk	[also BrE]
bobbles	puff balls	
changing room	locker room	
cinema	movies	[also BrE]
comprehensive	public school	[also BrE]
cooker	stove	[also BrE]
cracking	spanking good	
crumpets	English muffins	
cupboard	closet	[also BrE]

do his nut	go ballistic	[also BrE]
dressing gown	bathrobe	[also BrE]
dustbin	trashcan	
Father Christmas	Santa Claus	[also BrE]
football [the ball]	soccer ball	
football [the game]	soccer	[also BrE]
fortnight	two weeks	[also BrE]
glove puppet	hand puppet	
go to the loo	have a pee	[also BrE]
good on you	good for you	[also BrE]
group who …	group that …	[also BrE]
hamburger bars	hamburger restaurants	[also BrE]
he's got flu	he's got the flu	[also BrE]
holidaying	vacationing	
ice lolly	ice pop	
it's mad	it's ridiculous	[also BrE]
jacket potato	baked potato	[also BrE]
jelly	jell-o	
jumper	sweater	[also BrE]
lavatory seat	toilet seat	[also BrE]
letter-box	mail slot	
mad	crazy, insane	[also BrE]
matron	nurse	[also BrE]
motorbike	motorcycle	[also BrE]
multi-storey car park	multilevel parking garage	
mum	mom	
mummy	mommy	
newsreader	reporter	[also BrE]
next day	the next day	[also BrE]
next moment, Fred Weasley had chucked	a moment later, Fred Weasley chucked	[also BrE]
nobbled	clobbered	[also BrE]
notes	bills	[also BrE]
nutter	maniac	[also BrE]
packet of crisps	bag of chips	[also BrE]
pop my clogs	kick the bucket	[also BrE]
prevent them using	prevent them from using	[also BrE]
puddings	desserts	[also BrE]
queuing	lining up	[also BrE]
revising	studying	[also BrE]
roundabout	carousel	[also BrE]
row /raʊ/	fight	[also BrE]
rowing /raʊɪŋ/	arguing	[also BrE]
sack [verb]	fire [verb]	[also BrE]
sellotape	scotch tape	

September the first	September first	
set books	course books	[also BrE]
shan't	won't	[also BrE]
sherbet lemon	lemon drop	
straight away	right away	[also BrE]
sweets	candy	
tank top	sweater vest	
timetable	course schedule	[also BrE]
tinned soup	canned soup	[also BrE]
toilet	bathroom	[also BrE]
torch	flashlight	
trainers	sneakers	
trolley	cart	[also BrE]
tuck in	dig in	[also BrE]
twenty-foot-high	twenty feet high	[also BrE]
video	VCR	
wardrobe	closet	
waste bin	waste basket	[also BrE]
wellington boots	rubber boots	[also BrE]
whilst	while	[also BrE]
wonky	crooked	[also BrE]

*[also BrE] means that the American term is also used in UK.

American and British pronunciation: comparing GA with RP

As we paid attention to the RP accent in the last chapter (pp. 125–8), it is now time to focus more on GA, using RP as a point of reference. Apart from differences in consonants and (especially) vowels, we also examine differences in stress and in the pronunciation of particular words.

- In GA the letter *r* is pronounced in all positions: *heard* /hɜːrd/, *speaker* /ˈspiːkər/. This is a **retroflex r**, in that the tongue curls and bunches somewhat upward and backward in the mouth, rather than a trilled or tapped *r* such as is found in Scottish English (p. 143). In words like *girl* or *bird*, the /r/ is not so much a separate sound, as a burr-sound colouring the whole vowel. (In RP, by contrast, *r* is not pronounced after a vowel, see p. 125.)
- In words such as *after, aunt, can't, dance, glass, last, path* GA has the 'front *a* sound' /æ/ as in *cat* while RP has /ɑː/ – but GA has /ɑː/ in words with final *r*: *bar* /bɑːr/, *hard* /hɑːrd/.
- The RP diphthongs /ɪə, eə, ʊə/ are not found in GA, so the pronunciation is: *beard* /bɪrd/, *hair* /her/ and *pure* /pjʊr/.
- In GA the diphthong /oʊ/ or the single vowel /oː/ corresponds to the RP diphthong /əʊ/ in words such as *both, rose, grow*.

Rhotic and non-rhotic accents

Accents with *r* pronounced after vowels are called **rhotic** (after the Greek letter *rho*). The interesting thing about rhotic accents is that they are associated with different attitudes in parts of America and Britain. In England the rhotic accent of the West Country is under threat as the influence from RP, Estuary English (see p. 130) and other **non-rhotic** accents spreads more widely: the stereotyped user of the West Country burr is an agricultural worker, a 'country bumpkin'. In contrast, in the eastern United States, it is the non-rhotic accent that is losing ground and prestige (see box on p. 166). In a famous study of speakers of different classes in New York City, the great American sociolinguist William Labov found that the traditional non-rhotic accent (memorably mocked in such New Yorker spellings as *goil* for 'girl' and *woiks* for 'works') was used less by salespeople in 'upmarket' stores like Saks than in 'downmarket' stores like Klein's. Moreover, people when asked to repeat a phrase would introduce the *r* in a more careful pronunciation. Labov also observed that younger people used the *r* pronunciation more than older people. This suggested a declining trend in the use of the traditional New York *r* – something confirmed by later studies.

In all the above differences, GA reflects an older pronunciation: RP shows innovations that took place in Britain after the founding of the American colonies.

- GA has a longish /ɑ/, corresponding both to the short RP-vowel /ɒ/ in words like *bomb, bottle, cod, spot*, and to the long RP-vowel /ɔ:/ in words such as *bought, daughter, law, laundry, saw, tall, water*.
- GA has /u:/ (not the /ju:/ often found in RP) in words such as *due, new, suit, tune, pursue, resume*: 'doo', 'noo', 'toon' etc. Yet the /u:/ pronunciation (known as **yod-dropping**) is by no means unknown in England, where /su:t/ for *suit* is now more common than /sju:t/. (In some parts of England, such as East Anglia, yod-dropping is even more widespread than in the US.)
- In GA the *t*-sound between vowels is pronounced more lightly than in RP and tends to sound like a quick /d/ ('a voiced tap'). This means that *writer* and *rider, latter* and *ladder* are pronounced the same. We symbolize this American feature phonetically as /ɒ/.
- Like the Scots and the Irish, most Americans distinguish between *witch* /wɪtʃ/ and *which* /hwɪtʃ/, *weather* /'weðər/ and *whether* /'hweðər/ – they pronounce /hw/ in words spelled with *wh*. In RP, however, the single consonant /w/ is generally used in both *witch* and *which, weather* and *whether*.
- Adjectives ending in *-ile* usually have a reduced 'schwa' vowel /ə/ in GA, but not in RP:

	GA	RP
docile	/'dɑ:səl/	/'dəʊsaɪl/
fertile	/'fɜ:rɒəl/	/'fɜ:taɪl/
fragile	/'frædʒəl/	/'frædʒaɪl/
hostile	/'hɑ:stəl/	/'hɒstaɪl/
missile	/'mɪsəl/	/'mɪsaɪl/

- It is worth noting differences in assigning stress between GA and RP. In words ending in *-ary*, *-ery*, or *-ory* GA has a full vowel with secondary stress (indicated by ˌ), while RP has a reduced schwa vowel, or else the vowel may not be pronounced at all. This is signalled below by the raised symbol ᵊ:

	GA	RP
commentary	/ˈkɑmənˌteri/	/ˈkɒməntᵊri/
cemetery	/ˈseməˌteri/	/ˈsemətᵊri/
inventory	/ˈɪnvənˌtɔri/	/ˈinvəntᵊri/

- In French loanwords GA often assigns stress to the last syllable, as in the original French word:

	GA	RP
attaché	/ˌæɒəˈʃeɪ/	/əˈtæʃeɪ/
ballet	/bæˈleɪ/	/ˈbæleɪ/
detail	/dɪˈteɪl/, /ˈditeɪl/	/ˈdiːteɪl/
frontier	/frʌnˈtiːr/	/ˈfrʌntɪə/

- In some polysyllabic words, there is variation in the placing of the main stress. In GA there is usually only one option, but in RP, the 'American' pronunciation co-exists with a 'British' pronunciation:

MAINLY AmE	BrE ONLY	MAINLY AmE	BrE ONLY
applicable	*applicable*	*fragmentary*	*fragmentary*
aristocrat	*aristocrat*	*hospitable*	*hospitable*
controversy	*controversy*	*premature*	*premature*

- Apart from such general differences in pronunciation, certain particular words are pronounced differently in GA and RP. Some of them are listed below.

Different pronunciation of some individual words

English word	GA	RP
advertisement	ædvəˈraizmənt	ədˈvɜːrtismənt
ate (past of *eat*)	eɪt	et, eɪt
buoy	ˈbuːi	bɔɪ
café	kəˈfeɪ	ˈkæfeɪ
clerk	klɜːrk	klɑːk
data	ˈdæɒə, ˈdeɪɒə	ˈdeɪtə
dynasty	ˈdaɪnəsti	ˈdɪnəsti
garage	gəˈrɑːʒ	ˈgærɑːʒ
inquiry	ˈɪnkwəri	ɪnˈkwaɪᵊri
laboratory	ˈlæbrəˌtɔri	ləˈbɒrətri
leisure	ˈliːʒer	ˈleʒə
lever	ˈlever	ˈliːvə
lieutenant	luːˈtenənt	lefˈtenənt
moustache	ˈmʌstæʃ	məˈstɑːʃ

nephew	ˈnefjuː	ˈnefjuː, ˈnevjuː
process	ˈprɑːses	ˈprəʊses
progress	ˈprɑːgrəs	ˈprəʊgres
route	raʊt, ruːt	ruːt
schedule	ˈskedʒʊl	ˈʃedjuːl, ˈskedʒʊl
shone (of *shine*)	ʃoʊn	ʃɒn
tomato	təˈmeɪDoʊ	təˈmɑːtəʊ
vase	veɪs	vɑːz
vitamin	ˈvaɪDəmɪn	ˈvɪtəmɪn, ˈvaɪtəmɪn
z (the letter)	ziː	zed
zebra	ˈziːbrə	ˈzebrə, ˈziːbrə

Presidential voices

In his book *Presidential Voices*, the American linguist Allan Metcalf discusses speaking styles from George Washington to George W. Bush – how American presidents have spoken to the American public and how the American public has wanted its presidents to speak:

> *It's an understatement to say that the Atlantic Coast remains politically and economically influential to this day. But a funny reversal has happened: Instead of the East serving as a model of cultivation for the rest of the country, influencing would-be cultivated speakers from other areas to drop their r's, as used to be the case, the rest of the country now is influencing many Bostonians, New Yorkers, and Southerners to pronounce their r's. This reflects a shift in prestige from r-lessness: Where once it seemed elegant to drop the r, now it seems pretentious, at least for those who grow up r-ful. … Like other Americans, presidents now are normally r-ful.*

According to John Wells, R-Dropping 'has remained in American eyes an anglicism, an easternism, or a southernism'.

President George W. Bush's nickname is *Dubya*, which comes from his pronunciation of his middle initial. This extract from Metcalf's book shows how experienced speakers adapt their speaking styles to formal and informal situations:

> *Dubya's speech is r-ful. His part of Texas, like Lyndon Johnson's, and like Clinton's Arkansas, is well beyond the limits of r-less Southern territory. But more than Johnson's, though less than Clinton's, Bush's speech has the Southern and Texan ah for i. It's not pure ah in words like lives and child and mind, but it's not a strong Northern long i either. He also has a folksy style that sometimes changes –ing to –in' in words like talkin' and gettin', and that leaves out some syllables and consonants. He will say lemme and gotta and gonna – not in prepared remarks, but freely in press conferences and interviews.*

American vs. British grammar

In the standard language, there are only slight differences in grammar between American and British English. Gunnel Tottie writes: 'most of the time,

Americans and British speakers have the same grammars, with the same inventory of forms and the same rules, but that application of the rules differs between the dialects'. Perhaps the most noticeable difference of form is the American word *gotten*, as a past participle of *get*: 'She's *gotten* into trouble in school' where, in BrE, *got* would be used instead.

Other differences are found in meaning and in the way grammatical forms are used, rather than just in the fact of their existence in one variety rather another. For example, AmE has a useful construction to refer to a period of time:

> The tour lasted *from May through August*. [AmE]
> The tour lasted *from May to August*. [BrE]

In AmE, *through* in the sense of 'up to and including' is crystal clear, while in the BrE construction, it is open to doubt whether August is included. To clarify this, *inclusive* can be added: *from May to August inclusive*.

In the written language, grammar often involves people in problems of 'correct' and 'incorrect' usage, and arguments about which of two or more choices is preferable. One of the observations made about grammar is that American users are more 'grammar conscious', and more careful in following grammatical rules. Thus an American visitor might flinch on seeing the following headline in a British newspaper:

ARSENAL DEFEAT MANCHESTER UNITED

This appears to break the rule of agreement: because Arsenal is a singular noun, it should be followed by a singular verb: *defeats*. However, in BrE a football (soccer, that is) team can be treated as plural, which is not wholly unreasonable as each side has eleven players. In a similar way, singular collective nouns such as *team, audience, board, committee, government, the public* can be treated as plural in BrE, whereas the singular is normal in AmE: 'The committee *has* voted in favour of the bill'.

Another point where AmE seems to be more 'correct' is the choice of verb construction in an example like this:

[*a*] They insist that she *accept* the offer. (preferred in AmE)
[*b*] They insist that she *should* accept the offer. (getting unacceptable in AmE)
[*c*] They insist that she *accepts* the offer. (not accepted in AmE)

This construction is found with verbs like *insist, recommend* and *suggest*; also with some nouns like *recommendation* and some adjectives like *important*:

> There is a proposal that this tax *be* reduced.
> It is important that every house *have* its own water supply.

AmE has a preference for the subjunctive verb, as in [*a*]. BrE nowadays treats [*a*] and [*b*] as more or less equal options, whereas AmE nowadays avoids this 'quasi-subjunctive' use of *should*. The third option [*c*] is found in BrE, but is avoided in AmE. Once again, AmE seems careful of its grammar, using the traditional construction [*a*]. This subjunctive, which has been declining over the centuries, became virtually obsolete in BrE around the 1950s. It is an interesting case of re-importation – like the expression *I guess* which Chaucer used and which survived in the United States – and is now being borrowed in BrE. In both cases the New World has preserved an older usage now making a comeback in Old World English. Contrary to belief, the subjunctive is not on its deathbed in Britain, but is being resuscitated. This is a case where an Americanization process seems to be affecting BrE grammar.

However, the idea of the Americans being more 'grammar conscious' doesn't always hold up – at least not in the spoken language. Americans are more likely to use adjective forms as adverbs, a habit which is frowned on as non-standard in Britain:

They pay them pretty *well*.	They pay them pretty *good*.
You'll have to speak *slowly*.	You'll have to speak *slow*.
She's *awfully* thin.	She's *awful* thin.
I *certainly* hope it's temporary.	I *sure* hope it's temporary.

Here the left-hand examples show a standard use of adverbs like *well*, while the right-hand ones show matching adjective forms which would be considered non-standard in BrE, but are common and relatively acceptable in spoken AmE.

Another case where AmE seems more 'broad-minded' in interpreting grammatical rules is the use of *like* as a conjunction, introducing a clause with its own verb:

It seems *like* we've made another mistake.
Looks *like* the weather might be decent.

In standard BrE *as if* would be preferred to *like* here. *Like* as a conjunction is traditionally judged to be a non-standard construction.

When we look at dialectal variations, one of the most interesting features of American dialect grammar is the use of second-person plural pronouns like *you all* in the South. Because of the demise of the second-person singular pronoun *thou* in early Modern English (see p. 55), *you* is the only pronoun for the second person in standard English today. Whether you are addressing one person or more than one, there is no second-person counterpart to the first-person distinction between *I* and *we*. So there is a kind of semantic gap: how can we make it clear that when we say *you*, it refers to all the people present, or just one addressee? This doesn't usually cause problems, but it's fascinating that two American dialects have come up with a plural form of *you*: **you all** (pronounced and often written *y'all*) belongs to the South, and *yous* (or *youse*) belongs to the Northeast, especially New York City: 'I'll see *y'all* later', 'How much did *yous* want?' *Y'all* is held in high regard in the South, and cannot be considered non-standard. *Yous* is less acceptable, but has a dialect provenance that goes back to Ireland and some other parts of the British Isles. In spoken AmE generally it is noticeable that another plural of *you* is making headway: *you guys*. As *guys* is now a very general informal term to use for 'people', whether male or female, old or young, the combination *you guys* means 'you people', but it is so commonly used that it almost seems to have taken over the grammatical role of a second-person plural pronoun. Yet in a more formal setting, *you folks* or *you people* might be used instead.

**Some other grammatical differences between
American and British English**

In addition to such features as the use of *gotten* already mentioned, AmE and BrE differ in grammar in these ways:

- In AmE the past tense rather than the perfect can be used for the recent past: *Dolly (has) just finished her homework*. AmE often omits the *has* here. BrE prefers the perfect, in cases like this. Compare: *Did you eat yet?* [AmE], *Have you eaten yet?* [AmE and BrE].
- Prepositions are sometimes used differently in AmE and BrE. *Out* and *off of* are commonly used as prepositions in spoken AmE: *I always look out the window* (BrE usually *out of the window*); *He wants to get off of the sofa* (BrE usually *off the sofa*).
- AmE more freely allows past tense forms like:

  dove (alongside *dived*), as in 'She dove under the table'
  fit (alongside *fitted*)
  pled (alongside *pleaded*)
  rung (alongside *rang*)
  sung (alongside *sang*)
  sunk (alongside *sank*)
  snuck (alongside *sneaked*)
  swum (alongside *swam*), as in 'Dad swum across the lake'

AAVE – Black English – Ebonics

In the United States, many blacks in the inner cities speak a form of English which differs sharply from American Standard English, sometimes to the point of being misunderstood. A sentence like 'Dey ain't like dat' can easily be misinterpreted as 'They aren't like that' while it actually means 'They didn't like that'. Language can be a class-marker, and those who do not meet the general American standard are often branded as underachievers. There are different opinions about how this variety, commonly referred to as *Black English*, should be regarded. Is it a language? A dialect? A form of slang? An accent, or what? And how should the school system and society at large deal with this language issue? Should it be used and taught in school, or should students speaking this tongue be taught to adapt to the standard language? How does the low status commonly accorded to this variety affect the prospects of such students to function in a society dominated by speakers of a socially accepted standard language?

The term preferred by linguists to denote the variety of English spoken by many African Americans is **African American Vernacular English**, abbreviated as AAVE. Common but more controversial terms are **Black English** and **Ebonics** (from *ebony*). *Black English* can be controversial because not all blacks use AAVE: many are speakers of standard American English. *Ebonics* is controversial because it is associated with the claim that AAVE is a distinct language from English.

The situation here is not unlike the situation regarding non-standard dialects in other parts of the English-speaking world. However, in the case of AAVE, there is an additional issue (which we met in Chapter 7 regarding Scots, and will meet again in Chapter 9 regarding Jamaican Creole) as to whether this variety of language is actually a separate language from English.

In 1996 the Oakland School Board in California decided to recognize the language variety spoken by many African American students and to take it into account in teaching Standard English. The students' home language was to be accorded the status of a language separate from English, rather than a variety of vernacular English. In this school district some 27,000 students were Black and AAVE was their 'primary language' – the variety of English they had learned from their parents and used in the home and with their friends. The School Board thought that the students' education would improve if their 'primary language' was accepted as their own school language. But this suggested reform caused enormous controversy. If implemented, the reform could have led to a situation where students did not acquire the language of the larger community.

In fact, the linguistics experts in the United States supported the view that AAVE was not a distinct language, although it was recognized that AAVE has features derived from West African languages which reached American through the slave

---

Linguistic Society of America (LSA): resolution on the Ebonics issue (extract)

The variety known as 'Ebonics', 'African American Vernacular English' (AAVE), and 'Vernacular Black English' and by other names is systematic and rule-governed like all natural speech varieties. In fact, all human linguistic systems – spoken, signed, and written – are fundamentally regular. The systematic and expressive nature of the grammar and pronunciation patterns of the African American vernacular has been established by numerous scientific studies over the past thirty years. Characterizations of Ebonics as 'slang,' 'mutant,' ' lazy,' 'defective,' 'ungrammatical,' or 'broken English' are incorrect and demeaning.

trade. Eventually the resolution of the Oakland School Board was overturned., but it is of interest in this regard to read the carefully worded resolution of America's most influential body of linguists, the Linguistic Society of America (see box).

To illustrate the 'systematicity' emphasised by the LSA's resolution, here are some grammatical differences between AAVE and Standard English:

- Speakers use multiple negation, also called 'double negation': *He didn't do nothing* instead of *He didn't do anything* or *He did nothing*. (Such double negation is also common in many non-standard English varieties, in the US, in the UK, and elsewhere.)
- The verb is often used in its base form where standard English has a different form, for example *They be driving* instead of *They are driving* and *She like it* instead of *She likes it*.
- The verb *be* or one of its forms is omitted in sentences like *She busy*, instead of *She is busy*.
- *Be done* occurs instead of *will have done* in expressions like *We be done this job tomorrow*.
- *It* replaces *there* in a sentence like *It's no gas in the tank* instead of *There's no gas in the tank*.
- The past tense form *went* replaces the past participle *gone*: we find *The students had went to the gym* instead of *The students had gone to the gym*.

Vocabulary also differs from standard AmE. New uses of words can often be traced back to black jazz musicians and the culture of popular music: *bad* meaning 'wonderful, attractive, sexy', *mean* 'excellent, skillful' (*a mean game*), *wicked* 'strikingly good, effective' (*a wicked solo*). Yet many such words and expressions of African American origin are now part of mainstream American English, and indeed have become common colloquialisms throughout the English-speaking world: for instance, *chill out* 'relax', *gig* 'job', *cool* 'excellent'. A sample of idioms:

> *Stop bugging me.* 'Don't bother me'
> *Catch you later.* 'Good-bye, speak to you later'
> *Get out of my face.* 'Leave me alone'
> *Get real.* 'Face reality'

The pronunciation of AAVE has some characteristics like those of the Southern accent (see pp. 81–2), and some characteristics shared by creoles, such as Jamaican creole, which we discuss in Chapter 9. This is not surprising in view of the history of a black population tracing its ancestry back to slavery in the southern states and ultimately to West Africa. 'Southern features' include the omission of *r* after vowels, and the simplification of the /aɪ/ diphthong in *high* to /a:/ 'hah'. The features shared by creoles include the omission of consonants at the end of a word: *chil'* instead of *child*, *wes'* instead of *west*, and so on; also, the replacement of the 'th' sounds by /t/ or /d/ (for example *dat* for *that*) or sometimes by /f/ or /v/ (for example *bruvver* for *brother*). But such features are also found in white varieties of pronunciation, so it is too easy to suggest a direct link between AAVE and creoles.

If we accept the LSA's view that AAVE is a variety of English, rather than a separate language, it is easier to explain a continuum of usage linking it to standard English. Nevertheless, for many black speakers, there is a sense of being bilingual – of being able to switch from the variety associated with ethnicity to the standard variety of AmE. It has been observed that, generally, black speakers are moving closer to standard AmE, but also that some young speakers are using more characteristic AAVE forms than their elders, as if to emphasise their ethnicity.

Educationally, in the United States, as elsewhere in the English-speaking world, there are benefits in maintaining vernacular speech varieties just as there

---

Minority populations in the United States

In 1492 Christopher Columbus set out from the Canary Islands believing that the earth was round and that he could reach the East by sailing West. To his dying day, he was convinced he had found the sea route to the Indies. The people on the Caribbean islands that his ships visited he called *Indios* or *Indians*. Today the word *Indian* is ambiguous in that it can refer either to a person from India or to a person who belongs to the indigenous population of the Americas. In the latter sense, *Indian* is firmly rooted in such common terms as *Plains Indian, French and Indian War*, and *Indian Territory* and the term is in continuing use among American Indians themselves. It is however potentially offensive and is these days replaced by **Native American**.

Recent surveys show that most Black Americans prefer the term **African American** to **Black**, and it is widely used in the media. The term *negro* (from the word which means 'black' in Spanish and Portuguese) is however seen as offensive and can be used only in a historical context such as the slave trade.

Hispanic and *Latino*, though often used interchangeably in American English, are not identical terms. **Hispanic**, the term adopted by the US government for official documents, is by many considered inaccurate (because of the suggestion that it refers to people whose ancestors came from Spain). Among the multicultural population of Latin American origin living in the United States, the most frequently used term is **Latino** (for male) and **Latina** (for female). A third term, **Chicano/Chicana** (an alteration of *mexicano*), is more politically charged and can nowadays have associations of political activism.

White is still used for Americans of European extraction, but **Caucasian** often appears in the media and in legal jargon. Still, there is considerable confusion over the designation *white* or *Caucasian*. Increasingly, the term *white* is becoming a default category, denoting that part of the population not covered by the following classifications: Native Americans, African Americans, Hispanics, East Asians, Pacific Islanders, and other ethnic communities.

are different benefits in acquiring and using standard English. So the enlightened solution is emerging whereby the study and awareness of dialectal varieties and minority languages goes hand-in-hand with the acquisition and study of the standard language. In upholding 'language rights', the aim is to cultivate, and welcome, linguistic diversity – above all in a country like the United States, with such an ethnically and linguistically diverse population.

9
From Caribbean English
to Creole

This is my ocean, but it is speaking
Another language, since its accent changes around
Different islands.

Derek Walcott, *New Yorker*
(14 March 1983)

This chapter has two themes: first, the English language in the Caribbean, and second, the English-based creole languages on the islands of the West Indies and elsewhere in the world. These themes are closely related: although English-based creoles are widely spread across the tropical or subtropical parts of the world, they are concentrated most densely in the Caribbean, and their historical development cannot be better exemplified than by Jamaican Creole in that region. The first question to answer is 'What is a creole?' But before that, here is a little Caribbean history. (The word *Caribbean* can be pronounced with two stress patterns: usually with the stress on the third syllable as *Caribbean*, but in connected speech also as *Caribbean* – a phenomenon known as 'stress shift'.)

The Caribbean is a tropical sea nestling between the three land masses of North, Central and South America. In addition, in general usage, the name applies to the islands of the West Indies which enclose this sea, together with countries on the continental seaboard, such as Guyana /gaɪˈænə/ and Belize /bɪˈliːz/. Actually, Christopher Columbus did not reach North America in his expeditions of 1492–98: he first reached the Bahamas, a large group of small islands that are part of the Caribbean chain. Then he discovered many of the islands we now recognize as part of the English-speaking world. While the largest islands – Cuba and Hispaniola – remain Spanish-speaking and

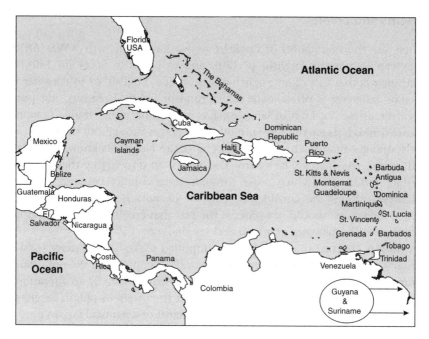

Figure 9.1 The Caribbean and Central America (for the circled countries, Jamaica, Guyana and Suriname, see separate maps, pp. 178, 181)

French-speaking to this day, most of the remaining islands eventually became British. Indeed, the Caribbean islands have a confusing patchwork history of colonization, with different islands being seized and fought over by the principal European colonizing powers – the Spanish, the Portuguese, the British, the French and the Dutch. On top of this, the colonizers imported large populations to work the plantations. In the sixteenth to eighteenth centuries, these were slaves forcibly brought in inhuman conditions from West Africa. After the abolition of slavery in the nineteenth century many indentured workers came from India. The resulting mixture of cultures and languages accounts for the rich diversity of life and traditions in the Caribbean. But, more important for our story, it accounts for a new set of variations on the theme of the English language. In fact, the intermingling of languages, and the special nature of the contacts between them, gave rise to truly 'mixed' languages, known as pidgins and creoles. Despite this, the Anglophone territories of the Caribbean are to be considered a part of the Inner Circle of largely native-speaking countries – the only part of the Inner Circle that has a largely Black population.

Pidgins and creoles

Where are the boundaries of English? As we have seen with AAVE (African American Vernacular English, p. 170), and earlier with Scots (p. 140), the decision whether to call an English-based tongue 'English' or to consider it a separate language is often made for cultural or political reasons, not purely linguistic ones. The English language has undergone some strange metamorphoses through its encounters with other languages throughout the world, and none stranger than in the creation of composite languages known as pidgins and creoles, to which we now turn. The jury is out on whether these so-called **contact languages** (which arose through close contact between unrelated languages) should be considered 'English' or not. However, calling them 'mixed languages' should not obscure the fact that creoles are fully developed languages with their own grammar and vocabulary.

A **pidgin** /ˈpɪdʒɪn/ is a reduced and simplified makeshift language used for contacts, especially trading contacts, between people who do not share a common language. The word *pidgin* is widely considered to be an alteration of *business*, but there are conflicting ideas about the origin of pidgin languages. According to one theory they are the descendants of a nautical jargon used for communication among seamen of different backgrounds. This in turn could have been a relic of *Sabir* /səˈbɪə | səˈbɪˀr/, a lingua franca based on Romance languages which can be traced back to the time of the Crusaders. Sabir was one of the earliest known pidgins, its main lexical influence being from Portuguese.

If a pidgin language is transmitted from parents to children it may become the mother tongue of a community and so turn into a **creole** /ˈkriːoʊl/. In other words, a pidgin has no native speakers, while a creole has become native to some of its speakers, and has therefore extended its communicative functions to those of a fully-fledged language. Creole languages in the world today consist to a large extent of words derived from other languages and are usually classified as Spanish-based, English-based, Dutch-based, and so on. There are some thirty English-based creoles in the world, most of them spoken in the Caribbean, West Africa and the West Pacific. English-based creoles found in the Caribbean developed during the slave trade and draw on various African languages.

In some regions where creoles and Standard English live side by side, such as Jamaica and Guyana in the Caribbean, the creole language and the standard language form a continuum of variation, where the 'highest' variants are the Caribbean versions of Standard English. Linguists draw distinctions between varieties that run from **acrolect** (closest to the standard language) via **mesolect** (intermediate) to **basilect** (closest to the creole). Here is an example from Guyana:

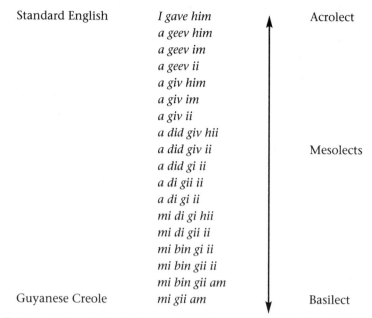

Standard English	*I gave him*		Acrolect
	a geev him		
	a geev im		
	a geev ii		
	a giv him		
	a giv im		
	a giv ii		
	a did giv hii		
	a did giv ii		Mesolects
	a did gi ii		
	a di gii ii		
	a di gi ii		
	mi di gi hii		
	mi di gii ii		
	mi bin gi ii		
	mi bin gii ii		
	mi bin gii am		
Guyanese Creole	*mi gii am*		Basilect

First, we take a look at the acrolects, the more standard varieties of Caribbean English. As far as pronunciation goes, there is variation among the scattered island nations, but some common features can be noticed:

- The number of vowel phonemes is smaller than in most varieties of Standard English: /a/ and /ɒ/ are not distinguished, so that *pat* and *pot* sound the same. Also the diphthongs /ɪe/ and /eə/ often merge, so that *here* and *hair* sound alike.
- Similarly, the *th*-consonants, a bugbear to learners in so many parts of the world, are frequently pronounced /t/ and /d/, so that *three* sounds like *tree*, and *though* like *dough*.
- The diphthong /eɪ/ of GA (General American, see pp. 163–6) and RP (Received Pronunciation, see p. 125) is rendered as a pure vowel /e:/. Similarly, the GA /oʊ/ diphthong becomes the pure vowel /o:/. However, in Jamaican English a different diphthong, the reverse of the GA diphthong, is used in both these cases: /ɪe/ and /ʊo/. So *pay* is pronounced like /pɪe/ and *go* like /gʊo/.
- Some Caribbean varieties, such as that of Barbados, pronounce the *r* after a vowel, while others, such as those of Trinidad and the Bahamas, don't.
- As in AAVE, consonant clusters are often simplified at the end of a word: *ol'* for *old* and *mos'* for *most*.
- Caribbean English is inclined to be **syllable-timed**, whereas the normal rhythm for American or British English is **stress-timed**. This means that, instead of basing the rhythm of the language on roughly equivalent

intervals between stressed syllables, Caribbean English will tend to even out the individual syllable lengths, so that these three West Indian names – *Trinidad, Jamaica, Bahamas* – sound like (a) rather than (b):

(a) Syllable-timed: *Tri̱-ni̱-da̱d Ja̱-ma̱i-ca̱ Ba̱-ha̱-ma̱s*
(b) Stress-timed: *Tri̱nidad Jama̱ica Baha̱mas*

Connected with this smoothing-out of the values of syllables is a tendency to avoid the schwa vowel /ə/ which is so common elsewhere in Inner Circle English. Instead, in Caribbean English, unstressed syllables are pronounced with the same vowels as are used for stressed syllables. Thus in Jamaica *matter* will often be pronounced /'mata/, with the same vowel in each syllable. In other cases the vowel in the word's spelling will be reflected in pronunciation, as in *government* /-mɛnt/, *woman* /-man/. This is a trait that links Caribbean to West African English (p. 116), as does also the melodic intonation typical of the Caribbean. Many of the acrolect characteristics of Caribbean English distantly reflect basilect features – those of the creole language(s) – which in turn reflect some characteristics of the ancestral West African languages.

In grammar, one of the characteristics is that Caribbean speakers prefer to ask questions without reversing the order of subject and verb or using *do*. Instead of *Do you like this music?* they will say *You like this music?*, using a rising interrogative intonation. (This is typical of the question word order of creoles.)

The vocabulary of Caribbean is rich, inventive and diversified. The various island nations seem to pride themselves on differences of vocabulary, lexical resources coming from other European languages or from West African languages. New coinages also abound – supremely in rastafarian language from Jamaica, with words like *attaclapse* 'a very big event', *bandulu* 'bandit, criminal' and *downpressor* 'oppressor'. It's worth mentioning here that writers from the Caribbean have produced some of the greatest literature in English of post-colonial years, including the poets Derek Walcott and Edward Brathwaite and the novelist V. S. Naipaul.

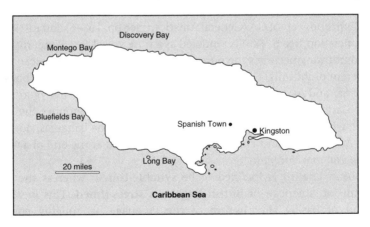

Figure 9.2 Map of Jamaica

Jamaican creole

Jamaican creole, often called 'patois' ('patwa'), is the classic example of a creole, having the largest and oldest body of oral literature in the Caribbean. It is making headway in commercials and entertainment programmes on the island's radio and television, although standard English dominates in news

Here are a few examples of Jamaican creole:

Jamaican creole	Standard English
Mi siik	*I am sick*
Mi nuo	*I know*
Mi da sing	*I am singing*
Him bad	*He is bad*
We yu a go?	*Where are you going?*
Di man dem a plaant kaan	*The men are planting corn*
Na nyam mi a nyam	*I am indeed eating*
Dis man breda bring faiv buk com gi mi yeside	*This man's brother gave me five books yesterday*
Mi sik so mi naa sing	*I am not well so I won't be singing*
Mi fren dem wen plan fi vizit mi bot mi tel dem se dem no fi bada kom	*My friends had planned to visit me but I told them not to bother to come*

Figure 9.3　Scene from a Caribbean wedding

Here is short text of mesolect Jamaican creole, *Sweet and Dandy*, a wedding song written by Frederick 'Toots' Hibbert, with transcription and notes by Peter L. Patrick:

> *Eh-eh! Ettie inna room a cry*
> *Mama seh she mus' wipe 'er h'eye*
> *Papa seh she no fi foolish like*
> *She neva been to school at all*
>
>> *It is no wonder*
>> *A perfect ponder*
>> *While they were dancin' in dat ballroom las' night*
>
> *Eh-eh! Johnson inna room a fret*
> *Uncle seh 'im mus' wuol' up 'im head*
> *Auntie seh 'e no fi foolish like*
> *Is not time for his weddin' day*
>
>> *It is no wonder*
>> *Is a perfect ponder*
>> *While they were dancin' in dat ballroom las' night*
>
> *One poun' ten for de weddin' cake*
> *Twenty bokkle of cola wine*
> *All di people-dem dress up inna white*
> *Fi go h'eat off Johnson weddin' cake*
>
>> *It is no wonder*
>> *Is a perfect ponder*
>> *While they were dancing' in dat ballroom las' night*
>
> *... But they were sweet an' dandy, sweet an' dandy,*
> *Sweet an' dandy, sweet an' dandy*
> *They were sweet an' dan-deh ... sweet an' dan-deh ...*

A few explanations:

eh-eh! An exclamation of surprise.

h'eye The spelling *h'* here and elsewhere signals an *h* that would not occur in standard English, but is added here, often for emphasis.

a cry and a fret 'is crying and fretting'

no fi foolish 'ought not to be foolish'

bokkle 'bottle'

fi go 'to go'

people-dem The plural *s* of standard English is not pronounced, but plural can be optionally expressed by *–dem*.

inna 'in, inside'

programmes and newspapers, as well as in education and the print media. Jamaican creole has gained widespread international exposure through reggae /'regeɪ/ music and its offspring dub poetry (*dub* is popular music in which audio effects and spoken or chanted words are imposed on an instrumental reggae background). However, the popularity of Jamaican creole causes linguistic problems and mixed allegiances: although Jamaicans generally regard Standard

English as their target variety, many creole-speakers do not use it. Instead, their English variety is straddled midway on the continuum between creole and the standard language, i.e. they speak some kind of mesolect. Recently, however, there has been a strong movement to recognize the status of the creole as a distinct language, with equal status to English.

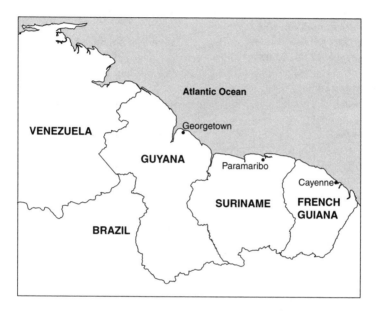

Figure 9.4   Map of Suriname, Guyana and French Guiana

Sranan

Suriname, formerly Dutch Guiana, is a country on the north-east coast of South America which became an independent republic in 1975. The population is of mixed origin and has been described by the linguist Herman Wekker as 'a fruit salad rather than a melting pot'. First colonized by the British, the region was ceded to the Dutch in 1667 in exchange for New Amsterdam (New York City). Shortly after that, most English speakers left Suriname, but the vocabulary of the country's lingua franca, Sranan /'sra:nən/, has remained basically English, although it has existed alongside Dutch for more than 300 years, and the Dutch language has been a major influence.

In Suriname there are various creole languages: Sranan, Saramaccan, Ndjuka, Boni, Paramaccan and Mataway. Sranan, also known as Sranan Tongo, is spoken by at least 95 per cent of the Surinamers, irrespective of ethnic background. It arose through contacts between the British and West Africans during the slave trade. Here is the National Anthem of Suriname, *Opo Kondreman* 'Rise, countrymen'.

Opo Kondreman	
Sranan with English word-for-word translation	**Standard English**
Opo kondreman un opo Rise countrymen you rise!	Rise, countrymen, rise!
Sranan gron e kari un. Surinamese ground call you.	Suriname, your country, is calling you.
Wans ope tata komopo From where ancestors came-up	Wherever our ancestors came from
We mu seti kondre bun. We must put country right	We must put things right in our country.
Strei de f'strei. Fight be for-fight	The fight has to be fought.
Wi no sa frede. We not shall be afraid	We shall not be afraid.
Gado de wi fesiman. God be our leader	God is our leader.
Eri libi te na dede. Whole life until to death	Our whole life until death.
Wi sa feti gi Sranan. We shall fight for Suriname	We shall fight for Suriname.

Explanations

opo from English *up*

kondreman is derived from *countryman*, with the same form in singular and plural: *wan kondreman, tu kondreman*

un has West African origin and is used as a plural form of address

gron from English *ground*

e is a grammatical marker corresponding to the progressive (*is calling*) in English

kari from *call*

tata 'ancestors' is of West African origin

mu from Dutch *moet(en)* 'must' (auxiliary verb)

seti from the Dutch verb *zet(ten)* 'to set'

bun from Portuguese *bon* 'good'

strei from the Dutch noun *strijd* 'fight'

no is a negative particle 'not' and is placed before the verb

sa from English *shall*

frede from English *afraid*

gado from English *God*

fesiman is derived from a compound *fesi* + *man*, which literally means 'first man', i.e. leader

eri from Dutch *heel* 'whole'

libi from English *life*

te na is a combination of the prepositions *te* (corresponding to English *until*) and *na* (English *to*)

dede from English *death*

feti from English *fight*

gi comes from the English verb *give* but is here used as a preposition meaning *for*

The life cycle of a creole

There is a basic similarity between creole languages in different parts of the world, both English-based and non-English-based. There is also a family resemblance between English-based creoles in terms of their grammar, their vocabulary and their phonology. These characteristics of creoles have been studied in detail, and there is no doubt that creoles are systematically structured like any other natural language. There are scholarly dictionaries and grammars, for example, of Jamaican creole, which also has an established oral literature of folk stories, proverbs and the like. But creoles are quite different in fundamental ways from the languages from which they draw most of their vocabulary – what is sometimes called their **lexifier** language. What we call English-based creoles have English as their lexifier, but they also have West African **substrate** languages (see p. 135), which have influenced much of their basic grammar and pronunciation. And yet creoles have characteristics all of their own – particularly a simple word structure, without the grammatical endings of singular and plural, present and past forms, for example, which may be found in the lexifier language. (Even so, creoles have their own distinctive ways of marking most of these grammatical features.) So creoles are genuinely **mixed languages**, which emerged from the blending together of two or more different languages. (There has even been a suggestion that standard English goes back to a creolization period a thousand years ago, when the Vikings and the Anglo-Saxons intermingled and Old English lost the complexity of grammatical endings found in other Germanic languages, ending up with the simple grammatical structure it has today (see p. 39–40).)

Terms like **creolization, decreolization** and **post-creole continuum** are now bandied about by linguists studying the case histories of creole languages. We have already explained the creolization process whereby a makeshift trade language, a pidgin, became the mother tongue of a new generation of speakers, and then acquired the full range of communicative functions that a native language needs. Let's put this in the context of the expansion of European trade and colonization in the seventeenth to nineteenth centuries.

Creoles in many cases came into being as a result of a traumatic upheaval of populations. The slaves transported across the Atlantic to work the plantations were forced into a situation where they had lost touch with their own language community and where they had to communicate with other people without the benefit of a common language. These were fellow slaves who spoke other African languages, and sailors, overseers and traders who spoke English or some other European language. In these circumstances the slaves picked up the pidgin English that was the general lingua franca of the trade routes, and their children were the first native speakers of a new language (perhaps their only language), a creole inheriting the simplified characteristics of the pidgin.

This is the kind of scenario we must imagine for the miraculous birth of a new language. We call this a 'miraculous birth' because, unlike the normal gradual evolution of new languages from old that we mentioned in Chapter 2 (English and German evolving from a common ancestor, and so forth), this is a new language that came into being possibly within one generation. One controversial view, that of Derek Bickerton, is that creoles come into existence through a 'bioprogram' – a special, genetically inbuilt process for learning language that children possess. Only such an explanation as this, he argues, could explain how creoles are so similar, particularly in grammatical structure, wherever they come into being. (The example he studied was Hawaiian creole, arising in very different social circumstances and in a part of the world remote from the Caribbean, so it was harder to explain the similarities as spreading out from a single common pidgin or creole language.)

Once the creole was formed it would go its own way. In the Caribbean, for example, in the early days the white colonists were a relatively small number, and little communication would take place between native English speakers and the speakers of the creole, so the connection between the English-based creole and British English would be effectively broken. However, an interesting contrast can be drawn here between the two creoles we have just illustrated. Sranan was a creole established in a colony which the Dutch got from the British in 1667. After that Suriname had little contact with English speakers, and Dutch remains its official language to this day. So Sranan has developed independently of its lexifier language for over 300 years, and is now for all reasonable purposes a separate language from English. But Jamaican Creole, in contrast, has developed for that same period side by side with the British colonial administrators, colonists and sailors speaking British English. After the abolition of the slave trade in 1807 and of slavery itself in 1833, there was gradually more and more communication between English speakers and the black speakers of creole. English, as the language of education and administration, was firmly planted among the black population.

In these circumstances a so-called **post-creole continuum** developed. What this means is that, instead of two independent languages (standard and creole) side by side, we find a continuum similar to that of the 'pyramid of standardization' discussed in Chapter 7 (p. 128). At the bottom of the continuum, the basilect (the creole) is linked to the acrolect (standard English) through the many variants of the mesolect.

But why should this creole-standard continuum be called a ***post*-**creole continuum? Surely the creole doesn't cease to exist? The idea behind this term is that once the discontinuity between the creole and the standard is broken, then the autonomy of the creole is broken; it can no longer be regarded as a separate language. When a continuum of dialectal variation exists, then there is no point at which we can say 'here is the boundary of the English language, and on the other side of the boundary is creole'. And, as education and national media reinforce the influence of standard Caribbean English, there is a tendency for people to move towards the more prestigious standard variety, and the creole begins to lose its distinctive character. This is where a new piece of terminology finds its place: **decreolization**. It is partly to prevent this decreolization – the decline of creoles through the influence of the standard language – that the movement to establish Jamaican Creole as an official language has been gathering momentum, and is supported, for example, by Hubert Devonish, Professor of Linguistics at the University of the West Indies. Another reason for arguing for a separate language is to give the creole more status. Some would prefer the language to be called 'Jamaican' – putting it on a par with independent languages like Dutch or Maori – rather than 'Jamaican Creole'.

Jamaican Creole is central to a culture with its own religious traditions and literature, intimately connected with other art forms such as music, dance and drama. The motives for preserving it against the dominant influence of standard English are the same as those that fuel movements for the preservation of native and vernacular languages throughout the world, whether in Wales, Scotland or Jamaica.

The Atlantic creoles and their characteristics

It is useful to use the term **Atlantic creoles** for the English-based creoles that developed in Africa, the Caribbean and North America, through the slave trade and other trading links along the West African coast and across the Atlantic. At the African end of the trade routes, there are a number of English-based creoles including Kamtok in Cameroon, Krio in Sierra Leone, Kru English in Liberia and Aku in the Gambia. In these countries and in the largest English-speaking country along this coast, Nigeria, there is a widely used lingua franca called **West African Pidgin English** (WAPE), used by people who speak other languages, but also closely linked to the creole languages already mentioned. Based on WAPE, creole communities are still being formed in the towns; it is noticeable here that creolization does not have to be a sudden process, as we assume it was in Jamaica. Although called a pidgin, WAPE is more like a complex of varieties incorporating both native and non-native speakers.

Across the Atlantic, in the Caribbean, apart from Jamaican Creole, there are other creoles such as **Bajan** /ˈbeɪdʒᵊn/ (in Barbados) and **Trinbagonian** (in Trinidad and Tobago). Last of all, we should mention the **Gullah** /ˈgʌlə/ creole spoken on the Sea Islands and coastal marshes of the southeast coast of the

United States. Spoken by an isolated island Black community, this appears to be a genuine Atlantic creole sharing features with the West African and Caribbean creoles. It also shares some features with AAVE, African American Vernacular English (see p. 170): the word *juke* 'disorderly', coming from Africa to Gullah, also came into AAVE, and eventually into world English in the word *jukebox*. Gullah provides a kind of missing link between AAVE and Africa.

The following are among the grammatical features shared in general by the Caribbean creoles, and also to a great extent by other Atlantic creoles:

- There is no variation of endings on the verb, so that *He love di pikni* 'He loves the child' has no ending on *love*.
- The verb *be* is omitted: *Di pikni sik* 'The child is ill'.
- So-called serial verbs, one following another (like '*Go fetch*'), are common: *I used to walk come down de road. Dem go try get it.*
- Adjectives are normally used instead of adverbs: *She sing real sof'* ('soft').
- Nouns often do not have a plural *-s*: *two book, dem creature*.
- There is no 'apostrophe *s*' to show possession: *dat man car* for 'that man's car'.
- In pronouns, there is no distinction between *I* and *me* and *my*, *we* and *us* and *our*, so we may meet *we music* 'our music'.
- There is a plural second-person pronoun, such as *unu* (compare the discussion of *y'all* and *yous*, pp. 168–9).
- There is often no distinction between *he* and *she*.
- Little words ('markers') before the verb do the work performed by endings (like the *-ed* of the past tense) and constructions (like the *is -ing* of the progressive) in Standard English.
- There is a special word for the past tense: for example, *been walk* instead of *walked*.
- *Da, de, a*, among others, are used to signal progressive or imperfective meanings: *Mi a nyam.* 'I am eating'.
- Negation is expressed by words like *no, naa* in front of the verb: *Ai no wahn a ting.* 'I want nothing'.
- Reduplicated forms and expressive repetitions are frequently used: *picky-picky* 'choosy'; *big-big* 'huge'.

Since it is easiest to use Standard English as a point of reference for describing creole grammar, the emphasis tends to fall on features which are absent from creoles, and so it is tempting to imagine that creoles are simplified or even deficient languages by comparison with other languages. However, this is a misleadingly negative view: looking at things from the opposite point of view, the last five features in the list above show some of the systematic structural features of creoles not shared by standard English.

Turning to pronunciation, creoles tend to have simplified vowel systems, in comparison with American or British pronunciation. The vowels tend to be pure, without diphthongization, and schwa /ə/ is little used. This resembles the comparatively simple vowel systems typical of West African languages. On the whole, too, the *r* following vowels is not pronounced: as in *pati* for 'party'.

Tok Pisin

For our last excursion into creole languages, we travel a long way east to the island state of Papua New Guinea, where one of the official languages is **Papua New Guinea Pidgin**, since 1981 officially called **Tok Pisin**. The name, pronounced /tɒk ˈpɪzɪn/, is derived from English *talk pidgin*. Papua New Guinea has over 700 native languages, but Tok Pisin is the single most widely used language, spoken by over a million people. It is used on radio and television and can be read in the weekly magazine *Wantok* (from *one talk*, i.e. 'one language'). As it is now spoken as a native tongue, *Tok Pisin* has become a creole rather than a pidgin, but the name has stuck.

Tok Pisin is one of the more than 2,000 languages into which the New Testament of the Bible has been translated. In Chapter 4 we gave examples of Bible translations from different periods of the English language. Here is the same Bible text in Tok Pisin, followed, for the sake of easy comparison, by the present-day English version that we quoted in Chapter 4 (p. 59):

> Na 6-pela de i go pinis, na Jisas i kisim Pita na Jems wantaim brata bilong en Jon, na em i bringim ol i goap long wanpela maunten em i antap moa. Na ol tasol i stap. Na bodi bilong Jisas em i senis long ai bilong ol, na em i kamap narakain. Na pes bilong en em i lait olsem san, na laplap samting bilong en em i kamap waitpela olsem lait. Na Moses wantaim Ilaija tupela i kamap na ol i lukim tupela i toktok wantaim Jisas. Pita i lukim dispela na i tokim Jisas, i spik, 'Bikpela, mipela i stap hia, em i gutpela. Sapos yu laik, orait mi ken wokim tripela haus hia. Wanpela bilong yu, na wanpela bilong Moses, na wanpela bilong Ilaija.'
>
> (from *Nupela Testamen*)

> Six days later, Jesus took with him Peter and James and his brother John and led them up a high mountain, by themselves. And he was transfigured before them, and his face shone like the sun, and his clothes became dazzling white. Suddenly there appeared to them Moses and Elijah talking with him. Then Peter said to Jesus, 'Lord, it is good for us to be here; if you wish, I will make three dwellings here, one for you, one for Moses, and one for Elijah.'
>
> (from the *New Revised Standard Version*)

A few explanations:

- *em* 'he, him'; *mi* 'I, me'; *ol* (from *all*) 'they, them'; *na* 'and'; *orait* 'all right'; *sapos yu laik* (from *suppose you like*) 'if you wish'
- The element *-pela*, which turns up in many words, comes from English *fellow*. It is found in *wanpela* (from *one + fellow*) 'a, one'; *gutpela* (from *good + fellow*) 'good'; *bikpela* (from *big + fellow*) 'the Lord'. Also: *naispela haus* 'a nice house', *wanpela meri* (*meri* from *marry*) 'a woman'
- The ending *-im* makes a verb transitive: *wok* 'work' but *wokim tripela haus* 'make three huts'
- *Bilong* (from English *belong*) indicates possession and corresponds to the genitive in *bodi belong Jisas* 'Jesus' body'. The word can be combined in different ways: *pul bilong kanu* ('pull of canoe') 'paddle of a canoe', *pul bilong pisin* ('pull of bird') 'bird's feather', *pul bilong pis* ('pull of fish') 'fish fin'.

We started this chapter by asking 'Where are the boundaries of English', and there is little doubt that Tok Pisin is on the other side of those boundaries: although its vocabulary is almost entirely from English, it is a foreign language for English speakers coming from other parts of the world. In the final chapter, Chapter 12, we will move back to the global level and ask 'Where is the English language heading?' But first, in Chapter 10, we look at 'The Standard Language Today' and, in Chapter 11, at 'Linguistic Change in Progress' in the current language.

Part III
A Changing Language in Changing Times

10
The Standard Language Today

> 'We may say, in short, that Standard English is that kind of English
> which draws least attention to itself over the widest area and through
> the widest ranges of usage.'
>
> Randolph Quirk and Gabriele Stein, *English in Use* (1990, p. 123)

It is a paradox of late Modern English that the language seems to have been
changing *more*, and yet it seems to have been changing *less*. The speed of
change seems to have been accelerating, if we look at the massive growth of
variation in English worldwide. With geographical spread have come divergences, especially in the form of new Englishes and creoles, as we saw in
Chapters 6 and 9. But if we look only at standard English, the language seems
to have been changing more slowly.

To see the force of this, we need to go back in history to around 1700, when
writers and scholars were thinking of setting up an English Language Academy
to 'ascertain' and 'fix' the language, to stop it from changing (p. 64). Poets like
Waller (1606–1687), Dryden (1631–1700) and Pope (1688–1744) were particularly worried that their poems would not be read or understood by succeeding
generations: in Pope's words,

And such as Chaucer is, shall Dryden be.

What he meant was that the language had changed so much since Chaucer's
time that Pope's contemporaries could no longer understand or appreciate his
poetry. The fear was that the same would happen to Dryden, Pope and their
contemporaries for future generations.

The strange thing is that this did not happen. Although no one succeeded in
setting up an English Academy and 'fixing' the language for all time – a futile
goal – the poets of 1700 can still be understood rather well in 2000. To see this,
consider these extracts from Chaucer (who died in 1400) and Dryden (who died

in 1700), in the original orthography:

Chaucer (the beginning of *The Pardoner's Tale*):

> In Flaundres whilom was a compaignye
> Of yonge folk, that haunteden folye

Modern rendering by Nevill Coghill:

> In Flanders once there was a company
> Of youngsters, haunting vice and ribaldry

Dryden (the beginning of *Mac Flecknoe*):

> All human things are subject to decay,
> And when fate summons, monarchs must obey.

In the three centuries following Chaucer's death (1400–1700), the language changed much more than it did in the next three centuries (1700–2000).

Why did the rate of change of English appear to slow down? One likely reason is that the eighteenth century saw the triumph of standard English: the variety of English associated with prestige, polite society and literature. The focus on 'correct' use of the standard language meant that non-standard and provincial forms of language were treated with disfavour. Typical sentiments of the mid-eighteenth century are those of Lord Chesterfield, Samuel Johnson's unhelpful patron in his dictionary project:

> I had long lamented that we had no lawful standard of our language set up, for those to repair to, who might chuse to speak and write it grammatically and correctly ... I cannot help thinking it a sort of disgrace to our nation, that hitherto we have had no such standard of our language.
> Lord Chesterfield, letter to *The World*, 28 November 1754

Also in the same period we see a focus on London and the university cities of Oxford and Cambridge as the source of the best 'most standard' spoken English:

> The language ... of the most learned and polite persons in London, and the neighbouring Universities of Oxford and Cambridge, ought to be accounted the standard of the English tongue, especially in accent and pronunciation.
> James Beattie, The *Theory of Language*, 1788

In Britain today, London, Oxford and Cambridge still form what is enviously called the 'Golden Triangle', the supposed source of wealth, influence and high culture in south-east England. Ironically enough, James Beattie, philosopher, poet and contemporary of Robert Burns, was born and lived in Scotland, where the tradition of separate linguistic and literary development was strongest, as we saw in Chapter 7. Yet linguistically, he could not resist the magnetic pull of the south-east.

The standard language underwent what we earlier called **codification** (see p. 67) – the description of the language in dictionaries and grammars, which again served to conserve and bolster existing approved usage. Later, when mass education took off in the nineteenth century, the teaching of literacy and writing again inculcated the standard language. The resulting power of the standard language put a brake on linguistic development. This is evident most of all in the standardizing of spelling, but also in pronunciation and grammar. The standard language was, of course, primarily written rather than spoken. But around 1800 we see an increase of **spelling pronunciations**, or pronunciations which changed to conform to spelling.

Ever since the sixteenth century, the gradual standardizing and stabilizing of spelling meant that spelling and pronunciation were on divergent paths: new changes in pronunciation would no longer be reflected in spelling. Eighteenth-century pronunciations which diverged from spelling, like 'obleege' for *oblige*, ''umble' for *humble* and 'weskit' for *waistcoat*, lost status and came in the nineteenth century (as we see in Dickens's novels) to be regarded as uneducated pronunciations, to be laughed at. Instead, pronunciation matching the spelling – *forehead* /'fɔːhed/ and *waistcoat* /'weɪskəʊt/ – came to be thought correct. Spelling pronunciation still exerts its power today: in many people's speech, *often* is pronounced /'ɒftən/ as the /t/, lost in the earlier pronunciation /'ɒfᵊn/, has been reintroduced through the influence of spelling.

Since the telephone, radio and television began to have a big part in our lives, it might be argued that the written language is now losing some of its influence: that we live in an 'oral' rather than a 'literate' culture. It certainly appears that the pendulum is swinging somewhat in the direction of speech. Yet we must also remember that the spoken language, since the arrival of national and international broadcasting networks, is itself beginning to feel the pull of standardized language (see p. 227). This might, like standard language in the written medium, put a brake on language change in the spoken medium. So if we focus on the standard language, and not on the vernacular varieties, English must be changing more slowly than it was up to the time of Dryden.

Standard English – the written language

In this chapter, we concentrate on the standard language and, since standard English finds its home in the written medium, we begin with the written language. Standard English began in the written language of late medieval England; it was exported to other Inner Circle countries, among them the

A world standard English?

In print, leaving aside the occasional difference of spelling between the US and the UK standards, English varies remarkably little from one region of the world to another. In fact, it is often hard to determine – apart from local names and local allusions – whether a text was written in Sydney, New Delhi, Anchorage or Edinburgh. Look at the four press cuttings below. In which of the above cities were the articles written? Our guess is that you will find no linguistic clues for the part of the world each text comes from: if you are able to locate these passages, it will be because of cultural rather than linguistic differences. Answers are given on p. 265 in the section Notes: Comments and References.

Text A

If gardening is a religion, seed racks are the alters [*sic*] of our church. They emanate a mystical power that attracts the gardener to worship, and every spring we stand before them, fingering the rosary of vegetable and flower packets.

We confess our innermost horticultural dreams and desires and contemplate the horticultural sins that resulted in past failures. We deal with jealousy, envy, hubris, laziness, competitiveness, anger, joy and the rest of human emotions. The experience gives us hope, and we are buoyed enough to buy a few packets, demonstrating our faith and renewing our horticultural commitment.

And if seed racks are our altars, seeds must be the first miracle of our faith. Contemplate that a seed is not alive. There are no metabolic processes taking place inside the seed. Yet when it comes into contact with three things – water, the right temperature and aerated soil – a seed begins a process that leads to the very essence of life itself.

Lots of new gardeners are afraid to plant seeds, and others consider themselves possessed by a demon known as Brown Thumb or Unskilled. This demon is easily exorcized by a better understanding of what seeds are all about and how they work.

Text B

Board examinations sometimes can be alarmist in nature for students who take the exams and the parents who go through the motions of preparing and appearing for a virtual exam. Despite having appeared for quite a few examinations in our lives, only a few of us have learnt to take examinations with the lightness they deserve.

Ideally, a year-long study and balanced approach to time-management would ease the anxiety, tension and heart-burn. Parents, however, are anxious, as they want children to do well. It's only after they ensure what they feel is a good education for their children that they relax and heave a sigh of relief.

Quite often, the communication between parents and children is quite weak and they are not able to get across the fact that they care too much. Often, it appears that they are foisting their ambitions on their children.

I think we would need to evolve a culture where we treat our children as friends and less as domineering parents. Children tend to be better informed and more adult than they were ever before. They are able to think out issues and problems. They have a point of view. So, it's important when they are in their teens that we treat them as young adults and perhaps try and understand their anxieties and stresses.

Text C

Many object to any human embryo research in principle, regardless of the medical benefits, because it's like killing live human beings for research.

But for those who, like me, do not see all embryos as ethically equivalent to babies, this case still raises special issues. ...

In EU countries where embryo research is permitted, most can only use 'surplus' embryos created from IVF treatments which would be destroyed anyway. It is one thing to use these for compassionate research into treatments for degenerative diseases. It is quite another to create embryos just to get cells out of them.

To create embryos simply as a resource to obtain cells, little remains of a 'special status' on which the current legislation was based. Slowly, by degrees, many fear that human embryos will become like research mice, hardly more than items in a scientific supplies catalogue.

Cloned embryos pose special problems because they could also be used for reproductive cloning. This is no 'slippery slope' because certain maverick scientists clearly want to use any research to make cloned babies in countries without regulations, regardless of major risks and ethical objections.

Text D

NOTE to self: Wednesday: celebrate the right of women to be treated as equal to men; Thursday: cheer for the right for women to be treated differently; Friday: sort through conflicting messages scattered about by modern feminists on what women want.

Some weeks just leave you exhausted. On Wednesday, all the talk was about equality for women in the home. Pru Goward, the Sex Discrimination Commissioner, said we needed a national conversation to drag men back into the home, to cook, clean and care for children and elderly parents. Women are doing a triple shift, said Goward, and this 'cold war going on in private time' was damaging families and women's careers. Equality at home is the answer, apparently.

Then, on Thursday, the talk was all about treating women differently because, well, women are different. Unions are trying to secure 12 days' menstrual leave per year for female Toyota workers in addition to the 10 sick days available to all workers.

So what's the problem with women darting between two agendas? Apart from showing the philosophical inconsistency that afflicts feminism – do we want to be treated equally or differently – the danger is that going too far down either route may ultimately lead women to places they don't want to go.

United States, and finally, it has been exported to the world. Nevertheless, historically, standard English comes from the Inner Circle, and it is on the Inner Circle native-speaking world that we mainly concentrate in this chapter.

These four texts suggest that standard English, at least in newspapers, is homogeneous. But that doesn't mean that it lacks **variety**. It is time to dispose of one misleading connotation of the word 'standard'. In modern life there is an idea, encouraged by the use of 'standard' in such phrases as *the standard equipment, the standard format, the standard procedure*, that standard English is monolithic: that it offers no options, permits no variation. This is far from the truth. Standard English offers us many choices between equivalent expressions, both in vocabulary and in grammar. Consider words such as *philanthropist,* *benefactor* and *do-gooder*. Standard English is full of such near-synonyms, in this case offering a choice between a Greek term (*philanthropist* = 'lover of people'), a Latin term (*benefactor* = 'well-doer') and a Germanic term (the elements *do, good*, and *-er* all derive from Old English). In grammar, too, standard English offers us choices – say between the *s*-genitive *the Queen's arrival* and the prepositional *of*-phrase *the arrival of the Queen*. Consider now these sentences:

(a) There are many friends to whom one would hesitate to entrust one's own children.
(b) There are lots of friends that you would never trust with your own children.
(c) There's lots of friends you'd never trust with your own children.
(d) There's loads of pals you'd never trust with your own kids.

All four sentences have roughly the same meaning, but they express it in very different ways. Sentence (a) is in a style often called **formal** – it is used in a situation where people are on their best linguistic behaviour, communicating in public and probably in an intellectually serious publication. At the other end of the scale, (d) is **very informal**, and although it can easily occur in the written medium (in an e-mail, for instance), it is more likely to be heard in speech. Sentences (b) and (c) are somewhere **intermediate** between the other two. Some of the differences are in choice of words – between *many, lots of* and *loads of*, also between *children* and *kids*. Other differences are grammatical, such as the use of *would* in preference to its contracted form *'d*; also the use of the relative clause beginning with a preposition (*to whom*) as contrasted with the relative clause with the *who(m)* or *that* omitted. Some highly grammar-conscious people might argue that (a) and (b) are the only 'standard English' forms, and that (c) and (d) are non-standard, for example because of the use of *There's* in (c) and (d), instead of the 'correct' plural *There are*. But since *There's* + plural is such an everyday usage, especially in speech, there is no reason to regard any of the four options as unacceptable in standard English.

What examples (a) to (d) show is that standard English is no straitjacket: it doesn't prevent us from expressing ourselves in a variety of ways according to the impression we want to give. The differences we have illustrated may be termed differences of formality, (a) being a formal option, and (b)–(d) being, to varying degrees, informal or colloquial. The difference between them is generally a matter of degree, rather than absolute contrast. For example, the *of*-construction in *the arrival of the Queen* is more likely to occur in serious written texts, compared with *the Queen's arrival*, but both constructions could be used in a single text. Similarly, the *wh*-relative (*who, whom, which*) illustrated by *whom* in (a) above is less likely to occur in informal contexts, such as everyday speech, but is certainly not impossible.

Vocabulary – combining the North Sea and the Mediterranean

Often the difference between 'formal' and 'informal' choices in standard English today can be traced back to different historical layers of the language, rather like the different strata of an archaeological dig. The oldest and most basic layer is Germanic, and we can think of the various waves of borrowing – in particular from French, from Latin, and from Greek – as strata superimposed on this foundation (see pp. 36–8, 49–50).

It may be surprising to learn that the bulk of modern English vocabulary is not Germanic, but of Romance (largely French or Latin) origin. So, it is reasonable to ask: is English really a Romance or Germanic language? The answer is 'essentially Germanic', because its grammar, the structural frame of the language, is largely Germanic, and so more closely related to, say, German and Danish than to French and Spanish. Also, English words of Romance origin are on average less frequent than words of Germanic origin, as we will discuss below.

The vocabulary of a language can be roughly divided into **content words** – like nouns, adjectives and main verbs, which convey most of the information content of any text – and **function words** – words that have a grammatical function, rather than a lexical content. Function words include prepositions like *of*, determiners like *the*, pronouns like *she*, conjunctions like *if*, and primary/auxiliary verbs like *be*, *have* and *can*. For example, words like *the*, *of*, *are* and *if* have hardly any content on their own: they make sense only if they are combined with content words in a grammatical construction like *If thousands of people are delayed* .... The important thing to notice is that almost all English function words are Germanic in origin.

If we look at a list of the 50 most common words in English, they are all function words and all of Germanic stock. Here they are in order of frequency:

the, of, and, a, in, to, it, is, to, was, I, for, that, you, he, be, with, on, by, at, have, are, not, this, but, had, they, his, from, she, that, which, or, we, 's (verb), an, -n't, were, as, do, been, their, has, would, there, what, will, all, if, can

On the other hand, if we go to the middle of the frequency list, taking 50 words occurring approximately once in every 10,000 words, the picture is very different:

dark, event, thousand, involved, written, park, 1988, returned, ensure, America, fish, wish, opportunity, commission, 1992, oil, sound, ready, lines, shop, looks, James, immediately, worth, in terms of, college, press, January, fell, blood, goods, playing, carry, less, film, prices, useful, conference, operation, follows, extent, designed, application, station, television, access, Richard, response, degree, majority

(The shaded words are of Romance (French or Latin) origin; words in unshaded boxes are of mixed Germanic and Romance origin, or else uncertain origin; the underlined words, or parts of words, are of neither Germanic nor Romance origin; words with no shading or underlining are Germanic.)

It is clear, in this example, that these words of middle-order frequency (one occurrence in 10,000 words) are more likely to be Romance than Germanic, and this trend gets stronger as one moves down the frequency list to rarer, more specialized and technical vocabulary. We also notice that the Romance words are, on the whole, longer than the Germanic words, and belong to a more 'cultivated' stratum of vocabulary.

In Chapter 3 we saw why this is. For over 300 years after the Norman Conquest, French became the language of the ruling class, and English was enriched with thousands of French words (see pp. 37–9). Latin has also been a generous word donor to English throughout the history of the language: from Old English, to Middle English and up to the latest Modern English (see pp. 21, 49). However, as one scholar has put it: 'French acted as the Trojan horse of Latinity in English, the sluice gate through which Latin was able to pour into English on a scale without any equivalent in any other Germanic language'. The combination of French and Latin words created a new English vocabulary, 'the Romance stratum', with many thousands of words from Latin, French and other Romance sources. A new stage was reached when Romance vocabulary 'went native', and new words were created within English, using such French/Latin elements as *dis-, de-, mal-, super-, sub-, -ation, -ify, -ble*. They were often added to native Germanic elements, producing 'hybrid' words such as *dislike* (*dis-* from Latin, *-like* from Old English). The opposite happened too: Germanic affixes were added to Romance stems – as in *beauty* + *ful* making *beautiful*. The different strata of vocabulary these days are closely intermeshed, but the feeling for their difference of tone still remains when we compare key political terms like *freedom* (Germanic), *liberty* (Romance) and *democracy* (Greek).

By increasing the wealth and size of English vocabulary, the combination of the North Sea (bordered by Scandinavian and west Germanic languages, see Figure 2.1, p. 14) and the Mediterranean (bordered by French and other Romance languages) has, on one level, caused problems for the non-native learner of the language, who has to learn to distinguish so many near-synonyms. But from another viewpoint, it has no doubt contributed to the learnability and spread of English as an international language. Words such as *agent, aquarium, candidate, document, information, international, generous, literary, manual, number, project, rational, session, torture, vocabulary* feel familiar to many speakers of other first languages than English. For example, the word *information* has corresponding words *information, informação, información* and *informazioni* in French, Portuguese, Spanish and Italian.

> ### 'Yes Prime Minister'
>
> The main characters in the British comic TV series *Yes Prime Minister* are Prime Minister James Hacker and the top civil servant Sir Humphrey. Sometimes it seems as if they aren't speaking the same language. Sir Humphrey has a marked preference for uncommon Romance words while the minister prefers monosyllabic Germanic words. In his diary Hacker remembers the occasion when Sir Humphrey explained that he was moving to another department (Romance words are highlighted in white):
>
> > Humphrey had said that 'the relationship, which I might tentatively venture to aver has not been without a degree of reciprocal utility and even perhaps occasional gratification, is approaching the point of irreversible bifurcation and, to put it briefly, is in the propinquity of its ultimate regrettable termination'.
>
> I asked him if he would be so kind as to summarize what he'd just said in words of one syllable.
> He nodded in sad acquiescence. 'I'm on my way out', he explained.

If we can say (as we often can) that Romance vocabulary belongs to a more 'sophisticated' stratum than Germanic vocabulary, then we can say that the Greek stratum is even more so, belonging mainly to a learned or scientific level of usage. This can be illustrated with the word *vocabulary* we have just used. Like *dictionary*, it is a word of Romance origin. But more technical terms used in linguistics, such as *lexicon*, *lexicography* (the writing of dictionaries) and *thesaurus* (literally a 'treasury'), are all from Greek. Digging down into the Germanic stratum, we find no everyday term for 'a collection of words' derived from Old English, although we do sometimes meet *wordstock* and *wordhoard* – *wordhoard* is actually used in the Anglo-Saxon poem *Beowulf* (see pp. 30–2) in the sense 'a treasure or store of words'.

However, the notion of separate layers of vocabulary can be taken too far: elements originally from more 'cultivated' strata have continually found their way into the core vocabulary of the language. So *use*, originally from French, is one of the most common verbs in the language. And the element *tele-* (from a Greek word meaning 'far') has become thoroughly at home in English even for the youngest of its speakers: we find it in *Teletubbies*, the name of the British cult television show for pre-school children.

A spectrum of usage – from speech to writing

The idea of **a scale** or **continuum of language variation** will have become familiar to readers of this book, for example in continua of dialect variation. We now have yet another scale to introduce – within standard English, we can identify a scale between spoken and written language, which we will call **a spectrum of usage**.

On the face of it, spoken language and written language are utterly distinct: speech communicates from mouth to ear by sound waves, and writing communicates to the eye by marks on paper or on some other visible surface. This is true, and yet when we reflect on the different functions and limitations of language in these two channels, we are not surprised to observe a scale running from the most typical spoken style of language to the most typical written style, by which we mean the type of writing (such as in official documents) that is most remote from speech. At this point, we are thinking of features of language such as vocabulary and grammar, which are common to both the spoken and the written modes of communication. Figure 10.1 illustrates this.

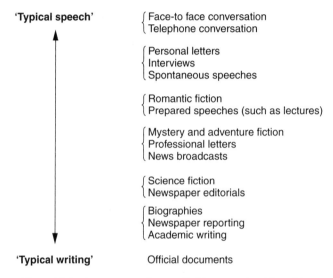

Figure 10.1   A spectrum of usage linking speech with writing

The figure shows a scale with selected language varieties, ordering them by their tendency to be **involved** or **interactive** as is typical of speech, or **informative** as is typical of writing. One thing we notice is that some written text types (such as personal letters) are much closer to 'typical speech' than some spoken varieties, such as prepared speeches. Other points to notice are that different spoken varieties can be ordered by how close (on average) they are to written style:

WRITING → News broadcasts → Prepared speeches → Spontaneous speeches → Conversation

Conversely, written varieties can be ordered by how close they are to spoken style:

SPEECH → Personal letters → Romantic fiction → Academic writing → Official documents

Here are examples of the kinds of discourse that belong to opposite ends of the spectrum in Figure 10.1.

Passage A

Part of **a face-to-face dialogue**: A is serving in a picture shop in the US, and B and C are customers:

A: Okay, so we have two separate ones, or do you want that one?
B: No, two, I'll, I'll, how much are those? Eighteen, well here's a twenty – twenty-one, plus tax – so put that towards her bill.
A: Okay.
C: Ooh, that's a neat picture.

Passage B

Part of **an official document** (from the 2004 Annual Report of the Australian Museum):

The sustainability of cultural heritage and biodiversity now requires a different response from natural history museums. Scientists are rightly concerned about the decline in researchers in anthropology and taxonomy. The causes of this decline are complex and beyond the scope of this message but the solution is as much in the hands of natural history museums as it is in the hands of the governments who fund such institutions.

If we look at the general impression of each passage on the page, Passage B looks much denser – the words are longer and more complex, and this reflects their origin. Once again we use grey shading to show which words come from Romance, as opposed to Germanic, sources. Words from Greek are shown in dark grey. But differences in grammar and in discourse features are also evident (see the box below).

The language of spontaneous speech, compared with written language

Here, we list the social and psychological characteristics of spoken language, together with the linguistic features associated with them. In the right-hand column, we note the contrasting characteristics of written language. To illustrate, we make use of Passages A and B above, and Passage C below.

- Spoken language takes place in a context that speaker and hearer share (**shared context**)

SPOKEN LANGUAGE	WRITTEN LANGUAGE
This means that in conversation we use a large number of pronouns and other words whose meaning points to the situation: among them *we, one, ones, I, you, her, that, those* in Passage A. In face-to-face conversation, speakers and listeners would know what these small words referred to. But readers often find transcriptions of speech difficult to interpret – because of their lack of this contextual knowledge.	In contrast, writers of typical written texts do not share common knowledge of context with their readers, and they have to be more explicit in making their meaning clear.

- Speakers avoid elaboration or specification of meaning (**lack of specification**)

SPOKEN LANGUAGE	WRITTEN LANGUAGE
Speakers are happy to leave information out, partly because of the shared context already mentioned, and partly because they are operating in real time, and have to get their points across quickly. So in speech we often use 'incomplete' sentences (such as structures without verbs) and snatches of syntax, as in:	In contrast, most forms of written language are relatively explicit and exact.

Passage C

> A: Oh just as easy to um
> B: What go by car?
> A: Go by car.
> B: Oh
> A: It takes about … well
> B: About two ticks, ya. All right.

Another aspect of this lack of specification is the habit speakers have of being blatantly imprecise: vague expressions like *sort of, kind of, and stuff, or something* are useful conversation-fillers where being too exact would be inappropriate and could cause delay.

- Spoken language is interactive (**interactiveness**)

SPOKEN LANGUAGE	WRITTEN LANGUAGE
Conversation takes place in a dialogue situation, where the hearer has an active role, and can respond to what you say. This is one reason why speakers can get away with vague and incomplete utterances, knowing that hearers can seek clarification if need be. Some of the common linguistic features of talk reflect this to-and-fro activity of dialogue. Questions and imperatives are common in speech: Passage A has *How much are those?* and *put that towards her bill*. Small words like *Okay, No, Well, All right* (see Passages A and C) are also important in speech – they are rather like traffic signals indicating the way the speaker wants the conversation to turn.	A written text lacks this interactiveness, and so the features just mentioned are uncommmon in writing. None of them occurs in Passage B.

- Spoken language expresses personal emotion and attitude (**emotive expression**)

SPOKEN LANGUAGE	WRITTEN LANGUAGE
Speech often contains polite formulae such as *Sorry, Thanks*, and greetings *Hi there!* as well as of familiar forms of address (vocatives) like *honey, dad, guys*. Exclamatory words like *Ooh* (Passage A) also express personal feelings, as do expletives like *Fuck* or *My gosh*.	Again, these highly personal features are generally absent from written texts: none are in Passage B.

- Spoken language takes place 'on line', in real time (**on-line processing**)

SPOKEN LANGUAGE	WRITTEN LANGUAGE
Spoken language unfolds in real time: it's a rapid and fleeting process, while a written text is usually a considered end-product. Handwritten manuscripts may provide us with a glimpse of the creative writing process with its deletions, additions and alterations. But these days, when we work with word processors, all early versions disappear into a large electronic black hole: they are (or rather were) for the writer's eyes only. In speech, by contrast, there is no 'delete' key: the editing process is plain for all to hear, including reformulations, repetitions, mixed-up sentence constructions, hummings and pauses. We see some of this disfluency, marked in bold face in this piece of Passage A:	Producing writing, on the other hand, takes place off-line, and the disfluent features of speech are edited out.

*No, two, **I'll, I'll**, how much are those? Eighteen, well here's **a twenty – twenty-one**, plus tax – so put that towards her bill.*

Using a metaphor from computers, we can say that producing speech is an on-line activity.

- Spoken language is more repetitive and has a restricted repertoire (**low lexical density**)

SPOKEN LANGUAGE	WRITTEN LANGUAGE
Because of the pressures of on-line language processing, in speech we tend to rely on repetitive phrases like *Can I have a ...?* or *Do you know what ...?* These are easy to retrieve from memory. For the same reason, conversations tend to have a rather limited vocabulary. For example, speakers use certain favourite conjunctions like *if, because* and *when*; favourite modal verbs like *can, will, would*; and favourite adverbs like *then, just, so*.	Partly as a consequence of this, speech is less dense in its information content than writing.

Is spoken English grammatical?

It's time to debunk the common myth that spoken language has no grammar. The grammar of spoken and written English is essentially the same, but the two channels make very different use of their common grammatical resources. Here is one construction from everyday speech, the typically English **tag question**:

A: It's cold today.
B: Yes it's freezing, *isn't it?*

Tag questions are a <u>highly typical interactive</u> feature of casual conversation. Speaker B's tag question <u>encourages speaker A to share ideas and experiences</u>, and prompts A to continue the conversation. But tag questions are a difficult aspect of English grammar to learn. Whereas in other languages a single form like German *nicht?* or Japanese *ne?* will do, in these standard English tag questions we have to match the tag to the preceding statement, as these examples illustrate:

Rita sang like an angel, *didn't she?*
You're joking, *aren't you?*
We've met before, *haven't we?*
She lives alone, *doesn't she?*
He's not very friendly, *is he?*
I couldn't go home without her, *could I?*
She doesn't live alone, ...?

You will be able to choose the missing tag in the last example. But if you should happen to choose the wrong match, as in **She doesn't live alone, is she?*, the result is an ungrammatical sentence. It is no wonder that learners of English get impatient with these complicated rules for tag questions, and some – as happens also in some native-speaking dialects (see pp. 135–6) – resort to some general tag that they can apply to any statement, like *isn't it?, right?, eh?* or *huh?* The rules for tag questions are an example of grammatical rules for standard English, but they are rules which operate almost entirely in spoken English. So there is something we can call spoken standard English – and it has a grammar!

Another type of grammatical structure that is typical for spoken English (as of the spoken variety of other languages) is found in these examples:

<u>North and south London</u>, *they*'re two different worlds ...
<u>This little woman</u>, *she's* ninety years old.

The pronoun (in italics) acts as a kind of substitute subject for the rest of the sentence, while the 'real subject', in terms of meaning (underlined), stands on its own, at the beginning. This construction has been called **left-dislocation**, for obvious reasons, although it is rather inappropriate to talk in terms of 'left' and 'right', as the construction is very rarely found in written English, it belongs almost entirely to the grammar of spoken language.

The opposite of the above construction, where the noun phrase stands at the end, has unsurprisingly been given the label **right-dislocation**:

It's nice <u>that table</u> anyway.
Oh ... *he* was a lovely man, wasn't *he*, <u>Doctor Jones</u>?

It is odd that left-dislocation is often noted to be a feature of creoles and New Englishes, as if it were foreign to other varieties of English. In fact it is found quite generally in spoken English, is not obviously restricted to any particular dialect, and is reasonably considered a feature of standard spoken English.

*   *   *

Of course, the answer to the question we posed at the beginning of this section is 'Yes – spoken English is grammatical'. In fact, written and spoken English largely make use of the same grammatical repertoire, but with very different preferences, according to different contexts of language use. Some constructions, such as the passive, are typical of writing, whereas others, like tag questions and left- and right-dislocations, are highly characteristic of speech. More generally, in this chapter we have seen that standard English is no monochrome variety of the language, but accommodates a wealth of variation.

11

Linguistic Change in Progress: Back to the Inner Circle

> Time changes all things: there is no reason why language should escape this universal law.
>
> Ferdinand de Saussure, *Cours de Linguistique générale* (1916)

If you ask native speakers of English how the language is changing today, after hesitation they will probably mention new vocabulary, or possibly some changes in pronunciation, but it is unlikely that grammar will appear on the agenda. This is probably for two reasons. First, most native English speakers are ignorant about the grammar of their mother tongue. Ask them about a grammatical problem, and they will dissolve into joking embarrassment. Second, grammar is an aspect of language that changes slowly, so it is popularly assumed to be unchanging, its rules set in stone. No one who has read this book, we are sure, will make that mistake. The grammar of standard English keeps changing, as it always has. However, within one generation there are likely to be few dramatic changes: what we can observe are changes of preference, of frequency. Interestingly, changes in recent English grammar tend to follow particular patterns, which we list as follows:

- **Grammaticalization** – Items of vocabulary are gradually getting subsumed into grammatical forms, a well-known process of language change.
- **Colloquialization** – The use of written grammar is tending to become more *colloquial* or *informal*, more like speech.
- **Americanization** – The use of grammar in other countries (such as the UK) is tending to follow US usage.

Grammaticalization

About 500 years ago, there developed a new class of English words, now known as **modal auxiliary verbs** (modals for short). The main members of this class are *can, could, will, would, shall, should, may, might* and *must*. They are called 'modal' because the meanings they express are in the area of modality (including such notions as possibility, necessity, obligation and prediction). These modals resulted from grammaticalization: after losing many of the forms and functions of main verbs, such as the ability to have infinitive or participle forms, they became special little grammatical items which normally have to be followed by a main verb (as in *can help*).

Gradually over the following centuries, a new class of 'modal verbs' arose: they include *be going to, have to, have got to, want to, need to, be supposed to*. Some of these **semi-modals**, as they have been called, such as *be going to, have to, need to* and *want to*, are becoming more frequent, especially in speech. Some of them have also been developing shortened, elided forms in speech, as is suggested by the informal spellings *gonna, gotta, hafta* and *wanna*. In casual conversation they are behaving almost like single function words. For example:

I just don't know how we *gonna* do this. ('how we are going to do this')
I *gotta* take this door to the dump. You *wanna* help me?

The meanings of these items are also gradually changing so that *be going to* (*gonna*) is developing a more neutral future meaning, and so competing with *will*. Especially in spoken American English, there is a strong preference for *be going to*.

Although evidence is difficult to come by, it's tempting to assume that the semi-modals, in taking a bigger role in expressing modality, are encroaching on the territory of the 'true modals' like *will* and *must*. For example, *have to* is now at least as frequent in speech as *must* and both verbs express the same concepts of obligation and necessity. This is all the more persuasive because the frequency of modals is generally declining. Some modals, like *shall, must* and *may*, are becoming rare, especially in American speech, and also in some other varieties, such as Scottish English. The decline of the modals in the period 1960–90 was overall about 10 per cent in written English and more in spoken English. But during the same period the loss of frequency of the rarer modals, like *shall*, was up to 40 per cent in some cases.

In spite of all this, it is difficult to argue that the rise of semi-modals is triggering the decline of modals, as modals are still much more common than semi-modals, especially in written English. Grammaticalization is perhaps just one cause of a changing balance between two methods of expressing modality. What we can observe today is significant in itself, but appears to be only a stage in an evolution which has been going on for centuries.

Colloquialization

As a general rule, changes in the grammar of English seem to come from the spoken language, then gradually spread into the written language. This appears to be what is happening in the rise of semi-modals and the decline of modals, as both trends are more advanced in speech. Looked at from the viewpoint of written English, this process can be seen as an aspect of **colloquialization** – the process by which written language is influenced by the norms of speech. The next box shows examples of colloquialization which were taking place in the recent past (1960–90), and are probably still doing so.

Written grammar affected by speech – likely examples of colloquialization

Increasing use in written English of:	Examples
'Semi-modal' verbs	*be going to, have to, need to, want to*
Present progressive constructions	*is walking, are eating, am telling*
Verb contractions and negative contractions	*it's, we're, they've, she'll, aren't, don't*
Relative clauses with *that* or 'zero'	*the shows <u>that I enjoy</u>, the shows <u>I enjoy</u>*

Decreasing use in written English of:	Examples
Passive constructions	*is eaten, was told, are divided (by ...)*
Relative clauses beginning with *wh*-forms (*who, whom, which*)	*shows <u>which I enjoy</u>, those <u>whom I admire</u>*

As this list shows, colloquialization has both a positive and a negative aspect. The negative side shows up when features of grammar typical of written styles become less frequent in writing as if they are giving way to the pressure of more speech-based constructions. However, both negative examples in the table (decrease of passives and of *wh*-relatives) also have another explanation. Both have succumbed to usage gurus – people who lay down the law about correct and incorrect usages. The passive has long been the target of usage manuals which portray it as a barrier to clear communication in 'plain English'. The relative pronoun *which* has also given offence to those who regard *that* as preferable, except when the relative clause follows a comma, expressing a 'separate thought'. These prohibitions largely come from prescriptive tradition in the US, where they are reinforced by publishers' editorial practices. But they are now almost certainly being spread around the world through the grammar-checking software of word processors.

Colloquialization is far from uniform in its effects. In one or two respects, it seems that written language is resisting the movement towards speech, and even increasing the distance between spoken and written language. An example of this contrary trend is an increase in writing of the occurrence of words of Latin or Greek formation: suffixes such as *-ism, -ist, -ion* and prefixes such as *trans-, inter-* and *hyper-* are on the increase in writing, although a trend towards speech would lead to their avoidance. Another example, probably connected with the last, is a trend towards greater **lexical density** – towards packing more information into a smaller number of words. We see this most characteristically in newspaper reporting (especially in headlines), where a sequence of several nouns without any intervening words is not unusual. Here are three different newspaper examples:

New York City Ballet School instructor
real estate tax shelter sales people
San Francisco Redevelopment Agency Executive Director Chuck Springfield

(To grasp this notion of lexical density, notice that we could make the meaning of the first example more explicit and 'spread out' by using prepositions like *at, for, of: an instructor at the School for Ballet in the City of New York.*)

The frequency of noun–noun sequences has increased quite substantially in written language generally, not just in the press. **Acronyms** or **alphabetisms** – words built out of initial letters of a longer expression – have also increased dramatically. These provide another way of condensing complex information into a smaller compass, as we recognize from fairly recent coinages which have become everyday words: *DNA* (*deoxyribonucleic acid*) and *AIDS* (*auto-immune deficiency syndrome*), *PC* (*personal computer*), *GM* (*genetically modified*), *SUV* (sport-utility vehicle).

An increase in the use of the 'apostrophe-*s*' genitive, at the expense of the corresponding *of*-phrase, is another trend towards greater density of information. Notice the greater compactness of *workers' compensation* compared with *the compensation of workers*, or of *the bill's supporters* compared with *the supporters of the bill.*

Liberalization?

In another direction, colloquialization seems to go with more liberal attitudes to grammatical rules. We have talked about the eighteenth century as the high noon of prescriptivism, when the language was extensively codified and leaders of opinion attached great importance to 'correctness' (see pp. 64, 67). But it is difficult, if not impossible, to suppress naturally occurring linguistic habits. It seems that some time-honoured usages rejected by grammatical authority 'went underground', surviving in the kind of language which was not subject to close scrutiny. Typically, this was spontaneous spoken language, which is the kind of usage benefiting from greater laxity – or perhaps ignorance – of grammatical 'standards'. We find that the use of pronouns like *me* and *them* after the verb to *be* – outlawed from the written language – is now more acceptable: *Hi, it's me.*

A: Who was that on the phone?
B: Marj and Bill.
A: Oh, I guessed it was *them*.

On a similar theme, *Who do you trust?* (George H. W. Bush's election slogan of 1992) – where traditional grammar dictates *whom* – is less likely to raise eyebrows or hackles nowadays, when people are more grammatically 'laid back'. The opposite phenomenon from *It's me* consists of expressions like *between you and I* (where orthodox tradition dictates *you and me*). It is interesting to note that Shakespeare was not averse to committing this 'grammatical crime' in dialogue passages:

> All debts are cleared between you and I (*Merchant of Venice* III.ii.321)

But nowadays this kind of departure from strict grammar is commonplace, even in writing. Still on the theme of pronouns, a singular use of *they*, long condemned by prescriptive grammar, is making increasing inroads into the written medium:

> **Any fool** can make up a story like that if **they** feel like it.

This breaks the rule which says that a singular cannot agree with a plural, but far from being a recent 'flaw', it dates back to before Shakespeare. The growing entrenchment of this form in modern written English, however, is evident in the occurrence since the 1970s of a new pronoun, *themself*:

> We are asking everyone to post a photo of *themself* on the notice board.

This is still only marginally acceptable, causing outrage in some quarters because it yokes plural *them* with singular *self* in one word.

Americanization

We have already noted one or two examples of British English (BrE) following American English (AmE) in the realm of grammar. First, the **mandative subjunctive** form has been increasing from a very low ebb (see p. 167):

> Hence it is important that the process *be* carried out accurately.

And, as we have seen in this chapter, the increasing use of **semi-modals** along with the declining use of the modals seems to be a change where AmE is leading the way. The same applies to the increasing use of **contractions** like *don't* and *it's* in written texts; also of ***that-* and zero-introduced relative clauses** – *the car (that) I saw* – versus the declining use of *wh*-relative clause – *the car which I saw*. In fact, the general picture is that AmE has been showing a more extreme or advanced tendency of colloquialization than BrE.

We mention finally an American-led change in BrE that was almost complete at the end of the twentieth century. The main verb *have* in BrE used to be treated like an auxiliary verb, in being placed before the subject in questions and before *not* or *n't* in the negative. AmE, on the other hand, treated *have* as a main verb, using **do-support** (as it is called technically) to form questions and negatives:

	A	B	C
	AmE (now also BrE)	BrE (more common than AmE)	BrE (now rare)
QUESTIONS	*Do you have a pen?*	*Have you got a pen?*	*Have you a pen?*
NEGATION	*I don't have any milk.*	*I haven't got any milk.*	*I haven't any milk.*

The 'American' construction (A) has largely displaced the 'British' construction (C) in present-day English. The middle construction (B) is found in both varieties, but less in AmE than BrE. It is an informal construction, largely confined to speech.

Is English becoming a more democratic language?

After our survey of present-day grammatical change, we are now moving on to more social developments in the language, reflecting human relations among its speakers. The claim is sometimes made that English is a 'democratic' language. It appears to lack the honorific forms that exist in other languages to signal relations of superiority or inferiority, deference or familiarity, between speakers. For example, languages such as Japanese and Korean have highly elaborate honorific systems manifesting traditional respectful relations and hierarchical values in society. Such languages also have special 'humble' forms, marking the lower status of the speaker. In most West European languages apart from English, there is at least one honorific marker – the use of a respectful pronoun very roughly comparable to *you* in Shakespeare's English (see p. 55) as contrasted with the familiar pronoun *thou*. French has *tu* and *vous*; German has *du* and *Sie*; Spanish has *tú* and *usted*. Standard English had more or less lost this distinction by 1660, so that the only second-person pronoun in general use was *you*. Since then, respectful forms of second-person address have been exceptional, almost fossilized, such as *your Honour* or *your Worship* (addressing a judge) or *your Grace* (addressing a duke, duchess or archbishop) – expressions ordinary citizens rarely, if ever, have occasion to use.

But this does not mean English is totally lacking in honorific forms. The address forms *Sir* and *Madam* or *Ma'am* are, in grammatical terms, **honorific vocatives**. These are getting rarer: apart from ritualized uses such as addressing officers in the armed services, their typical recipients in Britain tend to be ageing, imposing-looking people like ourselves. The typical users of *Sir* and *Madam*, on the other hand, are service providers such as sales assistants in an upmarket department store. However, an American correspondent (Julia Youst MacRae) writes that, in some areas in the Southern US, people use *Sir* and *Ma'am* more often than in the North: 'My cousins (who grew up in Texas) had to address their parents using *Sir* and *Ma'am*. They couldn't just answer a *Yes/No* Question with a simple *yes* or *no*. They had to say *Yes, Ma'am* or *No, Sir*. In other places throughout the U.S. I notice that *Sir* and *Ma'am* are still pretty commonly used when a sales assistant is trying to get someone's attention. It usually comes in the form *Excuse me, Sir/Ma'am.*'

Unlike familiar pronouns such as *tu* and *du*, though, vocatives are optional elements in any utterance. In this sense an English speaker does not have to 'declare' a particular relationship with the addressee: the most common kind of utterance in English is one that has no vocative. But vocatives can be used, where we wish, to signal the relationship between the speaker and the hearer – which may vary from respectful distance to familiarity.

By far the most frequent kind of vocative is one which addresses the person by name. And the choice of mode of address – such as using a first name (*Mary*) or a surname with title (*Mrs Mack, Doctor Ladd*) – is a way of calibrating the relationship we want to establish, or maintain, with the addressee. What has happened over the last hundred years or so is a massive change in habits of address, moving from the more distant and respectful to the more familiar and friendly end of the social scale. Generally, to be on *good* terms with someone in English in the twenty-first century, one needs to be **on first-name terms**.

Names of people

The names people address us by form part of our sense of identity. There are several different types of **proper names** used for individuals:

A **First names** (also called **given names** or **forenames**): *Alexandra, Alexander, Amber, Benjamin, Pamela, William*
B **Middle names**: John *Maynard* Keynes, George *Walker* Bush (often reduced to an initial: George *W*. Bush, hence humorously nicknamed *W* or *Dubya*, see p. 166)
C **Family names** (also called **surnames**): *Abbas, Brown, Cohen, Flanagan, Giuliani, Kim, Lakoff, MacDonald, Smith*
D **Nicknames** are familiar or shortened forms of proper names: *Fran* for Frances, *Liz* for Elizabeth, *Dick* for Richard. The ending *-y* or *-ie* adds a touch of friendly familiarity, especially popular in a girl's name: *Jackie* for Jacqueline. Nicknames can also be descriptive or joky names, such as *Curly* for someone with curly hair – or alternatively, with no hair at all.

Personal names are highly 'personal' and, mumbled at introductions, they are difficult to catch, spell – let alone, remember – especially for non-native speakers who also find it hard to know what nicknames go with what given names. Here's an example from the famous Kennedy family: *Joseph*, the father, was called *Joe*. His oldest son *Joseph Jr. Robert* was called *Bob* or *Bobby*, and *Edward* is known as *Ted*. *John Fitzgerald*, who became the 35th President of the United States, was known in the family as *Jack*. After his inaugural in 1961 President Kennedy (often referred to as *JFK*), let it be known that he didn't want to be known publicly as *Jack*. Familiarity may not be desirable for the world's most powerful person!

> ### 'Hi, Jill!'
>
> In Inner Circle parts of the English-speaking world, it's now much more common than it was to speak to, or about, people by their first names, especially among friends and young people: 'Hi Jill! How are you today?' In addressing a senior person, it's still quite usual to use the titles *Mr* and *Mrs* followed by the last name. If Jill is a teenager, she might say 'Hello Mrs Johnson! How are you today?' Mrs Johnson might then reply, 'Please, Jill, call me Maria.'
>
> Speaking of names, it's important to check how they are spelled – nobody wants to see their names misspelled. In English there is often a bewildering mix of ways of spelling names that are pronounced the same way: *McIntosh* or *Mackintosh, Stevenson* or *Stephenson, Davis* or *Davies, Catherine, Katherine* or *Kathryn, Graham* or *Graeme, Leslie* or *Lesley, Geoff* or *Jeff, Frances* (female) or *Francis* (male). Another source of confusion is the existence of 'unisex' names: a person answering to a name like *Charlie, Chris, Robin* and *Sam* can be either a man or a woman.

It seems that, recently, the whole ethos of forms of address in English (at least in western or westernized English-speaking culture) has been moving towards eliminating distinction and distance. **No distinction** means that the first-name relationship is ideally reciprocal: you call me *Nick* and I call you *Vicky*. It often exists mutually even between an adult and a child (though rarely when children address their parents). **No distance** means that the relation seems close and friendly. Even on first meeting, people will often get on first-name terms, without going through a previous stage of addressing one another as *Mr/Mrs/Ms/Miss X*.

But there are limits to first-name address. A female American reader says: 'Sometimes when a service provider uses my first name (especially if I've just met him) I get the feeling that he's trying to schmooze me. Something that's becoming more common in grocery stores is for clerks to read your receipt after a purchase and say *Thank you, Ms. MacRae* (receipts have your full name on them if you've used the store's club card, for example). Stores like Safeway train their employees in their special brand of customer service. The management has decided that addressing each customer by *Mr.* or *Ms.* + last name, as they leave the store, is one way to give good service. I think most customers find it very strange, especially when the clerks continue to mispronounce your name – it doesn't feel very polite when that happens and a little bit of an intrusion.'

We can suggest that the friendly feeling of 'camaraderie' has somehow been superseding the old model of polite respectful distance. One consequence of this is that it is important to use vocatives, for example in interacting with work colleagues. Here is a short extract from a dialogue between American office staff:

A: Good morning, *Ben*. You're on your own for two weeks.

B: Yeah, can you believe that, *man*. How do you get out of that?

A: So what's up *Ben*? There's no hot water in the house. I'm going nuts.

B: Did they? Oh my gosh. [*laugh*] Good morning *Betty*. Good morning *Mr* [*name*].

D: Hey *Ben* how are you?

Vocatives occur frequently – more frequently in AmE than in BrE – and one theory is that they are needed to maintain the friendly rapport between equals. This extends also to general vocatives like *man, dude, guys* which have a famil- iarizing effect. Omission of a vocative may have various negative implications, such as that the speaker is uncertain about the relationship with the addressee, or has forgotten the addressee's first name! In this context, we realize how important remembering people's names can be.

Another example of this trend is the popularity of the general plural vocative *you guys* or *guys* in AmE, now catching on in other Inner Circle countries. Although originally used as a term of address to males, it is now used generally

---

What's in a nickname?

The most common kind of nickname is a shortened and familiar version of a person's first name. Such nicknames are very commonly used nowadays, especially in the United States. The fashion is also growing for nicknames to be used as the basic, inde- pendent name, such as *Jill* (for *Gillian*), *Larry* (for *Lawrence*). Naming conventions also differ within the English-speaking world: for example, in the US (but not in the UK) *Charles* is often nicknamed *Chuck*. Finally, a gentle word of caution: don't assume that every *Tom, Dick* or *Harry* actually prefers to be called that outside their circle of family and friends, rather than *Thomas, Richard* and *Henry*. It is possible to be too familiar in addressing someone, as well as too formal. Some well-known cases of short names are as follows:

Female names	Male names
Alice ~ Ally	*Anthony ~ Tony*
Catherine ~ Kath, Kathy, Kate	*Christopher ~ Chris*
Christine ~ Chris	*David ~ Dave*
Diana ~ Di	*Douglas ~ Doug*
Gillian ~ Jill, Gill	*Edward ~ Ed, Eddy, Ned, Ted*
Josephine ~ Josie, Jo	*James ~ Jamie, Jim, Jimmy*
Margaret ~ Meg, Madge, Maggie	*John ~ Jack, Johnny*
Nicola ~ Nicky	*Joseph ~ Joe*
Patricia ~ Pat, Patty, Tricia, Trish	*Nicholas ~ Nick*
Samantha ~ Sammy, Sam	*Robert ~ Rob, Bob, Bobby*
Sarah ~ Sally, Sadie	*Thomas ~ Tom, Tommy*
Susan ~ Sue, Susie	*Timothy ~ Tim, Timmy*
Victoria ~ Vicky	*William ~ Bill, Will, Willie*

A different kind of nickname, as we noted earlier, is a descriptive name, such as *Tiger* (Eldrick Woods), *Ol' Blue Eyes* (Frank Sinatra) and *Tiny* (naming someone who is very small, or ironically, someone very large).

to address people of either gender. Also, an adult may address children as *guys*. We might argue that this is approaching the logical endpoint of a movement towards **no distinction** and **no distance**, where age and gender differences no longer count: where all people are *guys*. In this respect Inner Circle English, more particularly American English, has been progressively avoiding expression of relations of overt inequality in society, whether between male and female, senior and junior, old and young. Other linguistic habits contributing to this egalitarian ethos are various indirect forms of command or request: for example, utterances beginning *Why don't you* or *Do you want to* appear to be suggestions or invitations, but may really be disguised imperatives:

Why don't you put this in the office for me?
Do you want to hold this for a minute, Josh?

We can also call this a drive towards **individualism** – every member of society counts as an individual, as first-name address acknowledges. An important point to make, though, is that this trend in 'overt' democratization does not necessarily mean 'real' democratization. Covert inequalities exist and are understood, even if they tend to be disguised.

Is English becoming a non-sexist language?

To the ordinary user, grammatical change seems imperceptible and beyond human control – with one notable exception: since the 1960s, change has been taking place consciously and overtly through the efforts of the women's movement. Feminist campaigns, particularly in the period 1970–90, have been directed against **sexual bias in the language** in favour of men. The general goal was to make sure that women and men would be treated alike, eliminating built-in tendencies in the English language to give prominence or superiority to one gender at the expense of the other.

Consider this case: English has no **gender-neutral pronoun** for 'he or she', but according to a longstanding tradition, *he* has been used for this purpose:

Every writer would like **his** books to be read.

This seems to make the assumption that all writers are male. To get rid of this gender bias, various solutions have been proposed. One has been to invent a new pronoun, *s/he*, but it is not obvious how this word should be pronounced, nor how it could replace the oblique and possessive forms *him* and *his*. Another solution has been the use of a coordinated phrase: *he or she, him or her*, or, reversing the order, *she or he*, and so on:

Every writer would like **his or her** books to be read.

This has caught on, particularly in academic writing and lecturing, but can be wordy and awkward, especially if the coordination has to be repeated again and again. It has, though, led to an interesting new formation: the coordinated reflexive form, *himself or herself*, tends to be compressed into *him or herself*, where the suffix *-self* is grammatically attached to the whole phrase: *[him or her]self*.

Two other solutions have been more generally successful. One has been to favour the singular use of *they*, which we have already discussed above (see p. 210):

Every writer would like **their** books to be read.

Although condemned by purists as a grammatical mistake, this is getting more generally accepted these days, and is even found in educational publications (for example, in coursebooks for students). Finally, the most popular solution is probably a strategy of evasion. By recasting the whole sentence or passage in the plural, we can avoid both the problem of gender bias and the problem of mismatching singular and plural:

All writers want **their** books to be read.

Gender bias is also found in the area of vocabulary. English has a large number of human nouns with common gender, which cause no problem, such as *student, worker, doctor, guest*. But there are also nouns like *spokesman* and *hostess* which clearly declare themselves as masculine or feminine. The problem with such items is that they bring with them a lot of social and cultural baggage regarding typical roles of women and men. For example, in the past, spokesmen have typically been male, in keeping with traditionally masculine centres of power. Using the term *spokesman* where the gender is unknown can perpetuate this bias. Once again, there are a number of different solutions, but the use of *spokeswoman* (female) and *spokesperson* (gender-neutral) alongside *spokesman* (male) seems to fill the bill.

Words with overt female suffixes (*-ess, -ette*) are more discriminatory, because these suffixes are typically added to masculine nouns (*poet ~ poetess, actor ~ actress, usher ~ usherette*), treating the female role as if derived from, and lesser than, the male role. In fact, these gender suffixes have declined markedly in recent decades. The obvious solution here is to use the word without its suffix as a gender-neutral term. A woman can be a *manager*, just as a man can: the need for a separate feminine noun *manageress* is highly questionable. The few *-ess* words which remain popular in common usage today are nouns where the demeaning associations typical of nouns in *-ess* don't seem to apply. This may be

(a) because the role is a historical or mythical one, like *priestess* and *goddess*, or (b) because the word refers to an animal, like *lioness* and *tigress*, or (c) because the female role is distinctive and has favourable associations, like *princess, hostess* and *actress*. There are different preferences with the words *actor* and *actress*:

'The *actor* in me comes out when I'm in a group of people,' says Tunney.
The [London] Times 1999

The award marked Tunney out as an *actress* to be reckoned with …
The [London] Times 1999

Notice that in these extracts from the same newspaper report, Robin Tunney describes herself as an *actor*, but is described by the reporter as an *actress*.

Chairman, chairwoman, chairperson, chair

Today's society objects to antiquated gender-biased attitudes. Stereotypes are preserved through careless usage, although this may be due to ignorance rather than prejudice. When Neil Armstrong landed on the moon in 1969 he was first quoted as saying 'That's one small step for man, one giant leap for mankind.' This quotation, although famous, is somewhat difficult to interpret. According to one explanation, the radio transmission obliterated the indefinite article: 'That's one small step for a man, one giant leap for mankind' would make more sense. At the time Armstrong probably had other things on his mind, but had he been a woman he might have preferred to use *humankind, humanity* or *the human race* instead of *mankind*, which seems to allow no room in this epic achievement for the female of the species. Some people find *humankind* a ridiculous word, although it has existed since the seventeenth century. But there are other options: *human beings, society, men and women*. Some people try to root out all words with the element *man* even in cases like *manicure, manipulate, manoeuvre, manual, manufacture, manuscript*. But this is uncalled for, since in these cases the element comes from *manus* which is the Latin word for 'hand' and has nothing to do with English *man*.

In a world where there are at least as many women as men, even an unreformed sexist will realize that traditional masculine job titles, such as *foreman, spokesman, fireman, businessman*, can be both inappropriate and offensive. In many cases there are alternatives which focus on the job and bypass the gender of the person doing it. In practice both *congressman* and *congresswoman* refer to members of the House of Representatives, although technically the terms could also be applied to members of the Senate. A gender-neutral term is *member of Congress*.

A *chairman* may be either a man or a woman. To address a female person, *Madam Chairman* is used in formal, official contexts. But those who find that *chairman* is charged with undesirably strong male associations have the option of using *chairwoman* or *chairperson*. The latter is particularly appropriate when the sex happens to be unknown, for example when a post has yet to be filled: 'A new chairperson will soon be appointed'. One way to avoid the problem is simply to use the word *chair* – a common practice at international conferences: 'Address your remarks to the chair', 'Chair at the afternoon session: Professor Anna Brown'.

Gender-neutral terms

Below are listed a few traditional job titles which have been, or can be, replaced by gender-neutral terms. Some of the female words in square brackets are not often used.

Traditional male [or female] terms	Some gender-neutral terms
businessman [businesswoman]	*businessperson, executive, manager, entrepreneur*
cameraman	*camera operator*
cleaning woman/lady	*housecleaner, office cleaner, housekeeper, cleaner*
clergyman	*member of the clergy, cleric, minister, rabbi, priest, pastor, rector, vicar*
fireman	*fire-fighter*
forefathers	*ancestors, forebears, antecedents*
foreman	*supervisor*
housewife	*homemaker*
juryman	*juror*
layman	*layperson, non-specialist, non-professional*
mailman, postman	*postal worker, mail carrier, letter carrier, mail deliverer*
man (in the generic sense)	*human being, human, individual, person*
man hours	*working hours*
man in the street	*average person, ordinary person*
man-made	*manufactured, artificial, an artefact*
policeman [policewoman]	*police officer, law enforcement officer*
salesman	*salesperson, sales assistant, shop assistant*
spokesman [spokeswoman]	*spokesperson, representative*
sportsman [sportswoman]	*athlete, player, competitor, contestant, sportsperson*
steward, stewardess	*flight attendant*
weatherman	*meteorologist, weather officer*
workman	*worker, wage earner, employee*

Frequently the changes introduced through the women's movement have not so far succeeded in ousting targeted usages, but have led to a more complex situation of what is sometimes called **divided usage**, where a range of forms with differing associations is available. It is difficult to say whether this fluctuating variation in usage is likely to continue indefinitely, or whether, eventually, standard English will settle for one option or another as the most widely acceptable. But the language has changed – in particular, the generic use of *he* is no longer accepted by a wide range of native speakers of the language. There has never been an English Academy to regulate the language, but we have now seen how a powerful, committed change in public opinion can bring about a shift in the way the vocabulary and grammar of English are used, even changing the use of core English words like *he* and *man*.

Electronic English

We have left to the end of this chapter the greatest revolution affecting language use in the last twenty years: this has been the explosive burgeoning of new possibilities of communication through computer networks and the electronic channels they open up. For short, we will call this the **e-revolution.**

It is obvious that new electronic channels such as email and the World Wide Web have brought an enormous quantitative increase in the usage of English around the world. It can be said, in fact, that English had a headstart over other languages in this e-revolution, partly because the Internet was tailor-made for a language using the roman alphabet with no diacritics (like accents and umlauts), and English became the default language of the Net. However, the electronic revolution has also boosted the use of other languages: even endangered languages can benefit from the Internet, through dispersed networks of users who can now converse regularly around the world in a little-known tongue. Up to the late 1990s, it was estimated that the majority of text on the Internet was in English. Since then, although the use of English on the Net is still increasing immensely alongside that of other languages, the proportion of English in relation to other languages has decreased. Manifestly, the electronic revolution happening to English is also happening to other languages.

A more interesting issue is: How is the Internet affecting the language itself? What many people have noticed is that the Net is extending the range of written language further towards the pole of 'Typical Speech' (see p. 200) in allowing a much more interactive, 'on-line' version of written messages, for example in email, chat groups and Web logs. This shows up in an unprecedented degree of colloquial informality and ellipsis on the computer screen. It also leads to supplementary emotive means of communication, with symbols such as smiling faces ('smileys') and other imaginative combinations of symbols from the regular QWERTY keyboard.

This is not to deny that the Internet also fosters the dissemination of more formally and traditionally constructed written texts, such as formal letters sent by email or Web pages that have the character of legal or academic documents. Indeed, the Web provides by far the largest and most varied collection of English texts that has ever existed.

David Crystal argues that the Internet amounts to a new medium for language use: that alongside speech, writing and the third medium of sign language for the deaf, there is now a further medium, **Netspeak**. This, he says, is 'a development of millennial significance. A new medium of linguistic communication does not arrive very often, in the history of our race.'

True. But without diminishing the importance of the e-revolution in language, we can still argue that this revolution is not like the invention of writing – a totally new medium – but more of a technological leap forward like the introduction of printing in the fifteenth century. This, as we saw in discussing Caxton on pp. 43–5, had major repercussions on the language in spreading the availability of the written word and stimulating the evolution of a standardized language. It may be that the e-revolution is having even greater repercussions than did printing, and these show up in a radical extension of the range of possibilities of written communication, so that in particular the vehicle of writing invades a great deal of the territory of spoken communication without in any way supplanting the use of speech. In Chapter 10 we noted that **interactiveness, emotive expression** and **on-line processing** were three of the features that distinguished typical speech from typical writing, and the Internet enables users to go a long way towards attaining these features in the visual, written medium. Communication in the electronic age seems to be extending its capabilities by leaps and bounds – we recall here the new communicative opportunities of the cell phone (or mobile phone), with the accompanying capability of text messaging.

What we have said so far has suggested that the e-revolution brings new ranges of variation in the use of language. We must also take account of the way in which it has vigorously exploited and expanded the resources of the English language. The vocabulary of English has been extended in many ways. Here is a small sample:

Coinages of new words	*blog* (a shortening of *Web log*), *geek, nerd, netiquette*
Creating of new compounds	*download, inbox, mailbomb, voicemail*
Using specialized prefixes such as *e-*('electronic') *cyber-*, and *multi-*, and suffixes like *-ware*	*e-mail, e-cash, e-commerce, e-courses, e-training cyberspace, cyber-café, cyber-culture, multimedia, multi-tasking, multi-user, software, courseware, firmware, freeware, spyware*
Words converted from one class to another	The following are converted from nouns to verbs: *bookmark, boot, e-mail, flame, messag(ing), text(ing)*
New metaphorical uses of existing words	*browse, bug, chat, chip, client, cookie, dump, gateway, hack, link, menu, portal, spam, surf, virus, wizard*
Abbreviations, alphabetisms and acronyms	*Gb* (*gigabyte*), *IP* (*Internet protocol*), *FAQ* (*Frequently answered questions*), *ROM* (*read-only memory*), *MUD* (*Multi-User Dimension*)

The most noticeable innovations of e-communication are often in the area of writing conventions. Playing with the spelling of words and the visual forms of language generally creates foregrounded, abbreviated or affective forms of written language. Unlike ordinary written words, words in Netspeak can have internal capital letters and full stops which have special functions in Web addresses, email addresses and the like (*AltaVista, lastminute.com*) as well as symbols like @ ('at') and \ ('backslash') cropping up in unusual places: *lunch@Boots.yum* was a clever advertisement for a café. These eccentricities have been infiltrating playfully into other varieties of writing. So-called **emoticons** ('emotive icons') find their way into e-mails and text messages, the most popular being the 'smiley' :-) (a happy face) and its opposite :-((a sad face). But there is a large range of more exotic emoticons, some building on these well-known ones, for example, :-)) for 'very happy' and :-)))))))) for 'ecstatic'. Similar in spirit are impressionistic uses of repeated characters and capitalizations, as in *NOOooh!!!!! reEEALly???*. These are the nearest equivalent written language has to spoken-language features like voice quality, pitch range, and loudness – **paralinguistic** dimensions that the human voice can draw on as an extra expressive channel of communication. A few phrasal acronyms such as *aka* ('also known as'), *fyi* ('for your information') and *btw* ('by the way') have become widely used in workaday emails, but glossaries of 'Textspeak' (the language of texting) give hundreds of other, more inventive instances, building punningly on the phonetic quality of written symbols: for example, *BCNU* for 'be seeing you', *cu @ 7* for 'see you at seven', *cul8r* for 'see you later', *ICQ* for 'I seek you'.

People fear that these wayward practices will somehow undermine the standard language and the educational goal of learning to write good English prose. But if we take the view that Netspeak and Textspeak are essentially lively and versatile *additions* to the already rich tapestry of English language varieties, there need be no fear that they will *subtract* from the standard. In reality, the situation seems to be a mixture of pluses and minuses.

On the plus side, for a large proportion of young people using English, texting and browsing the Web have become second nature, almost as natural as speech. This cannot but ensure growing confidence in reading and writing, albeit of the racy vernacular variety of e-language that is the written analogue of colloquial conversation. On the minus side, educationists cannot help worrying that this vernacular writing will somehow become the normal form of literacy for new generations of native speakers, and that the transition to more formal literacy skills will become more difficult. Whatever will be the long-term outcome, let's finish by emphasising the positive: e-communication has brought to the English language a welcome infusion of vigour and creativity.

12
English into the Future

For last year's words belong to last year's language
And next year's words await another voice.

T. S. Eliot, *Four Quartets*

In this book we have followed the English language throughout its history over a period of some 1,500 years. It's a remarkable story: from a Germanic embryo came a small insular language, which in time grew into a world language. So what will happen to English now? Will there be many Englishes, or just one? Will the international use and learning of English continue to grow? Or will other languages take its place? It is difficult to predict the future of languages – some would say impossible. But at least we can examine the linguistic situation as it is developing today and try to make informed speculations about the future.

Although we cannot predict in what way English will change, we can be certain that change it will – that's in the nature of languages. It's only dead languages such as Latin or artificial languages such as mathematical notations that do not change.

One English or many Englishes?

The mention of Latin, the language of the ancient Roman Empire, brings us back to a question posed in Chapter 1. Latin was the nearest thing to a world language that western civilization saw until the rise of English. Yet Latin is now a dead language. Could English suffer the same fate? What happened to Latin shows some interesting parallels with the English language today. Its fate was not so much extinction as **diversification**: it split up into geographical dialects which eventually became different languages. The modern Romance family of languages was born. This happened especially with the disintegration of the

Roman Empire in the fourth to sixth centuries. There was no longer a unifying state, bureaucracy or culture. The different varieties of colloquial Latin – Vulgar Latin as it was called – eventually developed into the standard languages of France, Italy, Spain, Portugal and Romania.

We have seen modern parallels in the break-up of the British Empire, and the diffusion of varieties of English into 'new Englishes'. Significantly, tongues that were considered non-standard, provincial or offbeat dialects of English in an earlier age are now being seen as independent languages; the cases of Ulster Scots, Jamaican Creole, and Tok Pisin come to mind. Is this the slippery slope to the fragmentation of English into mutually unintelligible languages?

This 'Latin analogy' has found an echo in the views of leading language authorities since Noah Webster's prediction that American would become a different language from English (see p. 154). Although Webster later changed his mind, a similar view cropped up a century later in the writings of Henry Sweet, a renowned British phonetician and grammarian, the supposed model for Henry Higgins in Bernard Shaw's *Pygmalion* (see p. 129):

England, America, and Australia will be speaking mutually unintelligible languages, because of their independent changes of pronunciation.

Yet a century later, a similar view came from no less than the chief editor of the prestigious *Oxford English Dictionary*, Robert Burchfield, a New Zealander with a breadth of up-to-date knowledge of how the English language was developing internationally towards the end of the twentieth century.

But if we look more carefully, the destiny of Latin was not total **disintegration**. The classical or standard language more or less ceased to be a native language around the year 400, but continued as an important vehicle of international communication in succeeding ages, right up to the twentieth century. Changing little over the centuries, it became the revered language of the Universal Church. Up to recent centuries it remained the language of international scholarship (p. 63), and it remains even now the official language of Roman Catholicism. In a much diminished role, learned Latin still has some life in it today. As a 'dead language', as Tom McArthur says, it has been 'a lively and useful corpse'. Latin's continuing international life after death suggests that another international standard language like World Standard English today might survive the break-up of the English mother tongue.

But surely even this is giving too much mileage to the 'Latin analogy'. In many ways a better analogy would be Chinese, a language which through millennia of cultural and linguistic continuity has remained, in the eyes of its speakers, now numbering over a billion, a single language. The spoken language may have diversified into mutually unintelligible dialects, but the written language has maintained its unity, and nowadays the standard language Mandarin Chinese (or Putonghua, 'common language') is extending its influence in the spoken medium across the whole community of Chinese speakers, not only in China but around the world. This unity in diversity has maintained itself through the political, administrative and cultural continuity of Chinese civilization, as well as through an educational tradition placing high value on the linguistic and literary heritage of the written language. Over the centuries, the communication channels between Chinese speakers have been well preserved, whereas the speakers of Vulgar Latin largely lost contact with one another in speech and in writing.

Although the parallel is far from exact, we can learn from this example that sufficient continuity of communication can preserve the oneness of a language. The world has totally changed since Latin split up into various Romance languages. Today we have printed books, magazines, movies and television programmes in worldwide circulation, airborne travel, mobile phones, the internet and other new forms of communication. Given the enormous explosion of communicative potential over the past 25 years, it is difficult to imagine that the future world will not 'grow smaller and smaller' from the communicative point of view. David Graddol, in his book *The Future of English?*, gives a graphic illustration of this, tracking the plummeting cost of transatlantic telephone calls between 1927 and 1992 – a more than thousand-fold decrease of cost per talking minute. And as travel and tourism now make up the world's largest industry, cheaper and more frequent communication at a distance has been supplemented by much more frequent face-to-face communication between people living in different parts of the world. But more telling perhaps is the internet's potential for almost instantaneous communication among 'virtual language communities' through e-mail, chat groups, blogs and the like. In many respects, the immediacy of direct face-to-face communication can now be achieved through electronic channels. Virtual face-to-face interaction is likely to become even more of a future reality through advances in multi-modal communication in real time involving sound and vision as well as the written word.

Yet all this does not mean that there will be no further **divergence** among the world's local varieties of English. It means, rather, that the users of English in their localities throughout the world will still feel the pull from two opposite poles – **the need to identify with one's local community** and **the need for international communication**. The former need maintains the vigour of basilect and mesolect varieties (see pp. 176–7). The latter need maintains the importance of the acrolect and standard varieties. This is a recipe not for the disintegration of English, but for its **pluralization**: reminding us of the term 'language complex' (see p. 67) that Tom McArthur used to describe a tongue that is both singular and plural, both 'a language' and 'languages'. The title of his book on the subject, *The English Languages*, highlights the plurality of English at the expense of its oneness. In fact, we need to emphasize both.

The term **diglossia** has been used by sociolinguists for a division between two major varieties of a language: the 'High' or standard variety used for prestigious, literary, or religious functions versus the 'Low' or vernacular variety for everyday use. (This applies, for example, to Arabic in Egypt or German in German-speaking Switzerland.) In the case of English, though, it seems more appropriate to use the term **polyglossia** ('many-tongued-ness'), recognizing that many tongues are subsumed in a single one. An image we can use to represent the evolving situation is also McArthur's: he represents the worldwide map of English as a wheel containing three concentric circles – with World Standard English (WSE), a small circle, as the hub. Moving from the centre to the rim of the circle means moving to more and more diverse and localized varieties.

Polyglossia applies not just to the diversity of English, but to the repertoire of varieties that any one speaker of English can use. The monoglot village or small town community one finds in the US or the UK is far from the norm in the world at large. It has been estimated that two-thirds of the world's people grow up in some kind of bilingual community. Similarly, the plurality of English means that most members of an English-speaking community are likely to need more than one kind of English. One needs the English of one's local community, yes, but also the English of the international community, and no doubt something intermediate between those, something like a national standard. Already this need is beginning to be felt by native speakers as much as by non-native speakers. Both will feel the **centripetal force** tending towards the hub of the wheel, as well as the **centrifugal force** tending towards its rim. In the future, more than in the past, speakers will be **multidialectal**.

World English

Figure 12.1 on p. 226 is similar to that of McArthur, but we have tried to show it three-dimensionally, as a flattened cone, rather than as a two-dimensional circle. This relates it to the 'pyramid' diagram (Figure 7.1, p. 128) to show standardization and diversification of dialect in a single country.

Why is the base of the diagram shaped like a wheel?

WSE, the hub of the wheel, is small on the diagram, because here the amount of diversity is small: it is a rather uniform dialect (but nobody actually *speaks* WSE as their native dialect). On the other hand, at the rim of the wheel we have a vastly greater amount of variation between one part of the English-speaking world and another.

Why are there two concentric circles between the hub and the rim of the wheel?

These represent schematically the intermediate layers of generality of usage: showing the difference between regional standards and dialects or local vernaculars.

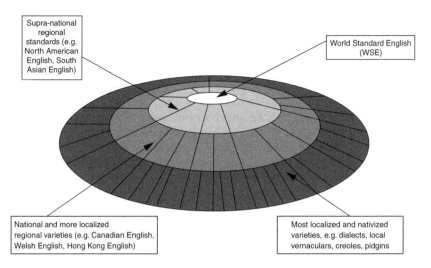

Figure 12.1   A model of world English

(These are called **acrolects** and **basilects** on p. 224). Distance on the spokes of the wheel actually represents a continuum of variation.

Why is the centre of the wheel higher up than the rim, representing a kind of cone?

This is meant to show the affinity between this diagram and the 'pyramid' of standardization we used before. The apex of the cone is a standard not only in being relatively uniform, but in carrying more prestige and being the goal of education. It is the form used for international communication: its goal is **intelligibility** across national and cultural frontiers. On the other hand, the local vernacular has the goal of **identity**. It is the variety people choose to show they belong to, and share the culture of, a particular community.

Why are the Inner Circle countries – Britain, the United States, and so on – found around the rim of the wheel, rather than at the hub?

Notice here a key difference between this diagram and the 'three circles' diagram presented in Chapter 1, showing the Inner Circle, Outer Circle and Expanding Circle countries (Figure 1.1, p. 2). A number of experts – including Braj Kachru himself, the inventor of the three-circles model – have pointed out that, as English becomes a global language, the differences between the circles are getting less clear, and also less important. At the same time, the native-speaking communities of the Inner Circle countries are arguably beginning to lose their status as the normative models for learning English around the world. So WSE, although strongly influenced by American English at the present time, cannot be identified with any native-speaker variety. (These points are discussed further in the next section.)

Is this diagram accurate?

No – it simply shows a 'conceptual model', omitting many aspects of variation. Also, it is not like a scale map: it makes no attempt to show accuracy in distance or area.

Is there a World Spoken Standard English?

David Crystal's opinion is that WSSE (**World Spoken Standard English**) 'is still in its infancy. Indeed, it has hardly yet been born'. But, he says, 'the foundation for such a development is already being laid around us'. One sign of this is the phenomenon of world TV channels – notably CNN International, founded in 1989. The speakers on this channel come from various nations in the world, predominantly, but not only, from Inner Circle countries. But although they speak with varying accents, these are not 'broad' enough to cause problems of intelligibility. The kinds of syntax and vocabulary they use – appropriate to international affairs – contain relatively few regionalisms.

Perhaps another sign of an emerging WSSE is the kind of public communication that takes place in international conferences where English tends to be the only language, or the main auxiliary language, for public discussion. Here the phenomenon known to sociolinguists as **accommodation** has a powerful influence. This is the process of adapting your own usage to the usage of other speakers, and it is often noticed in conference situations. People consciously or unconsciously try to suppress their regionally salient features of speech, in pronunciation and in idiomatic usage, adopting what they think is a more generally intelligible form. 'Foreigner talk' (*You sell stamps, yes?*), which native speakers use in talking to non-native speakers with limited command of their language, is one type of accommodation. 'Motherese' (*Now beddy-byes for little boys!*), which adult carers use in talking to their young children, is another. But in 'conference talk', accommodation is typically mutual, and more subtle.

The globalization of English

English is well on the way to becoming the first 'global language', and it is worth emphasising (as we did in Chapter 1) that this is not in any way due to the merits of the language itself, or to the merits of its speakers. To simplify matters, we can say that English benefited from three overlapping eras of world history. The first was the era of the **imperial expansion** of European powers, which spread the use of English – as well as of other languages, like Spanish, French and Portuguese – around the world. The second is the era of **technological revolution**, beginning with the industrial revolution in which the English-speaking nations of Britain and the United States took a leading part, and the later electronic revolution, led above all by the US. The third is the era of **globalization**. The world is beginning to behave like a single society, however complex, in terms of political, economic, environmental, communicative and other spheres of activity. These three processes have piggy-backed on one another so that, for example, the electronic revolution has given birth to the internet, and thereby generated e-mail, e-commerce, e-business and numerous other 'e-activities', which further globalization.

We can do no better than repeat approvingly here the four principles that Crystal enunciates at the beginning of his *English as a Global Language*:

- I believe in the fundamental value of multilingualism.
- I believe in the fundamental value of a common language.
- In my ideal world, everyone would be at least bilingual.
- In my ideal world, everyone would have fluent command of a single world language.

That English has turned out to be the most likely candidate for 'a single world language', as Crystal says, merely reflects the fact that English has been lucky enough to be 'in the right place at the right time': it has happened to be associated with power, and through power, with large populations.

In recent years, the 'globalization' of English has been accelerating, and the signs are that this acceleration will continue at least for a while. Crystal claims, on the basis of rough but reasonable estimates, that 'a quarter of the world's population is already fluent or competent in English ... In the early 2000s that means around 1.5 billion people'. He goes on to say, 'There are no precedents in human history for what happens to languages, in such circumstances of rapid change'.

More recent assessments of the global reach of English have been even more astounding. A report for the British Council in 2004 forecast that two billion people would be learning English in the next ten years, and that half the world's population could be speaking English by 2015. In 2005, a trailer for 'China week' on BBC television in the UK claimed that 300 million Chinese were learning English, a number almost as great as that of English native speakers in the whole world. However, such numbers are highly approximate and can be exaggerated. David Graddol, the author of the British Council report, injects some realism by pointing out that English is far from the only international language on the world stage: Chinese, Spanish and Arabic, for example, will be 'key languages' in the world's foreseeable future. It seems likely that the learning of English will reach a peak in the next decade or two and that, after that, the numbers of those learning will 'slump' to 500 million by 2050. According to this scenario, a saturation effect will set in: so widely will English be known and used that the demand from new populations of learners will decline.

This worldwide appetite for learning English has little to do with love of the language; it has much more to do with the opportunities for self-betterment a language of such international penetration can give, and the prestige it can carry.

McArthur explains this demand for English in human terms as follows: people 'can be positive, negative, calm, angry, neutral, mixed or unconcerned, but in the last resort they are *pragmatic'*.

Let's consider some indicators of the international penetration of English under various headings:

Political standing

English has various kinds of official or unofficial recognition as a leading language in various nations where it is a second language. This may vary from being the official language of the country, to having some auxiliary or significant unofficial status. According to McArthur, English is 'significant for one or more reasons in 183 out of 232 territories in the world'.

Business and commerce

In international trade, English is the most used language – notably between countries and regions whose languages are unrelated, say between East Asia and South America. But these days, transnational corporations (TNCs) are the giants of world trade, such that of the world's 100 largest economies, half are TNCs rather than nations. English is a primary language for these TNCs, some of the most powerful of which are in communications and travel industries, where business and language use go hand in hand (airlines, telecommunications, media). Some firms are adopting English as their working language: as one example, it is the lingua franca in a Toyota and Peugeot factory in the Czech Republic, between Czech, Japanese and French staff. It is also the working language of the Finnish telecommunications firm Nokia, based in Helsinki. The last 50 years have seen an enormous shift from primary industries (raw materials) and secondary industries (manufacturing) to tertiary, or service, industries. Communications are the very fabric of service industries, and here again, English has gained in currency and importance. A further global development that has favoured English is the growth in joint ventures between countries in the developed and developing parts of the world (for example, between Switzerland and Indonesia), where English comes in again as a lingua franca.

In all these respects, economic globalization increases reliance on an international language, with English as the leading contender.

Consumer culture

English has gained in prominence on the consumer's side of commerce, too. 'It's considered cool to speak English,' says MTV Asia's David Flack – speaking particularly of the Philippines – but his remark applies also elsewhere. 'Trendy' youth culture, in particular, recognizes the consumer appeal of English, which is copiously used in brand names, in advertising, in street signs and in popular media the world over. One fascinating symptom of this is the so-called **decorative use** of English on T-shirts, on shopping bags, and the like. Such uses of the language are not communicative but emblematic. Usages bizarre to native speakers crop up in such slogans as:

Never put off til [*sic*] tomorrow what you can do today. Let's sport.

But there is more to it than this. English has an enormous and growing impact on international youth today through movies, TV series, computer games and pop music. These come especially from the US but also from other countries, such as the UK, willing accomplices in the Americanization of popular culture. Other new media will also no doubt play a growing role. 'Those youngsters are bombarded with English all the time' is a comment that captures the spirit of the times.

Science and technology

The need for global communication in science and technology is self-evident, and here, as elsewhere, English has been gaining ground. One indicator, the share of English versus other major languages in journals of chemistry, has almost doubled from 43 per cent in 1961 to 82 per cent in 2000. Another indicator: 98 per cent of German physicists report English to be their working language. English has effectively become the lingua franca of science, and scientists who want their research to be known and discussed in a wide international arena have to use English. This contrasts with 40 years ago, when other major languages, such as Russian, German and French, had considerable international scientific currency. Significantly, the only major language apart from English whose share of scientific publication has increased since then is Chinese.

Communications, travel

In the 'old-fashioned' technology of books, 28 per cent of the world's publications are in English, compared with 13 per cent in Chinese and smaller percentages in other languages. Moving to more cutting-edge technology, the language of the internet has been English first and foremost. It is estimated that about 50 per cent of linguistic material on the internet is now in English (although other languages are taking a larger and larger proportion). A *Newsweek* article from 2005 claims that 80 per cent of the world's electronically stored data are in English.

Turning to the domain of international travel and transport, safety requires an agreed international linguistic code for control of air and sea traffic. To minimize accidents at sea, a restricted variety of English, known as 'Seaspeak' has been adopted since the 1980s as an international auxiliary language for maritime communication. English is also increasingly used as a lingua franca for air-to-air and air-to-ground communication, and the International Civil Aviation Authority has set strict standards for English to be used in flight and in air traffic control, to be attained by 2008.

Education

English itself has become a commercial commodity: the teaching of English has become an important global industry, and English is talked of as a product to be promoted and marketed. More generally, English is the beneficiary of vastly increased mobility in education. American, British and Australian universities compete to attract international students to their campuses, and (more recently) are engaging in joint ventures with campuses in other countries, such as China and Japan. In these collaborations, distance education through electronic media is becoming a major and essential ingredient. More recently still, countries of the Outer Circle, such as India and Malaysia, are beginning to enter the global education market in English as 'producers', rather than 'consumers'. Already, Inner Circle countries are beginning to lose their privileged status as providers of English-language tertiary education.

*   *   *

Education brings us back to the human aspect of the globalization of English. To the extent that English is at the forefront of international communication in academic, political, commercial and other spheres, the demand to learn English has been keeping pace with it. In most Outer Circle and Expanding Circle countries it is the first language to learn, after one's native language. One of the knock-on effects of this is that the English language is being learned at an earlier stage of education. Children in many parts of Europe are starting English education at an age of six, seven or eight. The mode of learning is also changing: children are exposed to spoken English from an early age (on television, in travel, and so on), whereas, formerly, learners met the language mainly through books. In gaining competence in English, countries like the Netherlands, Denmark and Sweden in Northern Europe already have a head start, because of their Germanic languages and their advanced tradition of English language learning. Another factor is exposure to the language: for example, TV watchers in these countries benefit from the use of film subtitles, instead of the dubbing used in many other countries. In the near future, it has been predicted that all Dutch speakers will be bilingual in Dutch and English. This situation also has a negative impact: the native languages of these countries are losing some of their functionality to English: the possibilities of publishing academic books and articles on (say) technology in Swedish is decreasing. So will Swedish in the future lack the vocabulary and the register for discussing technology? Such concerns about losing out to English in certain domains are worrying to countries where the main language, by global standards, has a relatively small number of native speakers.

In developing countries, increasing use of English is coming from the sector of the population that is growing fastest – among the professional classes, where English is seen as a ticket to advancement. Where middle-class couples with different mother tongues marry, English often becomes the language of the home. A strange phenomenon arises: for the babies of the next generation, English as a second language becomes the mother tongue, and they can no longer communicate with their grandparents.

There is little doubt that the globalization of English has produced an unprecedented situation, well beyond the scope of previous international language domination, such as the primacy in Europe of Latin during the Roman Empire or of French from the seventeenth to the nineteenth centuries. In this connection, Crystal makes two interesting claims. The first is this: 'if there is one predictable consequence of a language becoming a global language, it is that nobody owns it any more'. Perhaps we can envisage that the English, indeed the native speakers of English, will no longer have any special authority in how the English language is used and develops. Instead, speakers of English, whether native or not, will have a 'part ownership' in the language. Crystal's second claim is: 'English has already grown to be independent of any form of social control.'

English as a lingua franca

'English as a lingua franca' is a good illustration of what it means for native speakers of English to lose proprietorship of their native language. The term **lingua franca** (meaning 'Frankish language' in Italian) was originally used of a mixed Romance language used for trade in the Mediterranean in the Middle Ages. It has come to mean more generally a language that is used for communication between people who speak different languages – examples are Swahili in East Africa, or Hausa in West Africa. During the colonial era, the colonizers' European languages became lingua francas for the colonized peoples, for example, in Africa. There are examples, too, of English-based pidgins and creoles as lingua francas, such as West African Pidgin English and Tok Pisin (pp. 185, 187). Today, English acts as a lingua franca in many different parts of the world, and is the nearest thing there has ever been to a global lingua franca.

Let's take the example of continental Europe, and in particular the bureaucracy of the European Union (EU) in Brussels and elsewhere. There are plenty of jokes about 'Euro-English' or 'Eurospeak', the 'bad English perpetrated in Brussels'. But in reality the infiltration of English into European life is on a wider scale. The EU pursues a strong policy on equal language rights, as this extract from an EU document shows:

> All languages of Member States which have been recognized as official languages of the European Union shall be considered as equal as to their official treatment on the Union's level.

The acceptance of linguistic diversity is the price of democracy within a multi-ethnic community where everyone wants to keep and safeguard his/her cultural and linguistic identity.

Following this policy, the EU now has as many as 20 official languages, including major international languages such as French, German, English and Spanish, as well as lesser-known languages such as Estonian, Maltese and Slovenian. In addition, language rights are recognized for a large number of regional or local languages such as Welsh and Catalan. The EU is a hotbed of multilingualism. It has been calculated that there are 380 different directions for interpretation and translation, if every member country makes full use of its right to use its own official language for official purposes. At this rate, the cost of translation and interpreting is proving inordinately expensive. It is already said to account for one third of the costs of the European Parliament.

But EU politicians and administrators have to communicate also outside their official meetings, and the real practical language in the corridors of Brussels is usually English, of a somewhat flawed but obviously working variety. People familiar with the situation maintain that 'English, though not promoted in any way, permeates EU institutional activities and many areas of cultural and economic life more and more thoroughly'.

English, as an 'off-shore European language' would have hardly seemed a natural candidate for a lingua franca of continental Europe 50 years ago, at the founding of what would become the European Union. French and German, at the heart of the continent, would both seem to have stronger claims. Yet now it has been asserted that 'English is becoming the binding agent of a continent ... linking Finns to French and Portuguese as they move towards political and economic integration.'

But what sort of English model should Europe embrace? To adopt the norm of British English, giving precedence to one official language out of 20, would seem to go against the EU's principles of equal language rights between nations. As an uneasy solution to this problem, there are some signs that Europe is showing a preference for a so-called **Mid-Atlantic** variety of English. Twenty-five years ago, European teachers and educationists would make a conscious decision in favour of teaching British English or American English (usually the former) but now, according to one commentator, this choice represents an outmoded attitude. A recent study of Swedish speakers showed them in practice opting for a mix of American and British characteristics: for example, alternating between the American and British vowel in words like *last* and *bath*, and producing a weakened mid-Atlantic *r*, neither conspicuously American nor British, in words like *car* and *girl*.

When linguists these days talk about **English as a lingua franca** (or ELF for short) they are typically focusing on the use of English as an intermediary between people with different native languages, none of them English. The claim is that this type of English is developing its own systematic codes of usage, independent of the Inner Circle countries whose norms of usage have been so far regarded as the target for non-native speakers. A simple, already accepted example is the pronunciation of *three* as 'tree' in the international aviation code. The reason for this departure from standard English is obvious: the 'th' pronunciation is a notorious point of difficulty for non-native speakers. The substitution of /t/ or /s/ for /θ/, and of /d/ or /z/ for /ð/, is common in non-native speech, even among those whose competence in English is generally good. For a lingua franca, it makes sense to aid intelligibility in this way by replacing a 'difficult' sound, one rather rare among the world's languages, by an 'easy' one.

If this principle is extended to syntax, the following are among the features where ELF might replace 'eccentric' and 'difficult' areas of English with easier options, where intelligibility is not an issue:

- Dropping the third person -*s*, as in *She **cook** a great paella*.
- Omitting definite and indefinite articles where native speakers use them, as in *You have **new car?***
- Using invariant tag questions, as in *I'll see you tomorrow, **isn't it?***
- Using verb patterns like *want + that*-clause, which do not occur in native-speaker English, but have common parallels in other languages: *I want **that you visit** us*.

English language teachers are used to recognizing these as common errors in the **interlanguage** of foreign learners. ('Interlanguage' is a term used to describe the transitional system of a learner of a foreign language at any stage between beginner and advanced.) But many non-native speakers, the argument goes, communicate perfectly adequately without mastering the intricacies of WSE. When they are in international settings, talking to other non-natives without their English teacher looking over their shoulder and breathing down their neck, they can communicate and interact successfully. So why should they be bothered by issues of correctness in standard English?

It will be a long time before this conception of ELF gains general acceptance, if it ever does. But a start has already been made on a project of studying ELF by collecting samples and describing their regularities, with interesting implications for the future learning of English. Yet it will take a long time to overcome the weight of tradition favouring the teaching and testing of English using standard native-speaker norms. We can imagine a scenario where a codified ELF, based on observed usage, might serve as an auxiliary international English for certain functions – and the English native speakers would have to learn it too!

This scenario recalls the history of a search for an international auxiliary language lacking the irregularities and arbitrary details of real natural languages. Why should international communicators have to learn the weird spellings and irregular verbs of standard English? Attempted solutions to this problem have varied, from **artificial languages** like Esperanto to simplified versions of English like **Basic English** suggested by C. K. Ogden and I. A. Richards in the 1930s, and Randolph Quirk's proposal for a **Nuclear English** made 50 years later. For one reason or another, none of these proposals has taken off (although Esperanto has had modest and continuing success), perhaps mainly because these communicative systems were *invented*, and did not emerge from actual *natural* language behaviour. If ELF could emerge as a working international variety of language, the drawback of artificiality would have been overcome. Global English would have split, or diversified, in a new way: like the diglossia split in individual languages, there would be a split between the 'High' variety of WSE, and the 'Low' or demotic variety of ELF.

The conical diagram in Figure 12.1 on p. 226 has no place for ELF. We can imagine ELF as a flat circular base of the cone, undercutting WSE, providing another, less demanding, option for people wanting to communicate internationally. And perhaps there would be 'mesolect' varieties forming a scale between ELF and WSE, a kind of 'creole continuum' on a worldwide scale.

Now, the ELF project has advantages, but also problems. One problem is that this lingua franca will itself doubtless have regional 'dialects': for example, the ELF of Europe could be very different from the ELF of East Asia. It is likely, for example, that the European ELF would have articles (*the* and *a*), whereas the Asian ELF would not. Another problem is that teachers, educators, editors, administrators and even students worldwide will not readily turn their backs on the prestige of knowing a 'proper language', WSE. The providers of English as a Foreign Language (EFL) will not easily yield ground to English as a Lingua Franca (ELF).

'Reports of the death of the native speaker have been exaggerated'

For the immediate future and perhaps for longer, by far the most powerful influence on world English is likely to be its largest Inner Circle country, the United States. But this influence may be increasingly challenged in time.

Sardonic rumours that the 'native speaker is dead' have circulated since a book of that title was published by Thomas Paikeday in Canada in 1985. But, as Mark Twain (see p. 86) said of his own death, we must regard such reports as grossly 'exaggerated'. In view of the claim that the native speaker no longer 'owns' the language, a more appropriate heading for this section might be 'The toppling of the native speaker'. In the future, the native speaker may not automatically be regarded as the authority to which non-native speakers defer in determining what is correct or appropriate in the language.

Apart from the increasing use of English as a lingua franca between non-native speakers, there are good reasons for this. One is that, if we examine the Inner Circle and Outer Circle nations, the population of non-native (L2) speakers now comfortably exceeds the number of native (L1) speakers. Crystal's latest edition of *English as a Global Language* gives the figures 329 million for L1 speakers and 431 million for L2 – still not taking account of the hundreds of millions of learners and speakers of English in the Expanding Circle. In gross figures, the non-native speakers of English already vastly outnumber native speakers by three to one. Surely, with this demographic shift, there must also follow a shift in influence over the future of the language.

Another demographic factor is *increase* of population. Crystal's estimates indicate that the average increase of population per annum in L2 countries in 2003 was three times the average increase in L1 countries. At this rate, the gap between the world population of L2 speakers and that of L1 speakers is widening year by year. So, the native speakers of English could soon form a rather small proportion of the speakers of English world-wide. It has been speculated on this basis that the 'New Englishes' of the Outer Circle will increasingly make inroads into the native speaker-derived version of WSE that is now the authoritative norm. Perhaps, alongside the native speaker norm of a stress-timed pronunciation of English, there will grow up an alternative norm – the syllable-timed pronunciation

---

The native speaker no longer rules?

We live in a world where better English is often spoken and written by non-native speakers than by native speakers. At international gatherings, it is not an unusual experience to find that native speakers' English – particularly their pronunciation – is less intelligible than that of many non-natives. If you have to ask someone to repeat what they just said, it may be because their accent is from Liverpool or New Orleans, rather than from Delhi or Hong Kong. The following heartfelt appeal, expressed in impeccably persuasive English, comes from a Japanese speaker, Mikie Koyoi:

I have to live with this unfortunate fate: My native tongue is remote from European languages. Yet I believe I have the right to request that my Anglo-American friends who are involved in international activities not abuse their privilege, even though they do not do so intentionally. First of all, I would like them to know that the English they speak at home is not always an internationally acceptable English ... I sincerely believe there exists a cosmopolitan English – a lingua franca, written or spoken – that is clearly different from what native speakers use unconsciously in their daily life ... We non-natives are desperately learning English; each word pronounced by us represents our blood, sweat and tears. Our English proficiency is tangible evidence of our achievements of will, not an accident of birth. Dear Anglo-Americans, please show us you are also taking pains to make yourselves understood in an international setting.

predominant in the New Englishes (see pp. 121–3). It is even possible that native speakers, at least for international purposes, will eventually accommodate to this norm.

What is happening in the heartland of English?

Things could get even worse for those who, like Mikie Koyoi, plead for native speakers to adopt a more 'internationally acceptable' English. Noticeable changes

---

'It'll be a good night tonight, wunnit?'

Speaking of the English English of tomorrow, it's interesting to study the language of young people today. A survey by Anna-Brita Stenström, of Bergen University, showed some tendencies in the colloquial spoken language of teenagers in London. This is a conversation between John and Bill:

> *John*: I know four people who are going to the party and that's it. And they're not gonna stay with me, yeah? Just gonna go off. Yeah? With the girls, yeah? And I'll be alone.
> *Bill*: Well, don't go then! Fuck you!

Teenagers use more swearwords than adults, such as *fuck, God, shit* and *bloody*, and girls swear as much as boys (although with somewhat milder swearwords). In conversation, words such as *right, OK, innit* and *yeah* are used as tag questions (see p. 204), i.e. they are tagged onto a statement:

> You want to stay, *right?*
> With the girls, *yeah?*

Innit (as a reduced version of *ain't it*) is not used just as a standard tag where the choice depends on the grammatical form of the statement – for example, 'It's a fine day, *isn't it?*' contrasting with 'It was a good play, *wasn't it?*' Today, young people seem to use *innit* in almost all kinds of clauses:

> That man smart *innit?* (= isn't he?)
> She love her chocolate, *innit?* (= doesn't she?)

Short forms are common: *dunno* (= don't know), *wanna* (= want to), *gotta* (= got to), *gonna* (= going to), *cos* (= because). *Wunnit* can stand for both *wasn't it* and *won't it*:

> That was ages ago though, *wunnit?* (= wasn't it?)
> It'll be a good night tonight, *wunnit?* (= won't it?)

Forms of *be* and *have* are often omitted (a tendency even more common in American speech):

> Where you going, Liam? (= Where are you going, Liam?)
> That means you gotta do everything (= That means you have got to do everything.)
> What you gonna do? (= What are you going to do?)

taking place in England seem likely to make English in its mother country more remote from WSE and English as a lingua franca. For example, the substitution of /f/ and /v/ for the 'th' consonants (as in 'muvver' instead of *mother*), which is extending its influence in England out from the London area, has few parallels elsewhere in the world. Another feature associated with Estuary English (see p. 130) is the growing use of the glottal stop to replace /t/ (see p. 129). To judge from present trends, both of these features are likely to make spoken English English of the future less intelligible to the rest of the world.

Looking into the crystal ball in 1982, the British phonetician John Wells predicted the demise of Received Pronunciation (RP, see pp. 125–8):

> With the loosening of social stratification and the recent trend for people of working-class or lower-middle-class origins to set the fashion in many areas of life, it may be that RP is on the way out. By the end of the century everyone growing up in Britain may have some degree of local accent. Or, instead, some new non-localizable but more democratic standard may have arisen from the ashes of RP: if so, it seems likely to be based on popular London English.

Although this prophecy has yet to come true, Estuary English is clearly gaining ground in England, both socially and geographically.

The formerly 'cockney' heart of London, which, based on previous experience, is likely to influence the linguistic behaviour of the rest of the country, has been developing into a patchwork of varied ethnic groups with their own linguistic affiliations. Interestingly, a version of Jamaican Creole has established itself among the young black population in South London, as described in Mark Sebba's book *London Jamaican* (see box on p. 239).

It is intriguing to imagine what might happen to English English pronunciation over the next 50 years. Will Estuary English, fanning out into the areas more distant from London, begin to act as a non-region-specific accent – in effect a rival to RP? Will it gain increasing prestige, as Wells suggests? On the other hand, what will happen to the traditionally class-bound prestige accent, RP? According to Crystal:

> The number of people using a non-regionally tinged RP accent has fallen greatly … Estimates of usage in the 1980s were that between 3 and 5 per cent of the British population still used it – around 2 million. This must be now less than 2 per cent and falling.

Will there come a time when RP will survive only through a transcription system in dictionaries, grammars and learning materials published in the UK? In that case, rather like an approved school pronunciation of classical Latin, it may still be a 'reference accent' for learners, popular in some pedagogical circles, but will have no native speakers.

A London creole

The following is an extract from a dialogue Mark Sebba transcribed in the 1980s between two fifteen-year-old girls of Jamaican parentage. Notice how these Afro-Caribbean teenagers switch between Creole and the London English used by both black and white populations:

Key:
Underlining marks Creole pronunciation or grammar or both.
Non-underlined sections are London English.
? is the glottal stop (replacing /t/): it's typical of London English (see p. 129) but not of Jamaican creole: as in *par?y* 'party'
(1.0), (0.6), etc. represent the length of pauses in seconds

J: did you go to Jackie's par?y? (1.0)
C: who, Jackie <u>Lomax</u>?
J: yeah
C: no one <u>never invi?e</u> me
J: I heard that she had a really nice par?y an' Cheryl said there was a lo? of boys there (0.6) you know and they (were) playin' pass the parcel an' that
C: is it?
J: yeah
C: <u>she invite you?</u>
J: no
C: she <u>never invite</u> me neither an Leonie <u>'ave</u> one as well <u>never invite never tell</u> me <u>not'in'</u> (0.4) <u>me no business too!</u>
J: <u>Leonie have party</u>?!
C: <u>man</u> (1.0) <u>Leonie have party</u> (0.4) when? (1.2)

British creole (to give it a more general label) is flourishing as an Afro-Caribbean 'heritage language' alongside other inner city dialects, suggesting a British parallel to AAVE in the United States (see p. 169). According to some reports, it is even being imitated by younger white speakers of London English.

Changing American voices: Northern Cities Shift

Changes of accent have also been taking place in the United States, especially in the area marked 'the Inland North' on the map (Figure 12.2, p. 240).

Opinions vary among specialists about American speech areas and their subdivisions. However, a definitive current research project, the Regional Dialects of American English by William Labov, Sharon Ash and Charles Boberg at University of Pennsylvania, has produced a more detailed subdivision than that provided by our earlier map, Figure 5.2 on p. 81. The broad dialect area we have called 'General American' is there further divided into the Inland North (the area of the Northern Cities Shift, see pp. 240–1), North Central, the Midland and the West.

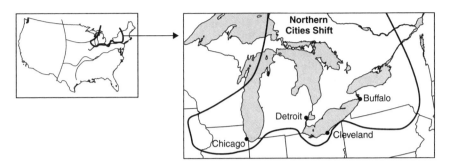

Figure 12.2   Dialect areas in the United States with the Northern Cities Shift

People of states like Michigan used to feel pride in their neutral pronunciation – the quintessential 'General American'. But recently, centred on the populous cities around the southern shores of the Great Lakes (Chicago, Detroit, Cleveland, Buffalo), there have emerged changes known collectively as **The Northern Cities Shift**. A report of a telephone dialect survey led by William Labov describes this as 'a revolutionary rotation of the English short vowels, which have historically remained stable since the 8th century'. Vowels have been migrating to new positions of articulation:

(1) /æ/, the vowel of *cat*, has been changing into a closer vowel /e/ or a diphthong /ɪə/ – so that *cat* sounds as if it were spelt *kee-yat*
(2) /ɑ/, the vowel of *cot*, has been moving towards /æ/, the vowel of *cat*
(3) /ɔ/, the vowel of *caught*, has been moving towards /ɑ/, as in *cot*
(4) /e/, the vowel of *bet*, has been moving towards /ʌ/, as in *cut*
(5) /ʌ/, the vowel of *cut*, has been moving towards /ɔ/, as in *caught*
(6) /ɪ/, the vowel of *kid*, has been moving towards a more central position near 'schwa' (/kəd/)

Collectively, these changes are represented in Figure 12.3 on p. 241.

This whole set of changes is a kind of phonetic chain reaction – a **chain shift**, as it is called – whereby one vowel moves into the position of a neighbouring vowel, which in turn shifts to a new position – the articulatory equivalent of a game of musical chairs. The Great English Vowel Shift (p. 61), which took place in the fifteenth to the eighteenth centuries, was another example of a chain shift, but it affected long vowels rather than short vowels.

The Northern Cities Shift seems to be a spreading pattern of sound changes. Perhaps it will colonize new areas of North American in the decades to come. Some signs of these changes can already be observed in neighbouring parts of

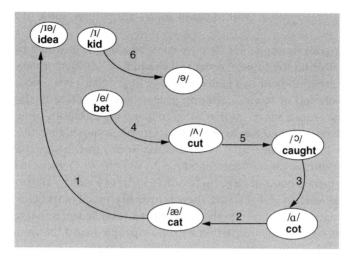

Figure 12.3 Northern Cities Shift

the United States, for example in Minnesota, St Louis, Missouri and the country districts around the Great Lakes. The survey of Labov and his team also reveals diverging accents in other parts of the US, and suggests that altogether the American pronunciation of English is definitely 'on the move'.

Taken together with the Estuary English phenomenon in the UK (p. 130), the Northern Cities Shift exemplifies how the two most populous Inner Circle countries are developing their own individual phonetic paths which will no doubt increase problems of intelligibility between speakers of US and UK English. Perhaps we are seeing, in these changes, one further step towards a divergence of native-speaker accents from a 'World Spoken Standard English' (p. 226) which may be the future target for international learners.

Sound changes often lead to a merger of different pronunciations, so that words no longer sound distinct, leading to a communicative loss (for example, in some parts of the United States, the vowels of *cot* and *caught* have merged). But as a chain shift generally preserves the distinctions between vowels, while changing their quality, it does not lead to this loss of distinctions. On the other hand, chain shifts can produce their own problems of intelligibility. A professor at the University of Michigan reports being asked why his son, Ian, had a girl's name. It turns out that *Ian* and the local pronunciation of *Ann* ('Eeyan') sound alike!

The English juggernaut?

In modern parlance, a juggernaut is something large and unstoppable: something likely to flatten or destroy anything in its path (see p. 119). Like globalization, global English has recently had a bad press in some quarters. Like anything apparently unstoppable, world English rouses antipathies, some of them well founded.

But *is* English unstoppable? Here we come to a debate in which two leading commentators on the topic, Crystal and Graddol, take different views. Talking about the establishment of a global language in general, Crystal says, 'it would take a revolution of world-shattering proportions to replace it'. He goes on: 'A language's future seems assured when so many organizations come to have a vested interest in it.' Also, as we have seen, he proposes that the future of English is now beyond social control. Presumably this means that, even if immense political power were mobilized to overthrow English, it could not succeed. Crystal's point of view, then, is that, short of a global catastrophe, once English has reached global status, there is little likelihood of its being replaced.

One intriguing possibility, perhaps a hundred years hence, is that technology in the form of machine translation will allow people round the world to communicate in real time in their own languages. For example, a Japanese speaker in Tokyo phoning a German speaker in Berlin, would speak a message in Japanese which the German speaker would 'hear' in German. It sounds a futuristic fantasy, but much research in Japan has already been conducted with such an ambitious goal in mind. If automatic interpreting and translation became successful and generally available, the need for English or any other language as a world lingua franca would decline (but hardly disappear – there will always be people without access to such sophisticated technological gadgetry).

On the other hand, Graddol does see English as stoppable to some extent: in his 1997 book he argued 'that the global popularity of English is in no immediate danger, but that it would be foolhardy to imagine that its pre-eminent position as a world language will not be challenged in some world regions and domains of use as the economic, demographic and political shape of the world is transformed'.

Graddol and others have pointed out various reasons why the English 'juggernaut' is unpopular, and might become more so. First, the same changes in society and in the globalization of communication that have enabled English to rise to unprecedented heights have led to a catastrophic decline and death of many other languages. It is estimated that anything from 50 to 90 per cent of the world's remaining languages – some 6,000 – could die out in the twenty-first century. This is at a time when language rights, such as those enunciated in our EU quotation on pp. 232–3, are coming to be considered an aspect of basic human rights. A language which, directly or indirectly, is seen as threatening the survival of other languages will not be favourably regarded. Graddol believes that ethical concerns might 'turn the world against English'.

Other arguments against English come from an anti-imperialist critique of its role as the language of the colonizers. The great Kenyan novelist Ngugi Wa Thiong'o at one point gave up writing in English, a language he saw as contaminated by colonial oppression, preferring to use his native language

Gikuyu. Another postcolonial writer, the Singaporean Edwin Thumboo, describes a Commonwealth literary conference in the 1960s in these terms:

> The Indians, West Indians, Pacific Islanders, Malaysians, Maltese, Africans and Sri Lankans ... discovered that they had learnt the same nursery rhymes, studied virtually the same selection of poems, the same plays and novels; read the same grammars, the same language series ... consulted the same collection of model essays; debated the same topics; had the same selection of History, Geography, and Hygiene texts; had gone through the same rituals on Empire Day – come sunshine or rain – and, in many instances, knew 'God Save the Queen' better than their recently adopted National Anthems.

Such reminiscences remind us that languages and cultures are closely intertwined, and that borrowing a language inevitably entails other kinds of cultural influence. This gives plausibility to a more radical anti-English stance illustrated by these quotations from Alastair Pennycook:

> [English's] widespread use threatens other languages; it has become the language of power and prestige in many countries, thus acting as a crucial gatekeeper to social and economic progress ...
> [I]t is also bound up with aspects of global relations, such as the spread of capitalism, development aid and the dominance particularly of North American media. ...
> [I]t is constantly pushing other languages out of the way, curtailing their usage in both qualitative and quantitative terms.

One step further brings us to the even more radical stance of those who see English as the vehicle of an 'English linguistic imperialism' promoting inequalities throughout the world. This stance can be rejected as an 'anachronism', based on the unjustified assumption that a language somehow acquires, by attraction, the guilt of its native speakers in the era of imperial expansion.

There is no doubt, however, that English does arouse strong and mixed feelings in former colonial countries like South Africa, where it has taken over functions – for example, in higher education – that would otherwise accrue to indigenous languages like Zulu, or for that matter to Afrikaans. It is a matter that affects self-worth and identity as well as economic power. At the same time, English in South Africa is the language associated with empowerment and internationalism. It was the language adopted by the African National Congress to represent pan-Africanism in the days of apartheid, and it remains the one language that can pretend to neutrality between the country's different ethnic communities (see p. 114).

Similarly, in Singapore, the link between English and imperialism seems to have been broken. As Phyllis Ghim-Lian Chew puts it:

> In Singapore, the position is stated very clearly: 'yes' to English and 'no' to western cultural values. Singaporeans like to think of their city as 'modern' but not 'western'. Similarly, while English is the official language of Asean [the Association of South East Asian Nations], Asean has not shown itself to be either pro-British or pro-American.

More generally, the argument that sees English as the vehicle of Western imperialism, particularly US imperialism, ignores the trend we have observed many times in this book: English, when exported to new territories and peoples, has soon become 'nativized', acquiring the ability to represent the cultures of its adopted speakers, or at least to act as a go-between, binding those cultures to the international world.

However, yet another factor on the negative side of the balance sheet is that English is tending to create élites, to draw a line between the haves and have-nots. In those L2 countries where English brings empowerment, lack of English can also spell deprivation for those who have not had the opportunity to learn it.

Franglais, Japlish, Spanglish, Englog and Manglish

One of the signs of a powerful language is that it exerts its influence on other languages, through borrowing and varied kinds of language mixing. This can be a cause of resentment and deep concern to the speakers of those other languages, who see the English 'juggernaut' encroaching on their mother tongue. But as we saw in Chapters 2–6, English itself has, throughout its history, borrowed heavily from the vocabulary and structure of other languages, notably French and Latin. Now the tables are turned, and French is borrowing more from English than English from French. The semi-humorous term **Franglais** (a blend of the French words for French and English) has been used to refer to a kind of mongrel French full of anglicisms. In 1992 France passed a law that an English word must not be used where a French equivalent is available, but the French supreme court ruled the law unconstitutional. Although the French language planners have had successes – *computer* and *software* have been generally rejected in favour of *ordinateur* and *logiciel* – the English 'juggernaut' still has its impact on French.

In the province of Quebec, bastion of French-speaking Canada, the measures taken to control the threat from English have been even more resolute. In 1977 a *charte* ('charter') for the French language was enacted requiring, for example, that advertising billboards and commercial signs be in French alone, and that all public bodies and businesses should address their employees in French. Education in English was to be restricted in various ways. If these measures appear draconian, it is worth remembering that the Quebec situation is one where French has been fighting to reclaim and maintain its status in a country (Canada) where English increasingly predominates (see pp. 93–5). The measures of the 1977 charter have since been relaxed to some extent.

Returning to Europe, we note that loanwords from English are common in all European languages. They have been studied extensively by Manfred Görlach, who has edited a *Dictionary of European Anglicisms*. As a sample, the following is Görlach's selective list (from a 1986 study) of English words borrowed by both French and German, as well as many other European languages:

> *aquaplaning, aftershave, babysitter, bestseller, blue jeans, camping, club, cocktail, container, cowboy, doping, flipper, gag, gangster, hobby, jet, job, kidnapper, lobby, make-up, pipeline, playboy, pudding, poster, pullover, pyjama, sex appeal, show business, sketch, star, transistor, western*

We notice the American flavour of many of these, as well as their belonging to areas like popular entertainment and the media. However, the largest class of anglicisms these days comes from the field of technology.

Like **Franglais**, terms such as **Japlish** (Japanese + English), **Spanglish** (Spanish + English) and **Englog** (English + Tagalog) have proliferated to represent the way English has infiltrated the vocabulary and fabric of other languages. Although these terms often have jokingly negative connotations, the 'anglicization' effect they refer to is real enough. It may take various forms: not only wholesale borrowing of words, but the borrowing of affixes, even of syntactic preferences. Japanese, which has borrowed thousands of English words since 1945, shows a particular tendency to shorten English words, and also to combine these shortened forms into compounds:

> *terebi* (= *televi-*, for 'television'), as in *terebi gēmu* 'video game(s)'
> *panku* (= *punc-*, for 'puncture, flat tire')
> *oke* (= *orche-*, for 'orchestra') in *karaoke* (literally, 'empty orchestra')
> *pokemon* from two abbreviated words, *poke* and *mon* (= 'pocket monster')

Karaoke and *pokemon* have, of course, been borrowed back into English. Japanese has a much simpler syllable structure than English, with each syllable ending in a vowel or /n/, and also has a smaller number of consonants and vowels. This is why the English words seem to undergo amazing transformations when they are borrowed into Japanese. The café menu in a Japanese hotel (= *hoteru*) will contain the following familiar items in an unfamiliar guise:

tsuna sando – tuna sandwich	*hamu sando* – ham sandwich
tsuna sarada – tuna salad	*chīzu omuretsu* – cheese omelette
orenji jūsu – orange juice	*gurēpu furūtsu jūsu* – grapefruit juice
kōhī – coffee	*roiyaru miruku tyī* – royal milk tea
dezāto – dessert	*kēki* – cake
purin – pudding (custard)	

Another kind of mixing together of two languages is the code-switching combined with borrowing found in **Malenglish** or **Manglish** (a hybrid of Malay and English). This example is from a Malaysian TV serial:

A: Thanks, Ita, for house-sitting for me.
B: No problem. Apartment kau lebih cantik darpada apartment apu. ['Your apartment is much more beautiful than mine.'] Anyway, it's all yours again.

And where is it all going?

Will widespread disapproval or resentment of the English language have any significant impact on its use? At present, there appear to be few signs of this. Perhaps the future of English is beyond all social control, and attitudes will count for little. It seems that many non-native speakers around the world have a love–hate relation towards English, like an equally noticeable love-hate attitude to the main powerhouse for present-day English, the United States. Whether it is in wearing baseball caps and jeans, or eating McDonalds's hamburgers and french fries, the habit of imitating American culture seems inescapable, especially among the young and even among those who deplore American politics, power and economic practices. In a similar way, using English is a desirable habit to be acquired and imitated around the world, even among those who dislike what English stands for, in terms of threats to other languages, promulgation of western culture and globalization of western values.

Yet what we can foresee at the moment is limited: we have a small window on a fast-changing world. It is said that the twentieth century was the century of US power and influence, culminating in the present situation where the US is the world's 'only remaining superpower'. If we project present trends into the future, the West's economic power seems set to decline, and the twenty-first century is shaping up to be China's century. Graddol may be right in proposing that, by the middle of the century, English could be facing a much more pluralized world language situation, in which other major players – not only Chinese, but Spanish and Arabic, for example – will have an extended international presence. It seems certain that Chinese, now with more than twice the number of native speakers of any other language, will gain a more and more powerful role in the world of the coming decades, along with the increasing power of the Chinese economy. On the other hand, it is conceivable, as Crystal puts it, 'that English, in some shape or form, will find itself in the service of the world community for ever'.

At the beginning of our story, we saw the English language emerging from an uncertain and misty past in the forests of continental Europe. At the end of our story, we cannot help reflecting that the future of English, as the world's first 'global language', is just as misty and uncertain.

Notes: Comments and References

In these notes, books and articles are mentioned by their titles and the names of authors (or editors). For details of the publisher, year and place of publication, and so on, see the list of References, beginning at p. 266.

Chapter 1: English – the Working Tongue of the Global Village

Many of the references in this and the following chapters draw on the following sources: *The Cambridge Encyclopedia of the English Language* by David Crystal and *The Oxford Companion to the English Language* edited by Tom McArthur. We have also made use of books for the general reader, such as *The Story of English* by Robert McCrum, William Cran and Robert MacNeil, *Mother Tongue: The English Language* by Bill Bryson; and *The Adventure of English: the Biography of a Language* by Melvyn Bragg. General works on English language (not particularly historical) are Randolph Quirk and Gabriele Stein, *English in Use*, and Stephen Gramley and Kurt-Michael Pätzold, *A Survey of Modern English*. A lively introduction is provided by David Crystal's *The English Language*.

p. 1

Marshal McLuhan introduced the expression 'global village' in his book *Understanding Media: The Extension of Man*.

p. 2

Braj Kachru explained his 'three circles' diagram in 'Standards, codification and sociolinguistic realism: the English language in the outer circle' (p. 12), and it has appeared in print many times since.

p. 3

Estimates for the number of speakers in Inner Circle countries are based on David Crystal's *English as a Global Language*, pp. 62–5. Figures for the Caribbean refer to populations of nations and associated states belonging to the Commonwealth of Nations: for example, including Jamaica but excluding Haiti.

p. 6

For a description of current editorial procedures, see John Simpson, Edmund Weiner and Philip Durkin, 'The *Oxford English Dictionary* today'. The quotation on the third edition of the *OED* is from Simon Winchester's *The Meaning of Everything: The Story of the Oxford English Dictionary*, p. 249. The web address of the OnLine edition is www.oed.com.

p. 7

The claim about the use of English in Russian business is by Vladimir Neroznak, a linguist who helps advise the Russian government on language policy – quoted in *Newsweek* (1 July 2002, p. 30). The permeation of EU institutions by English is discussed by Alan Forrest in 'The Politics of Language in the European Union'.

p. 9

Quotations are from David Crystal in *English as a Global Language*, p. xii, and Melvyn Bragg in *The Adventure of English*, p. 128.

Chapter 2: The First 500 Years

Covering the ground of this and the following four chapters are a number of good histories of the English language. We often make reference to Albert C. Baugh and Thomas Cable, *A History of the English Language* and N. F. Blake's book of the same title. Other books worth consulting are Charles Barber, *The English Language: A Historical Introduction*; Jeremy Smith, *An Historical Study of English: Function, Form and Change*; David Burnley, *The History of the English Language: A Source Book*; Dennis Freeborn, *From Old English to Standard English*; Thomas Pyles and John Algeo, *The Origins and Development of the English Language*. Recent books taking a fresh angle on the history of English are David Crystal, *The Stories of English*, and Richard Watts and Peter Trudgill, *Alternative Histories of English*. The multi-volume, multi-author *The Cambridge History of the English Language* (General Editor: Richard M. Hogg) has set a new standard of detail and scholarly depth in the historical study of English.

p. 14

This section draws on Albert C. Baugh and Thomas Cable, *A History of the English Language* and Gerry Knowles, *A Cultural History of the English Language*. Frank Stenton's *Anglo-Saxon England* is a good standard history of the period. Regarding the number of present-day speakers of Celtic languages, Tom McArthur in *The Oxford Companion to the English Language* gives the figure of 1.2 million (p. 202).

On the nomenclature of *United Kingdom*, *British*, etc., see Sidney Greenbaum and Janet Whitcut, *Longman Guide to English Usage* (p. 235).

p. 17

For this section we have benefited from, especially, N. F. Blake, *A History of the English Language* (pp. 53–6) and Gerry Knowles, *A Cultural History of the English Language* (pp. 21, 29–32), as well as other books mentioned at the beginning of this chapter's notes. For archaeological evidence, see *The Oxford History of Britain* edited by Kenneth Morgan, p. 62.

p. 18

On endangered languages (including Celtic languages), see David Crystal, *Language Death*. On the mixing of Celtic and Germanic sources of vocabulary, see Loreto Todd, 'Where have all the Celtic words gone?'

p. 19

This section is partly based on Otto Jespersen, *Growth and Structure of the English Language*, pp. 37–44; C. L. Wrenn, *The English Language*, pp. 38–41; John Ayto, *Dictionary of Word Origins*, as well as other books mentioned at the beginning of this chapter's notes. The term 'religious kaleidoscope' is from *The Oxford History of Britain* edited by Kenneth Morgan, p. 26.

p. 22

The section on the Viking influence is largely based on Julian D. Richards, *Viking Age England*; Peter Sawyer (ed.), *The Oxford Illustrated History of the Vikings*; and John Ayto, *Dictionary of Word Origins*.

p. 23

For Alfred's 'crash programme in education', see N. F. Blake, *A History of the English Language*, p. 83.

p. 24

The quotation on *thrive, ill, die,* etc. is from Otto Jespersen's *Growth and Structure of the English Language*, p. 74.

p. 26

The map of Viking place-names is based on that in Robert McCrum et al., *The Story of English*, p. 68.

p. 27

On Old English, see further Albert C. Baugh and Thomas Cable, *A History of the English Language*, pp. 48–9; N. F. Blake, *A History of the English Language*, pp. 3, 20, 75–104; Gerry Knowles, *A Cultural History of the English Language*, p. 38.

p. 31

The Old English text is from Fr. Klaeber (ed.), *Beowulf and the Fight at Finnsburg*; the phonetic transcription is from Randolph Quirk and C. L. Wrenn, *An Old English Grammar*.

p. 32

The first modern English translation is by John Porter, *Beowulf: Text and Translation*, and the second by Seamus Heaney, *Beowulf: A Verse Translation*.

Chapter 3: 1066 and All That

The chapter title comes from a classic of British humour, *1066 and All That: A Memorable History of England* by W. C. Sellar and R. J. Yeatman. This chapter, like the last, draws extensively on standard histories of the English language, especially N. F. Blake's *A History of the English Language*.

p. 33

The contribution from *The Oxford History of Britain* can be found in John Gillingham's chapter, 'The Early Middle Ages', p. 124.

p. 35

The figure of 'no more than 5 per cent' for native speakers of French is given by N. F. Blake, *A History of the English Language*, p. 107. The quotation (spelling modernized) from the Company of Brewers is taken from Simon Schama, *A History of Britain*, p. 228.

The quotation on *gaol* is from Pam Peters, *The Cambridge Australian English Style Guide*, p. 416. The list of words from French includes *because*, although only the second half of the word (*cause*) is actually from French. The first part is the Old English preposition *be*, modern English *by*.

p. 36

Ranulf Higden, a Benedictine monk of St Werburg's in Chester, wrote his history *Polychronicon* in 1352; it was translated from Latin into English by John of Trevisa in 1387, and printed by Caxton in 1482. The text is from Norman Davies, *The Isles: A History*, p. 429.

pp. 36, 37

The modern translation of John of Trevisa is from Charles Barber's *The English Language: A Historical Introduction*, p. 143.

p. 38

The Law French terms are from Tom McArthur (ed.), *The Oxford Companion to the English Language*, p. 591; see also Albert C. Baugh and Thomas Cable, *A History of the English Language*, p. 170. The comparison of 'hearty welcome' (from Old English) and 'cordial reception' (from French) can be found in Simeon Potter, *Our Language*, p. 37.

p. 39

The quotations come from Sir Walter Scott's *Ivanhoe*, the 1845 edition, p. 38; and from Robert Burchfield (ed.), *The New Fowler's Modern English Usage*, p. 18.

p. 40

The details about the pronunciation of *harass* are from J. C. Wells, *Longman Pronunciation Dictionary*. The Burchfield quotation is from *The New Fowler's Modern English Usage*, p. 349.

p. 41

The quotation 'because the French tongue ... is much unknown' occurs in the *Statute of the Realm* I.375.

p. 42

The text is from F. N. Robinson (ed.), *The Works of Geoffrey Chaucer*. The phonetic transcription of the Prologue is based on Helge Kökeritz, *A Guide to Chaucer's Pronunciation*, p. 20. See also Alan Cruttenden (ed.), *Gimson's Pronunciation of English* pp. 73–4. The modern rendering is by Nevill Coghill in *Chaucer's Canterbury Tales, translated into modern English verse*.

p. 43

The two books Caxton published on the continent were *Recuyell of the Historyes of Troy* (1475) and *The Game and Playe of Chesse* (1476). On Caxton's publications, see N. F. Blake, *Caxton and his World*, especially pp. 224–39, and George H. McKnight, *The Evolution of the English Language*, p. 68.

p. 44

The famous story about *eggys* and *eyren* is from Caxton's Preface to *Eneydos*. The whole passage is given in Albert C. Baugh and Thomas Cable, *A History of the English Language*, p. 196.

Chapter 4: Modern English in the Making

The general background for this chapter will be found in Albert C. Baugh and Thomas Cable, *A History of the English Language*; N. F. Blake, *A History of the English Language*; Gerald Knowles, *A Cultural History of the English Language*; Robert McCrum et al., *The Story of English*; David Burnley, *The History of the English Language*.

p. 48

The comparison of versions of the *Book of Common Prayer* is borrowed from David Burnley, *The History of the English Language*, pp. 399–407.

p. 50

Estimates of the population of English in the reign of Queen Elizabeth I vary considerably. Melvyn Bragg's figure, in *The Adventure of English*, is as low as three and a half million (p. 130).

p. 52

The passage on the London theatre is translated from a German original printed in an article by G. Binz, 'Londoner Theater und Schauspiele im Jahre 1599' in *Anglia* (Bd. XXII, NF., bd X, Halle, 1899). [Translation from Norton Topics Online www.nto/16century/topic4/tplatter.htm.

p. 54

See Randolph Quirk, 'Shakespeare and the English Language'. A general book on Shakespeare's English is N. F. Blake's *The Language of Shakespeare*. The document of 1574 is quoted in Erik Frykman and Göran Kjellmer, *Aspects of Shakespeare*, p. 40. The figure of 3,000 people is from Melvyn Bragg, *The Adventure of English*, p. 140.

p. 56

The quotation from Richard Mulcaster is dated 1582 and appeared in *The First Part of the Elementarie* (Menston: Scolar Reprint 219: 75); from Gerry Knowles, *A Cultural History of the English Language*, p. 78. The figure of 6,000 words per year is from Simon Winchester's *The Meaning of Everything*, p. 15. A fascinating account of the 2004 performance of *Romeo and Juliet* with the original pronunciation is given in Crystal, *Pronouncing Shakespeare*.

p. 57

The discussion of pronunciation and the phonetic transcription of the *Hamlet* extract are based on Helge Kökeritz, *Shakespeare's Pronunciation*.

p. 60

'God's teaching in homely English for everyman' – these are the words of Robert McCrum et al., *The Story of English*, p. 114. This section draws on N. F. Blake, *A History of the English Language*, pp. 236–71. The quotation beginning 'an anarchist springtime' is from J. K. Chambers, 'Three kinds of standard in Canadian English', p. 5. The variant spellings of

Shakespeare's name are reproduced in David Crystal, *The Cambridge Encyclopedia of the English Language*, p. 149.

p. 61

The table of vowel pronunciations is based on Alan Cruttenden (ed.), *Gimson's Pronunciation of English*, p. 75.

p. 62

The story about Churchill is well known: our direct source is Robert Burchfield, *The New Fowler's Modern English Usage*, p. 736. For the quotation from *Fowler's Modern English Usage*, p. 618. For the quotation from Edmund Waller, see Robert McCrum et al., *The Story of English*, p. 133. For the situation in England relating to the use of English versus Latin, see Charles Barber, *The English Language*, p. 175.

p. 63

The quotation from Alexander Pope is to be found in his *Epitaph: Intended for Sir Isaac Newton* (1730). The following quotation is from Dan Brown's *The Da Vinci Code* (New York: Doubleday, 2003), pp. 387, 392.

p. 64

The quotation from Jonathan Swift is taken from his *A Proposal for Correcting, Improving and Ascertaining the English Tongue* (1712). For further background, see Robert McCrum et al., *The Story of English*, p. 135.

p. 65

The quotation from Johnson's Preface is also from *The Story of English*, p. 139.

p. 67

On English as a 'language complex', see Tom McArthur, *The English Languages*, p. xvii; and 'World English, Euro-English, Nordic English?'.

Chapter 5: English Goes to the New World

This chapter draws not only on general histories of English (as in previous chapters) but on books on American English, especially Gunnel Tottie, *An Introduction to American English*; J. L. Dillard, *A History of American English*; Walt Wolfram and Natalie Schilling-Estes, *American English*. A recent important volume is John Algeo (ed.), *English in North America*. H. L. Mencken's *The American Language* is compellingly written, although now very dated. It is a historical document in its own right.

p. 71

The Bismarck quotation is from William H. Skeggs, *German Conspiracies in America* (London: T. Fisher Unwin, 1915, pp. 65–6).

p. 72

Matter relating to John Adams comes from Albert C. Baugh and Thomas Cable, *A History of the English Language*, p. 365; and Robert McCrum et al., *The Story of English*, p. 254.

The quotation from Arthur Barlowe is taken from 'Captain Barlowe's Narrative of the First Voyage to the Coasts of America', Henry S. Burrage (ed.), *Early English and French Voyages, Chiefly from Hakluyt, 1534–1608* (New York: Scribner & Sons, 1906), pp. 228–9.

p. 73

On matter relating to 'zummerzet', Chesapeake Bay and Tangier Island, see *The Story of English*, pp. 109–10.

p. 74

The quotation from James I on tobacco is taken from *The Minor Works of King James VI and I* (ed. by James Craigie) Edinburgh: Scottish Text Society, 1982. The quotation from James I on kingship comes from a speech to Parliament on 21 March 1609, in *Works* (1616). Reprinted in *The Political Works of James I*, New York: Russell & Russell, 1965, p. 307.

p. 76

The 'picaresque novel' quotation is from Bill Bryson, *Made in America*, p. 15; the story of Squanto is from Tad Tuleja, *The New York Public Library Book of Popular Americana*, p. 361.

pp. 77, 78

The details about Native American language families are from Gunnel Tottie's *An Introduction to American English*, pp. 233–4. The list of Native American terms is from *American Heritage Dictionary of the English Language* and Gunnel Tottie, *An Introduction to American English*, p. 121.

p. 79

The Mencken quotation came to us via Bill Bryson, *Made in America*, p. 172. The quotation about a 'veritable cemetery of languages' is from Alexandro Portes and Lingxin Hao, 'E pluribus unum: Bilingualism and loss of language in the second generation', and came to us via Gunnel Tottie, *An Introduction to American English*, p. 235.

p. 83

On Jefferson and the Declaration of Independence, see Jon E. Lewis (ed.), *The Mammoth Book of How It Happened in America*, pp. 97–8. The discussion and quotations are from Robert McCrum et al., *The Story of English*, pp. 254, 256.

p. 88

The quotation on the California goldrush is from *The Story of English* (above), p. 273.

p. 89

The story of the first American pizza is found in Bill Bryson, *Made in America*, pp. 225–6.

p. 90

The definitions (some simplified) of the Yiddish terms are from *American Heritage Dictionary of the English Language*.

p. 91

According to Kenneth R. Andrews, *Trade, Plunder, and Settlement*, the only safe statement about the area discovered by Cabot is that it lay between 42 degrees North and 54 degrees

North. The background to English in Canada is based on J. L. Dillard, *A History of American English*, pp. 2, 46.

p. 92

On French words borrowed into North American English, see Thomas Pyles, *Words and Ways of American English*, p. 47. On *Cajun, bayou*, etc., see Tad Tuleja, *The New York Public Library Book of Popular Americana*, p. 24. The figure of 25,000 comes from J. L. Dillard, *A History of American English*, pp. 45–6.

p. 94

The figures, which are based on *Statistics Canada*, are given in J. K. Chambers, 'Solitudes and solidarity: English and French in Canada', pp. 122–9. On endangered indigenous Canadian languages, see David Crystal, *Language Death*, p. 16. Usage regarding 'First Nation' and other terms is taken from the Government of Canada website at http://www.ainc-inac.gc.ca/pr/info/info113_e.html. Figures for language usage are from the *Ethnologue* (SIL) website.

p. 95

On Canadian English as a variety of Northern American English, see Jaan Lilles, 'The myth of Canadian English', pp. 3–9.

p. 96

The account of the pronunciation of English in Canada is indebted to J. K. Chambers, 'Three kinds of standard in Canadian English', pp. 11–12. The term 'Canadian raising' was coined by J. K. Chambers in 1973 (see Tom McArthur (ed.), *The Oxford Companion to the English Language*, p. 181). It is a convenient term for what may in fact be a non-lowering of certain vowels that are lowered in most other dialects.

p. 97

The J. K. Chambers quotation is from his 'Three kinds of standard in Canadian English', p. 8. The 'Canadian expletive' *eh* is explored in Elaine Gold, 'Canadian *Eh?*: A Survey of Contemporary Use'.

Chapter 6: English Transplanted

In addition to books mentioned in the Notes to Chapter 1, the next four chapters draw on a number of books dealing world varieties of English, especially in Tom McArthur, *The Oxford Guide to World English*, Laurie Bauer, *An Introduction to International Varieties of English*, and Gunnel Melchers and Philip Shaw, *World Englishes: An Introduction*. J. C. Wells, *Accents of English* is an excellent source for varieties of pronunciation around the world.

p. 99

On the history of settlement in Australia, see John Rickard, *Australia: A Cultural History*. These paragraphs draw on pp. 24–6. According to *The Concise Oxford Dictionary of Australian History*, 1,030 people went ashore from the First Fleet; and of these, 548 men and 188 women were convicts. On the origins of Australian English, see Neil Courtney, 'The nature of Australian'.

p. 100

The quotation about the inhabitants of the tavern comes from *The Story of English*, p. 319. The paragraph on the Gold Rush and the convicts draws on John Rickard, *Australia: A Cultural History* (p. 44) and Bill Bryson, *In a Sunburned Country* (p. 81).

p. 101

The statement of the seven-minute lifespan of Australian English is from George W. Turner, 'English in Australia', p. 303. On Captain Cook and the word *kangaroo*, see Michael Quinion, *Port Out, Starboard Home and Other Language Myths*, p. 172. Lang's poem is quoted in *The Story of English*, p. 309.

p. 102

On the endangered languages of Australia, see Tom McArthur (ed.), *The Oxford Companion to the English Language*, p. 95; also David Crystal, *Language Death*, pp. 15, 16, 20, 49–50.

pp. 102, 103

For help with the text version and glosses of *Waltzing Matilda*, thanks are due to Pam Peters, Macquarie University; also to the website of the National Library of Australia. On *flash language* see Michael Cathcart (ed.), *Manning Clark's History of Australia*, p.18. The quotation is from J. C. Wells, *Accents of English*, p. 593.

p. 104

The book *Let Stalk Strine*, with a putative author Afferbeck Lauder ('alphabetical order'), was published by Ure Smith in Sydney in 1965.

pp. 104, 105

The definitions are based on *The Macquarie Dictionary*.

p. 108

Details are from Tom McArthur (ed.), *The Oxford Companion to the English Language* (p. 696); and Laurie Bauer, 'English in New Zealand' (p. 386). On infiltration of American English into New Zealand English, see Janet Holmes, 'T-time in New Zealand'.

pp. 108, 109

Details of New Zealand pronunciation draw on Wells, *Accents of English*, pp. 605–10. Gunnel Melchers and Philip Shaw, *World Englishes*, pp. 109–13 quote Elizabeth Gordon and Tony Deverson, *New Zealand English and English in New Zealand* (p. 37) as the source of the 'Here's Dad' story.

p. 112

The recognition of Cape English, Natal English and General South African English variables derives from L. W. Lanham and C. A. Macdonald, *The Standard in South African English and its Social History*.

p. 113

The historical background draws on Vivian de Klerk (ed.), *Focus on South Africa*. On details of constitutional and national language policy, see William Branford, 'English in South Africa'. The quotation is from *Long Walk to Freedom: The Autobiography of Nelson Mandela* (Boston: Little, Brown and Company, 1994), pp. 15–16.

pp. 114, 115

Details of South African pronunciation come from Wells, *Accents of English*, pp. 610–22, and Gunnel Melchers and Philip Shaw, *World Englishes*, pp. 117–21. (The 'KIT Split' is Wells's term.)

p. 116

The classification of Englishes is due to Tom McArthur, 'English in the world, in Africa, and in South Africa'.

p. 117

For details of Indian English, we draw extensively on Braj B. Kachru, 'English in South Asia', and also on the website www.aegis.com/countries/India/html.

p. 118

As background to the quotation, see Agnes Scott Langeland, 'Rushdie's language'. The quotation comes from Salman Rushdie, 'Imaginary Homelands', *London Review of Books* (7–20 October 1982, pp. 18–19). The quotation from Oliver Wendell Holmes is found in Tad Tuleja, *The New York Public Library Book of Popular Americana*, p. 40.

p. 120

For features of Singlish, see Duncan Forbes, 'Singlish'; Christine C. M. Goh, 'The level tone in Singapore English'.

p. 121

On English in Hong Kong, see Joseph Boyle and Ruth Tomlinson, 'Job interviews in Hong Kong'; David R. Carless, 'Politicised expressions in the *South China Morning Post*'; Andrew Taylor, 'Hong Kong's English Newspapers'; Gregory James, 'Cantonese particles in Hong Kong students' English e-mails'; Martha C. Pennington, 'The folly of language planning; Or, A brief history of the English language in Hong Kong'. The Chinese boom in English may be followed up in Eva Lai, 'Teaching English as a private enterprise in China', and Keqi Hao 'The view from China'. The figure of *c.* 100 million Chinese children learning English comes from *Newsweek* (7 March 2005, p. 64). Also, in March 2005, the BBC claimed 300 million Chinese (presumably including adults) were learning English. These figures may be guesswork.

p. 122

Examples of Singlish are from the *Times-Chambers Essential English Dictionary*, National University of Singapore (1995, 1997), which contains the following footnote on the points of grammar: 'Note that these features belong to informal SME [= Singapore-Malaysian English]. When they are used in standard or formal SME, they are considered to be errors'. The sample dialogue is from Loga Baskaran, 'The Malaysian English mosaic', p. 28.

Chapter 7: English Varieties in the British Isles

On the subject of this chapter, the following are general books: Arthur Hughes and Peter Trudgill, *English Accents and Dialects: An Introduction to Social and Regional Varieties of British English*; James Milroy and Lesley Milroy (eds.) *Real English: The Grammar of English Dialects in the British Isles*; and Peter Trudgill (ed.) *Language in the British Isles*.

p. 124

Howard Giles and Peter F. Powesland, in *Speech Style and Social Evaluation*, investigated the pleasant or less pleasant associations of various accents.

p. 125

Lynda Mugglestone, in *'Talking Proper': The Rise of Accent as Social Symbol*, has traced the historical background to the rise of RP.

p. 126

The quotations are from John Sinclair, 'Models and monuments', p. 6; David Abercrombie, 'The Way People Speak'; and Melvyn Bragg, *The Adventure of English*, p. 235. For different perspectives on RP and its association with 'BBC English', see Randolph Quirk, *Style and Communication in the English Language*, pp. 5, 30; Robert McCrum et al., *The Story of English*, pp. 16–18 , 397–8; Beverly Collins, *The Early Career of Daniel Jones*, p. 363.

p. 127

On varieties of RP, see Alan Cruttenden (ed.) , *Gimson's Pronunciation of English*, p. 80, and J. C. Wells, *Accents of English*, p. 280.

p. 128

The quotation about 'Cocknies' is from Fynes Moryson, *An Itinerary* (1617), in Tom McArthur (ed.), *The Oxford Companion to the English Language*, p. 225. The Shaw quotation is originally in the preface to *Pygmalion*. On 'h-dropping' and its non-occurrence in the US: the point is made by J.C. Wells in *Accents of English*, pp. 253, 255.

p. 129

The glottal stop is described in Alan Cruttenden (ed.) , *Gimson's Pronunciation of English*, p. 154.

p. 130

John Wells's useful web address is http://www.phon.ucl.ac.uk/home/estuary/index.html. This quotation is from an article by Wells in *English Teaching Professional*, 1998.

p. 132

Peter Trudgill expresses this view in 'Received Pronunciation: sociolinguistic aspects', p. 11.

p. 134

The examples of West Country grammar are from Peter Trudgill and J. K. Chambers (eds.), *Dialects of English: Studies in Grammatical Variation*, p. 9. There is a discussion of forms of the verb *to be* in Ossi Ihalainen's contribution, pp. 104–19. The examples of vernacular grammar are from Douglas Biber et al., *Longman Grammar of Spoken and Written English*, pp. 1121–5, where there is a general account of vernacular or non-standard grammar.

p. 135

On Welsh English, see Alan R. Thomas, 'Welsh English', and Peter Trudgill and Jean Hannah, *International English*, pp. 32–6; on Welsh pronunciation, see J. C. Wells, *Accents of English*, pp. 377–93.

p. 136

The text and details of the Ruthwell Cross and *The Dream of the Rood* are in Dorothy Whitelock, *Sweet's Anglo-Saxon Reader in Prose and Verse*, pp. 153–9; see also Norman Davies, *The Isles*, p. 188.

p. 138

Details of Scots and Scottish English can be found in Tom McArthur, *The English Languages*, pp. 138–59.

p. 141

These welcoming messages were to be found on the Scottish Parliament's website, http://www.scottish.parliament.uk/vli/language/scots/, on 13 January 2005.

p. 143

Our source for the quotation of Robert Burns on *Auld Lang Syne* is Adrian Room (ed.), *Brewer's Dictionary of Phrase and Fable*, p. 75.

p. 144

The Irish in America – details are from Bill Bryson, *Made in America*, pp. 163–4. On Germanic contacts with Ireland, see Jeffrey L. Kallen, 'English in Ireland', p. 150.

p. 146

On limericks in general, see Tom McArthur (ed.), *The Oxford Companion to the English Language*, p. 605.

p. 149

Gunnel Melchers and Philip Shaw, *World Englishes* (pp. 71–7) is a good source for Irish English, and incidentally contains the anecdote about Shirley MacLaine.

Chapter 8: American and British English

The publications on English in North America listed at the beginning of Chapter 5, especially Gunnel Tottie's *An Introduction to American English*, are also relevant to this chapter. Another useful source is John Algeo, 'American and British Words'.

The epigraphs are from *Act of Legislature of Illinois* (ch. 127, section 178, 1923, quoted in Tom McArthur, *The English Languages*, p. 221) and William Safire's column 'Language' in *The New York Times* (as reprinted in *International Herald Tribune*, 23 August 1993, quoted from *The English Languages*, p. 225).

pp. 152, 153

The quotation is from Bill Bryson's *Mother Tongue*, pp. 170–1. The database mentioned is the Longman Corpus of Spoken American English. The number of separate words in the second edition of the *OED* (published in 1989) is quoted as 615,200 by Simon Winchester in *The Meaning of Everything*, p. 247.

p. 153

On lexical differences between AmE and BrE, consult John Algeo, 'American and British Words', and John Algeo, 'British–American lexical differences: a typology of interdialectal variation'.

p. 157

The quotation is from H. L. Mencken, *The American Language*, p. vi. Details of the early history of American English and of Americanisms are found in Albert C. Baugh and Thomas Cable, *A History of the English Language*, pp. 390–7.

p. 160

The Kipling quotation is from *From Sea to Sea* (1889), as cited in Tom McArthur's *The English Languages*, p. 220.

p. 161

The 'Harvard Yard' example is from Gunnel Tottie, *An Introduction to American English*, p. 209.

p. 163

The concept of a General American accent is criticized increasingly by those who feel it is necessary to make finer distinctions. Nevertheless, it is valuable as a point of reference. See Alan Cruttenden (ed.), *Gimson's Pronunciation of English*, p. 84 and, for more detail, J. C. Wells, *Accents of English*, pp. 467–73.

p. 164

For Labov's and others' studies of *r*-fulness in American accents, see the account in Gunnel Tottie, *An Introduction to American English*, pp. 215–17.

p. 166

The quotations are from Allan Metcalf, *Presidential Voices*, pp. 142, 158.

p. 167

On grammar, see John Algeo, 'British and American grammatical differences', and Gunnel Tottie, 'How different are American and British English grammar? And how are they different?'

p. 168

On adjectives used like adverbs: see Gunnel Tottie, *An Introduction to American English*, pp. 168–9.

p. 169

On AAVE, see John Russel Rickford and Russell John Rickford, *Spoken Soul: the Story of Black English*; also J. L. Dillard, *Black English: Its History and Usage in the United States* and

John Rickford, *African American Vernacular English: Features and Use, Evolution, and Educational Implications*. The example *Dey ain't like dat* is from William A. Stewart, 'Sociolinguistic Factors in the History of the American Negro Dialects', p. 195.

p. 172

On the usage of *black, African American*, etc. we consulted *The American Heritage Book of English Usage*, p. 190.

Chapter 9: From Caribbean English to Creole

The following books relate to the subject matter of this chapter: John Holm, *An Introduction to Pidgins and Creoles*; Mark Sebba, *Contact Languages: Pidgins and Creoles*; Loreto Todd, *Pidgins and Creoles*. The Derek Walcott poem from which this is an extract was published in *New Yorker* (14 March 1983, p. 48).

p. 176

For a fuller discussion of the etymology, see Loreto Todd, *Pidgins and Creoles*, pp. 20–3. For further background and reading, see Tom McArthur, *The English Languages*, pp. 160–73.

p. 177

The example of a Guyanese creole continuum is taken from Ronald Macaulay, *The Social Art: Language and its Uses*, p. 176. Caribbean pronunciation is described in considerable detail by J. C. Wells, *Accents of English*, pp. 560–91.

p. 179

Background to the Jamaican mesolect varieties is given in Monica E. Taylor, 'Jamaica and the economics of English'.

p. 180

For the text of Hibbert's *Sweet and Dandy*, with explanatory notes, we are indebted to Peter L. Patrick's excellent webpages on creoles, University of Essex: http://privatewww. essex.ac.uk/~patrickp/SweetAnDandy.htm

p. 181

On Sranan, see Herman Wekker, 'Creole words' and 'The English-based creoles of Surinam' (where *Ope Kondreman* appeared).

p. 184

Derek Bickerton's hypothesis is explained in his article 'The language bioprogram hypothesis'.

p. 186

On the grammatical characteristics of creoles: see David Crystal, *The Cambridge Encyclopedia of the English Language*, p. 347; Tom McArthur (ed.), *The Oxford Companion to the English Language*, p. 271; Gunnel Melchers and Philip Shaw, *World Englishes*, p.125.

p. 187

Peter Mühlhäusler has studied Tok Pisin in depth. See especially his book *Pidgin and Creole Linguistics*. See also David Crystal, *The Cambridge Encyclopedia of the English Language*, pp. 348–9; Stephan Gramley and Kurt-Michael Pätzold, *A Survey of Modern English*, pp. 343–7; Tom McArthur (ed.), *The Oxford Companion to the English Language*, pp. 1044–5. For a description of the local meaning of 'Wantok', see Mark Sebba, *Contact Languages: Pidgins and Creoles*, p. 18. The Biblical text is from *Nupela Testamen bilong Bikpela Jisas Kraist*, the Bible Society in Papua New Guinea, 5th edn, 1974.

Chapter 10: The Standard Language Today

p. 191

On the concept of Standard English, see James Milroy and Lesley Milroy, *Authority in Language: Investigating Standard English*; and Peter Trudgill, 'Standard English in England'.

p. 192

The modern rendering of the beginning of *the Pardoner's Tale* is from Nevill Coghill's *Chaucer's Canterbury Tales, translated into modern English verse*. The Lord Chesterfield and James Beattie quotations are both sourced in Tom McArthur's *The English Languages*, p. 120.

p. 196

Examples are adapted from Geoffrey Leech and Jan Svartvik, *A Communicative Grammar of English*, pp. 31–2.

p. 197

The frequency data are derived from the British National Corpus; and are published in List 2.1 in Geoffrey Leech, Paul Rayson and Andrew Wilson, *Word Frequencies in Written and Spoken English*, pp. 120–5.

p. 198

The 'Trojan horse' quotation is from Jean-Marc Gachelin, 'Is English a Romance Language?', p. 9; the idea of a Romance stratum is explored in Sylviane Granger, 'Romance words in English: From history to pedagogy', p. 105.

p. 199

The extract is from Jonathan Lynn and Antony Jay, *Yes, Prime Minister*, p. 16.

p. 200

Figure 10.1 is very roughly based on Douglas Biber, *Variation across Speech and Writing* (p. 128, Figure 7.1 'Mean scores of Dimension 1 for each of the genres; Dimension 1: Involved versus Informative Production'). The following paragraph also draws on the discussion in Biber's book. This dimension of variation is simply the most important of a number of stylistic dimensions statistically revealed in Biber's research on spoken and written English.

p. 201

The conversational extract is part of a longer passage quoted and discussed in Douglas Biber et al., *Longman Grammar of Spoken and Written English*, p. 10. The example of written language is from the webpages of the Australian Museum: http:www.amonline.net.au.

pp. 201–3

The discussion in this box is based on Douglas Biber et al., *Longman Grammar of Spoken and Written English*, pp. 1041–51. Passage C is from the same source.

Chapter 11: Linguistic Change in Progress

On recent history of the standard language, see Christian Mair, *Twentieth-Century English* and Christain Mair and Geoffrey Leech, 'Current change in English syntax'.

p. 207

Data and discussion on the declining modals are found in Geoffrey Leech, 'Recent grammatical change in English: data, description, theory'.

p. 210

On British grammar following in the footsteps of American grammar, see Geoffrey Leech and Nicholas Smith, 'Recent grammatical change in written English 1961–1992'. This article also includes discussion of the increasing use of the mandative subjunctive in British English. Data and discussion on the use of *don't have, haven't* (*got*), etc. are to be found in Douglas Biber et al., *Longman Grammar of Spoken and Written English*, pp. 161–2. See the same book, pp. 215–16, on the related issue of *do ... have, have ... got* in questions.

pp. 213, 214

For the dialogue example and a discussion of vocatives: see Douglas Biber et al., *Longman Grammar of Spoken and Written English*, pp. 1108–13.

p. 219

The main sources for the section on 'Electronic English' are two books by David Crystal: *Language and the Internet* and *A Glossary of Netspeak and Textspeak*. The quotation from Crystal is from *Language and the Internet*, p. 239; the examples *lunch@Boots.yum* is from the same book, p. 20.

Chapter 12: English into the Future

Three publications have been particularly valuable sources for this chapter: David Crystal, *English as a Global Language*; David Graddol, *The Future of English?*; and Tom McArthur, *The English Languages*. These books are identified below simply as Crystal, Graddol and McArthur.

pp. 222, 223

Tom McArthur has explored the 'Latin analogy', to use his term, in depth; see McArthur, pp. 180–96.

p. 223

The quotation from Henry Sweet is from his *Handbook of Phonetics*, p. 196 (see Crystal, p. 176). Burchfield's view on the disintegration of global English was reported by Randolph Quirk, who also drew attention to the comparable prediction by Henry Sweet (in Randolph Quirk, *Grammatical & Lexical Variance in English*, pp. 5–6). The quotation 'a lively and useful corpse' is from McArthur, p. 185.

p. 224

The plummeting cost of telephone calls is depicted by a graph in Graddol, p. 31.

p. 225

The term 'multiglossia' is used by Crystal (p. xi), whereas the term 'polyglossia' is mentioned (in the entry for *diglossia*) in Tom McArthur's *The Oxford Companion to the English Language*, p. 313. The estimated incidence of bilingualism is from Crystal, p. 17.

p. 226

On the circle of world English, see Tom McArthur, p. 97. Manfred Görlach has a similar diagram in *Studies in the History of the English Language* (see McArthur, p. 101).

p. 227

The quotations on WSSE are from Crystal, pp. 185–6. 'Accommodation' is a familiar term in sociolinguistics; the concept was developed by Howard Giles and Philip Smith in 'Accommodation theory: optimal levels of convergence'.

p. 228

For Crystal's four principles and his statement that English was 'in the right place at the right time', see Crystal, pp. xiii, 14. Claims on the numbers of Chinese speakers and learners of English came from Reuter's UK Report on-line, 9 December 2004 (reporting a British Council press release); and from *Newsweek*, 7 March 2005. Graddol's report 'The Future of English' was published at the British Council's 'Going Global Conference in International Education', in Edinburgh on 8 December 2004. The quotation is from Tom McArthur in 'World English, Euro-English, Nordic English?', p. 55.

p. 229

In *The English Languages*, McArthur surveys the role of English in the countries of the world, and comes to the conclusion that 'in the territories listed' English is 'significant for one or more reasons.' In some cases, the role of English is official, in others it is not (pp. 47–8). The following sections 'Business and Commerce', 'Education', etc. are based on Graddol, pp. 28–49. On the 'decorative' use of English, see John Dougill, 'English as a decorative language'; also McArthur, *Oxford Guide to World English*, pp. 368–9.

p. 230

On the scientific role of English, see Hikomaro Sano, 'The world's lingua franca of science'. Figures on book publication are from Graddol, p. 9. The claim about 80 per cent database use of English was made in *Newsweek*, 7 March 2005.

p. 231

The prediction about Dutch is in Tom McArthur, 'World English, Euro-English, Nordic English?', p. 58.

p. 233

The quotation about English permeating EU institutional activities is from Alan Forrest, 'The Politics of Language in the European Union', pp. 314, 318–19. The phrase 'an off-shore European language' is from Tom McArthur, 'World English, Euro-English, Nordic English?', p. 55.

pp. 233, 234

The language rights quotation came from the 'Basic Principles' of the 'Draft Charter on Fundamental Rights in the EU: EU Citizenship and Language Rights and Obligations of the Citizen', Brussels, 2000. Other assessments of the present and future standing of English in Europe are to be found in Robert Phillipson, *English-Only Europe? Challenging Language Policy*, and Jennifer Jenkins, Marko Modiano and Barbara Seidlhofer, 'Euro-English'. For different takes on Mid-Atlantic English in Europe, see Marko Modiano, 'The emergence of Mid-Atlantic English in the European Union' and Gunnel Melchers, ' "Fair ladies, dancing queens" – A study of Mid-Atlantic accents'. For the study and promotion of ELF, see Jennifer Jenkins, 'ELF at the gate: the position of English as a lingua franca'. Barbara Seidlhofer (who is working on the Vienna-Oxford corpus of ELF) wrote 'Closing a conceptual gap: the case for a description of English as a lingua franca'; and Anna Mauranen, on another ELF corpus project, wrote 'The Corpus of English as a Lingua Franca in International Settings'.

p. 235

The concept of Nuclear English is developed in 'International communication and the concept of Nuclear English', a chapter in Randolph Quirk, *Style and Communication in the English Language*, pp. 37–53. The proposition that 'the native speaker is dead' is discussed by P. Bhaskaran Nayar in 'Variants and varieties of English: Dialectology or linguistic politics?'.

p. 236

On the demographics of L1 and L2 populations, see Crystal, pp. 69, 171. There are several articles devoted to related issues in *English Today* 82 (April 2005): Abdulla Al-Dabbagh, 'Globalism and the universal language'; Carmen Acevedo Butcher, 'The case against the "native speaker" '; James E. Alatis, 'Kachru's circles and the growth of professionalism in TESOL'; Ross Smith, 'Global English: gift or curse?' The letter from Mikie Koyoi is abridged from Tom Arthur's *The English Languages*, p. 211; from 'Dear English Speakers: Please Drop the Dialects', *International Herald Tribune*, 3 November 1995.

p. 237

Our illustration and discussion of London teenage speech is based on material from Anna-Brita Stenström's COLT Corpus (the Bergen Corpus of London Teenage Language). See her paper *'Can I have a chips please? – Just tell me what one you want*: Nonstandard grammatical features in London teenage talk'.

p. 238

The quotation on the decline of RP is from Crystal, *The Stories of English*, p. 472. Quotations on the future of English from Crystal, p. 28; Graddol, p. 2; David Crystal, *Language Death*, pp. 18, 165; Graddol, p. 62. John Wells's quotation on the probable decline of RP is from *Accents of English*, p. 118.

p. 239

The extract is from Mark Sebba, *London Jamaican*, pp. 19–20.

pp. 240, 241

The most important source we have found for Northern Cities Shift is Labov, Ash and Boberg *A National Map of the Regional Dialects of American English*, http://www.ling.upenn.edu/phono_atlas/NationalMap/NationalMap.html, from whom we have borrowed the map and the vowel diagram (Figure 12.2) and the quotation about 'a revolutionary rotation' of vowels. Other useful webpages describing Northern Cities Shift are: http://www.ic.arizona.edu/~lsp/Northeast/ncshift/ncshift3.html (the Language Samples Project) and http://www.pbs.org/speak/seatosea/americanvarieties/midwest/. The latter of these (author: Matthew J. Gordon) tells the anecdote of Ian and Ann, attributed to linguistics professor John Lawler.

p. 243

Thumboo was describing a conference on Commonwealth Literature. This passage comes from Alastair Pennycook, *The Cultural Politics of English as an International Language*, quoting Edwin Thumboo, *Literature and Liberation: Five Essays from Southeast Asia*, p. 131. On the anti-imperialist critique of English, read Alastair Pennycook, *The Cultural Politics of English as an International Language*, especially pp. 13–14; also Robert Phillipson, *Linguistic Imperialism*. On attitudes to English in South Africa, see Penny Silva, 'South African English: oppressor or liberator?', p. 73 (also a quotation from Vivian de Klerk, (ed.), *Focus on South Africa*, p. 8). The quotation from Phyllis Ghim-Lian Chew is taken from her 'Linguistic imperialism, globalism, and the English Language' (p. 42), in *English in a Changing World* edited by David Graddol and Ulrike H. Meinhof.

p. 244

On Franglais, see René Etiemble, *Parlez-vous franglais?* Details of the Canadian French situation are from the webpages of Claude Bélanger, Department of History, Marianopolis College. Manfred Görlach's *English Words Abroad* provided the information about French law (p. 35).

p. 245

The list of English loanwords in French and German is also from the same source (p. 38). See also his *Dictionary of European Anglicisms*. Tom McArthur gives the 'Manglish' example of language mixture in 'World English, Euro-English, Nordic English?', p. 57. The example is from Andrew Preshous, 'Where you going ah?'

p. 246

The final quotation is from Crystal, p. 191.

Key to texts on pp. 194–5

Text A: Anchorage, Alaska, USA (*Anchorage Daily News*, 18 February 2005)
Text B: New Delhi, India (*The Times of India*, 14 February 2005)
Text C: Edinburgh, Scotland (*The Scotsman*, 11 February 2005)
Text D: Sydney, Australia (*The Australian*, 16 February 2005)

References

Abercrombie, David (1951) 'The way people speak', *The Listener*, 6 September, 385–6.

Alatis, James E. (2005) 'Kachru's circles and the growth of professionalism in TESOL', *English Today* 82: 25–34.

Al-Dabbagh, Abdulla (2005) 'Globalism and the universal language', *English Today* 82: 3–12.

Algeo, John (1988) 'British and American grammatical differences', *International Journal of Lexicography* 1: 1–31.

Algeo, John (1989) 'British–American lexical differences: a typology of interdialectal variation', in Ofelia García and Ricardo Otheguy (eds.) *English across Cultures; Cultures across English: a Reader in Cross-cultural Communication*. Berlin: Mouton de Gruyter, pp. 219–41.

Algeo, John (1996) 'American and British words', in Jan Svartvik (ed.) *Words*, 145–58.

Algeo, John (ed.) (2001) *English in North America (The Cambridge History of the English Language*, vol. 6). Cambridge: Cambridge University Press.

Andrews, Kenneth R. (1984) *Trade, Plunder, and Settlement: Maritime Enterprise and the Genesis of the British Empire, 1480–1630*. Cambridge: Cambridge University Press.

Australian Oxford Dictionary (2004), 2nd edn by Bruce Moore. South Melbourne: Oxford University Press.

Ayto, John (1990) *Dictionary of Word Origins*. New York: Arcade.

Bailey, Richard W. (1992) *Images of English: A Cultural History of the Language*. Cambridge: Cambridge University Press.

Barber, Charles (2000) *The English Language: A Historical Introduction*. Cambridge: Cambridge University Press.

Baskaran, Loga (1994) 'The Malaysian English mosaic', *English Today* 37: 27–32.

Bauer, Laurie (1994) 'English in New Zealand'. In Robert Burchfield (ed.), *The Cambridge History of the English Language*, vol. 5, 382–429.

Bauer, Laurie (2002) *An Introduction to International Varieties of English*. Edinburgh: Edinburgh University Press.

Baugh, Albert C. and Thomas Cable (2002) *A History of the English Language*, 5th edn. London: Routledge.

Biber, Douglas (1988) *Variation across Speech and Writing*. Cambridge: Cambridge University Press.

Biber, Douglas, Stig Johansson, Geoffrey Leech, Susan Conrad and Edward Finegan (1999) *Longman Grammar of Spoken and Written English*. London: Longman.

Bickerton, Derek (1984) 'The language bioprogram hypothesis', *Behavioral and Brain Sciences* 7, 2: 173–222.

Blake, N. F. (1969) *Caxton and his World*. London: Deutsch.

Blake, N. F. (1988) *The Language of Shakespeare*. Basingstoke: Macmillan.

Blake, N. F. (1996) *A History of the English Language*. Basingstoke: Macmillan.

Boyle, Joseph and Ruth Tomlinson (1995) 'Job interviews in Hong Kong', *English Today* 43: 36–9.

Bragg, Melvyn (2003) *The Adventure of English: The Biography of a Language*. London: Hodder and Stoughton.

Branford, William (1994) 'English in South Africa'. In Robert Burchfield (ed.), *The Cambridge History of the English Language*, vol. 5, 430–96.

Bryson, Bill (1990) *Mother Tongue: The English Language*. London: Hamish Hamilton.

Bryson, Bill (1995) *Made in America*. London: Minerva.

Bryson, Bill (2001) *In a Sunburned Country*. New York: Broadway Books.

Burchfield, Robert (ed.) (1994) *The Cambridge History of the English Language*, vol. 5, *English in Britain and Overseas: Origins and Development*. Cambridge: Cambridge University Press.

Burchfield, Robert (ed.) (1996) *The New Fowler's Modern English Usage*, 3rd edn. Oxford: Clarendon Press.

Burrage, Henry S. (ed.) (1906) *Early English and French Voyages, Chiefly from Hakluyt, 1534–1608*. New York: Scribner & Sons.

Burnley, David (2000) *The History of the English Language: A Source Book*, 2nd edn. London: Longman.

Butcher, Carmen Acevedo (2005) 'The case against the "native speaker" ', *English Today* 82: 13–24.

Carless, David R. (1995) 'Politicised expressions in the *South China Morning Post*', *English Today* 42: 18–22.

Cathcart, Michael (ed.) (1994) *Manning Clark's History of Australia*. London: Chatto & Windus.

Chambers, J. K. (1985) 'Three kinds of standard in Canadian English'. In W. C. Lougheed (ed.) *In Search of the Standard in Canadian English*, 1–15.

Chambers, J. K. (2004) 'Solitudes and solidarity: English and French in Canada', *Moderna Språk* XCVIII: 122–9.

Coghill, Nevill (ed.) (1963) *Chaucer's Canterbury Tales, translated into modern English verse*, rev. edn. Harmondsworth: Penguin Books.

Collins, Beverly (1988) 'The Early Career of Daniel Jones'. Dissertation, Utrecht University.

Courtney, Neil (1996) 'The nature of Australian', *English Today* 46: 23–9.

Cruttenden, Alan (1997) *Intonation*. Cambridge: Cambridge University Press.

Crystal, David (1990) *The English Language*. London: Penguin.

Crystal, David (2000) *Language Death*. Cambridge: Cambridge University Press.

Crystal, David (2001) *Language and the Internet*. Cambridge: Cambridge University Press.

Crystal, David (2003) *English as a Global Language*, 2nd edn. Cambridge: Cambridge University Press.

Crystal, David (2003) *The Cambridge Encyclopedia of the English Language*, 2nd edn. Cambridge: Cambridge University Press.

Crystal, David (2004) *The Stories of English*. London: Allen Lane.

Crystal, David (2004) *A Glossary of Netspeak and Textspeak*. Edinburgh: Edinburgh University Press.

Crystal, David (2005) *Pronouncing Shakespeare*. Cambridge: Cambridge University Press.

Davies, Norman (1999) *The Isles: A History*. Oxford: Oxford University Press.

Dillard, J. L. (1972) *Black English: Its History and Usage in the United States*. New York: Random House.

Dillard, J. L. (1992) *A History of American English*. New York: Longman.

Dougill, John (1987) 'English as a decorative language', *English Today* 12: 33–5.

Etiemble, René (1973) *Parlez-vous franglais?* [1st edn. 1964]. Paris: Gallimard.

Forbes, Duncan (1993) 'Singlish', *English Today* 34: 18–21.

Forrest, Alan (1998) 'The politics of language in the European Union', *European Review* 6: 3, 299–319.

Freeborn, Dennis (1992) *From Old English to Standard English*. 2nd edn. Basingstoke: Macmillan.

Frykman, Erik and Göran Kjellmer (1991) *Aspects of Shakespeare*. Lund: Studentlitteratur.

Gachelin, Jean-Marc (1990) 'Is English a Romance language?', *English Today* 23: 8–14.

Giles, Howard and Peter F. Powesland (1975) *Speech Style and Social Evaluation*. London: Academic Press.

Giles, Howard and Philip Smith (1979) 'Accommodation theory: optimal levels of convergence'. In Howard Giles and Robert N. St. Clair (eds.) *Language and Social Psychology*. Baltimore, MD: University Park Press, pp. 45–65.

Goh, Christine C. M. (1998) 'The level tone in Singapore English', *English Today* 53: 50–3.

Gold, Elaine (2005) 'Canadian *Eh?*: A Survey of Contemporary Use'. In *Proceedings of the 2004 Canadian Linguistics Association Annual Conference*, ed. Marie-Odile Junker, Martha McGinnis and Yves Roberge, http://www.carleton.ca/~mojunker/ACL-CLA/pdf/Bliss-CLA-2004.

Gordon, Elizabeth and Tony Deverson (1998) *New Zealand English and English in New Zealand*, Auckland: New House Publishers.

Görlach, Manfred (1990) *Studies in the History of the English Language*. Heidelberg: Winter.

Görlach, Manfred (ed.) (2001) *A Dictionary of European Anglicisms*. Oxford: Oxford University Press.

Görlach, Manfred (2003) *English Words Abroad*. Amsterdam: John Benjamins.

Graddol, David (1997) *The Future of English? A Guide to Forecasting the Popularity of the English Language in the 21st Century*. London: British Council.

Graddol, David and Ulrike H. Meinhof (eds.) (1999) *English in a Changing World: The AILA Review* 13. Oxford: Catchline.

Gramley, Stephen and Kurt-Michael Pätzold (2004) *A Survey of Modern English*, 2nd edn. London: Routledge.

Granger, Sylviane (1996) 'Romance words in English: From history to pedagogy'. In Jan Svartvik (ed.) *Words*, 105–21.

Greenbaum, Sidney and Janet Whitcut (1988) *Longman Guide to English Usage*. London: Longman.

Hao, Keqi (1988) 'The view from China', *English Today* 13: 50–2.

Heaney, Seamus (2002) *Beowulf: A Verse Translation*. New York: Norton.

Hogg, Richard M. (1992–2001) (general editor) *The Cambridge History of the English Language*. Cambridge: Cambridge University Press.

Holm, John (2000) *An Introduction to Pidgins and Creoles*. Cambridge: Cambridge University Press.

Holmes, Janet (1997) 'T-time in New Zealand', *English Today* 51: 18–22.

Huddleston, Rodney D. and Geoffrey K. Pullum (2002) *The Cambridge Grammar of the English Language*. Cambridge: Cambridge University Press.

Hughes, Arthur and Peter Trudgill (1996) *English Accents and Dialects: An Introduction to Social and Regional Varieties of British English*, 3rd edn. London: Edward Arnold.

Ihalainen, Ossi (1991) 'On grammatical diffusion in Somerset folk speech'. In Peter Trudgill and J. K. Chambers (eds.) *Dialects of English*, 104–19.

James, Gregory (2001) 'Cantonese particles in Hong Kong students' English e-mails', *English Today* 67: 9–16.

Jenkins, Jennifer (2004) 'ELF at the gate: the position of English as a lingua franca', *The European English Messenger* 13, 2: 63–9.

Jenkins, Jennifer, Marko Modiano and Barbara Seidlhofer (2001) 'Euro-English', *English Today* 68: 13–19.

Jespersen, Otto (1948) *Growth and Structure of the English Language*, 9th edn. Oxford: Blackwell.

Kachru, Braj B. (1985) 'Standards, codification and sociolinguistic realism: the English language in the outer circle'. In Randolph Quirk and H. G. Widdowson (eds.) *English in the World*, 11–30.

Kachru, Braj B. (1994) 'English in South Asia'. In Robert Burchfield (ed.) *The Cambridge History of the English Language*, vol. 5, 497–553.

Kallen, Jeffrey L. (1994) 'English in Ireland'. In Robert Burchfield (ed.) *The Cambridge History of the English Language*, vol. 5, 148–96.

Klaeber, Fr. (ed.) (1950) *Beowulf and the Fight at Finnsburg*, 3rd edn. Boston: D. C. Heath.

Klerk, Vivian de (ed.) (1996) *Focus on South Africa*. Amsterdam: Benjamins.

Knowles, Gerry (1997) *A Cultural History of the English Language*. London: Arnold.

Kökeritz, Helge (1953) *Shakespeare's Pronunciation*. New Haven, CT: Yale University Press.

Kökeritz, Helge (1954) *A Guide to Chaucer's Pronunciation*. Stockholm: Almqvist & Wiksell.

Labov, William (1966) *The Social Stratification of English in New York City*. Washington, DC: Center for Applied Linguistics.

Labov, William, Sharon Ask and Charles Boberg (1997) *A National Map of the Regional Dialects of American English*. University of Pennsylvania: the Linguistics Laboratory. http://www.ling.upenn.edu/phono_atlas/NationalMap/NationalMap.html

Lai, Eva (2001) 'Teaching English as a private enterprise in China', *English Today* 66: 32–6.

Langeland, Agnes Scott (1996) 'Rushdie's language', *English Today* 45: 16–22.

Lanham, L. W. (1996) 'A history of English in South Africa'. In Vivian de Klerk (ed.) *Focus on South Africa*, 19–34.

Lanham, L. W. and Macdonald, C. A. (1979) *The Standard in South African English and its Social History*. Heidelberg: Julius Gross.

Leech, Geoffrey (2004) 'Recent grammatical change in English: data, description, theory'. In K. Aijmer and B. Altenberg (eds) *Advances in Corpus Linguistics*: Papers from the 23rd International Conference on English Language Research on Computerized Corpora (ICAME 23) Göteborg 22–26 May 2002. Amsterdam: Rodopi, 61–81.

Leech, Geoffrey, Paul Rayson and Andrew Wilson (2001) *Word Frequencies in Written and Spoken English based on the British National Corpus*. London: Longman.

Leech, Geoffrey and Jan Svartvik (2002) *A Communicative Grammar of English*, 3rd edn. London: Longman.

Leech, Geoffrey and Nicholas Smith (2006) 'Recent grammatical change in written English 1961–1992: some preliminary findings of a comparison of American with British English'. In Antoinette Renouf and A. Kehoe (eds.) *The Changing Face of Corpus Linguistics*. Amsterdam: Rodopi, pp. 186–204.

Lewis, Jon E. (ed.) (2003) *The Mammoth Book of How It Happened in America*. London: Robinson.

Lilles, Jaan (April 2000) 'The myth of Canadian English', *English Today*, 62, 16(2): 3–9.

Lindquist, Hans, Staffan Klintborg, Magnus Levin and Maria Estling (eds.) (1998) *The Major Varieties of English* (Papers from MAVEN 97, Växjö 20–22 November 1997). Acta Wexionensia Humaniora No.1, Växjö University.

Lougheed, W. C. (ed.) (1985) *In Search of the Standard in Canadian English*. Kingston, Ontario: Queen's University.

Lynn, Jonathan and Antony Jay (2003) *Yes, Prime Minister: The Complete Collection*. London: BBC.

Macaulay, Ronald (1994) *The Social Art: Language and its Uses*. New York: Oxford University Press.

Mair, Christian (2006) *Twentieth-Century English: History, Variation and Standardization*. Cambridge: Cambridge University Press.

Mair, Christian and Geoffrey Leech (2006) 'Current change in English syntax'. In Bas Aarts and April MacMahon (eds). *The Handbook of English Linguistics*. Oxford: Blackwell, pp. 318–34.

Mauranen, Anna (2003) 'The Corpus of English as a Lingua Franca in International Settings', *TESOL Quarterly* 37, 3: 513–27.

McArthur, Tom (ed.) (1992) *The Oxford Companion to the English Language*. Oxford: Oxford University Press.

McArthur, Tom (1998) *The English Languages*. Cambridge: Cambridge University Press.

McArthur, Tom (1999) 'English in the world, in Africa, and in South Africa', *English Today* 57: 11–16.

McArthur, Tom (2002) *The Oxford Guide to World English*. Oxford: Oxford University Press.

McArthur, Tom (2003) 'World English, Euro-English, Nordic English?', *English Today* 73: 54–8.

McCrum, Robert, William Cran and Robert MacNeil (1992) *The Story of English*. London: Faber and Faber.

McKnight, George H. (1968) *The Evolution of the English Language: From Chaucer to the Twentieth Century*. New York: Dover.

Melchers, Gunnel (1998) ' "Fair ladies, dancing queens" – A study of mid-Atlantic accents'. In Hans Lindquist et al. (eds.) *The Major Varieties of English*, 263–71.

Melchers, Gunnel and Philip Shaw (2003) *World Englishes: An Introduction*. London: Arnold.

Mencken, H. L. (1936) *The American Language*, 4th edn. New York: Knopf.

Metcalf, Allan (2004) *Presidential Voices: Speaking Styles from George Washington to George W. Bush*. Boston: Houghton Mifflin.

Millward, Celia M. (1989) *A Biography of the English Language*. Fort Worth: Harcourt Brace.

Milroy, James and Lesley Milroy (eds.) (1993) *Real English: The Grammar of English Dialects in the British Isles*. London and New York: London.

Milroy, James and Lesley Milroy (1999) *Authority in Language: Investigating Standard English*. London: Routledge.

Modiano, Marko (1998) 'The emergence of mid-Atlantic English in the European Union'. In Hans Lindquist et al. (eds.) *The Major Varieties of English*, 241–8.

Morgan, Kenneth (ed.) (2001) *The Oxford History of Britain*, rev. edn. Oxford: Oxford University Press.

Mugglestone, Lynda (2003) *'Talking Proper': the Rise of Accent as Social Symbol*, 2nd edn. Oxford: Oxford University Press.

Mühlhäusler, Peter (1986) *Pidgin and Creole Linguistics*. Oxford: Blackwell.

Mühlhäusler, Peter (1997) *Pidgin and Creole Linguistics*. London: University of Westminster Press.

Nayar, P. Bhaskaran (1998) 'Variants and varieties of English: Dialectology or linguistic politics?' In Hans Lindquist et al. (eds.), *The Major Varieties of English*, 283–9.

Oxford English Dictionary [OnLine ed. www.**oed**.com]. Oxford: Oxford University Press.

Paikeday, Thomas M. (1985) *The Native Speaker is Dead!* Toronto: Paikeday.

Patrick, Peter [website, University of Essex, with Creole texts] http://privatewww.essex.ac.uk/~patrickp/SweetAnDandy.htm.

Pennington, Martha C. (1998) 'The folly of language planning; Or, A brief history of the English language in Hong Kong', *English Today* 54: 25–30.

Pennycook, Alastair (1994) *The Cultural Politics of English as an International Language*. London: Longman.

Peters, Pam (1995) *The Cambridge Australian English Style Guide*. Cambridge: Cambridge University Press.

Phillipson, Robert (1992) *Linguistic Imperialism*. Oxford: Oxford University Press.

Phillipson, Robert (2003) *English-Only Europe? Challenging Language Policy*. London: Routledge.

Porter, John (1991) *Beowulf: Text and Translation*. Pinner: Anglo-Saxon Books.

Potter, Simeon (1990) *Our Language*, rev. edn. London: Penguin.

Preshous, Andrew (2001) 'Where you going ah?', *English Today* 65: 46–53.

Preston, Dennis R. and Roger W. Shuy (eds.) (1979) *Varieties of American English: A Reader*. Washington, DC: Educational Communication Agency.

Pyles, Thomas (1952) *Words and Ways of American English*. New York: Random House.

Pyles, Thomas and John Algeo (1993) *The Origins and Development of the English Language*, 4th edn. Fort Worth: Harcourt Brace Jovanovich.

Quinion, Michael (2004) *Port Out, Starboard Home and Other Language Myths*. London: Penguin.

Quirk, Randolph (1974) 'Shakespeare and the English language'. In Randolph Quirk, *The Linguist and the English Language*, London: Edward Arnold, pp. 46–64.

Quirk, Randolph (1982) *Style and Communication in the English Language*. London: Arnold.

Quirk, Randolph (1995) *Grammatical & Lexical Variance in English*. London: Longman.

Quirk, Randolph and Gabriele Stein (1990) *English in Use*. London: Longman.

Quirk, Randolph and H. G. Widdowson (eds.) (1985) *English in the World: Teaching and Learning the Language and its Literatures*. Cambridge: Cambridge University Press.

Quirk, Randolph and C. L. Wrenn (1955) *An Old English Grammar*. London: Methuen.

Richards, Julian D. (2000) *Viking Age England*. Stroud: Tempus.

Rickard, John (1996) *Australia: A Cultural History*, 2nd edn. London: Longman.

Rickford, John R. (1999) *African American Vernacular English: Features and Use, Evolution, and Educational Implications*. Oxford: Blackwell.

Rickford, John Russel and Russel John Rickford (2000) *Spoken Soul: the Story of Black English*. New York: John Wiley.

Robinson, F. N. (ed.) (1957) *The Works of Geoffrey Chaucer*, 2nd edn. Boston: Houghton Mifflin.

Room, Adrian (ed.) (1999) *Brewer's Dictionary of Phrase and Fable*. 16th edn. New York: HarperCollins.

Sano, Hikomaro (2002) 'The world's lingua franca of science', *English Today* 72: 45–9.

Saussure, Ferdinand de (1916) *Cours de Linguistique générale* [Translated from the French by Wade Baskin as *Course in General Linguistics* (1974). London: Fontana].

Sawyer, Peter (ed.) (1997) *The Oxford Illustrated History of the Vikings*. Oxford: Oxford University Press.

Schama, Simon (2003) *A History of Britain: The Fate of the Empire 1776–2000*. London: BBC.

Sebba, Mark (1992) *London Jamaican: Language Systems in Interaction*. London: Longman.

Sebba, Mark (1997) *Contact Languages: Pidgins and Creoles*. Basingstoke: Palgrave Macmillan.

Seidlhofer, Barbara (2001) 'Closing a conceptual gap: the case for a description of English as a lingua franca', *International Journal of Applied Linguistics* 11, 2: 133–58.

Sellar, W. C. and R. J. Yeatman (1930) *1066 and All That: A Memorable History of England*. London: Methuen.

Silva, Penny (1998) 'South African English: oppressor or liberator?' In Hans Lindquist et al. (eds.) *The Major Varieties of English*, 69–77.

Simpson, John, Edmund Weiner and Philip Durkin (2004) 'The *Oxford English Dictionary* today', *Transactions of the Philological Society*, vol. 102: 3, 335–81.

Sinclair, John (1988) 'Models and monuments', *English Today* 15: 3–6.

Smith, Jeremy (1996) *An Historical Study of English: Function, Form and Change*. London: Routledge.

Smith, Ross (2005) 'Global English: gift or curse?', *English Today* 82: 56–62.

Stenström, Anna-Brita (1997) '*Can I have a chips please? Just tell me one you want*: Nonstandard grammatical features in London teenage talk'. In J. Aarts, I. de Mönnink and H. Wekker (eds.), *Studies in English Language and Teaching*. Amsterdam: Rodopi, pp. 141–52.

Stenton, F. M. (1989) *Anglo-Saxon England*, 3rd edn. Oxford: Oxford University Press.

Stewart, William A. (1979) 'Sociolinguistic Factors in the History of the American Negro Dialects'. In Dennis R. Preston and Roger W. Shuy (eds.), 194–205.

Svartvik, Jan (ed.) (1996) *Words: Proceedings of an International Symposium, Lund, 25–26 August 1995*. Stockholm: Almqvist & Wiksell International.

Svartvik, Jan (1999) *Engelska – öspråk, världsspråk, trendspråk*. Stockholm: Norstedts.

Sweet, Henry (1877) *A Handbook of Phonetics*. Oxford: Clarendon Press.

Taylor, Andrew (1989) 'Hong Kong's English newspapers', *English Today* 20: 18–24.

Taylor, Monica E. (1996) 'Jamaica and the economics of English', *English Today* 48: 25–31.

The American Heritage Book of English Usage (1996) Boston: Houghton Mifflin.

The American Heritage Dictionary of the English Language (2001) 4th edn. Boston: Mariner.

The Concise Oxford Dictionary of Australian History (1994) 2nd edn. by Jan Bassett. Melbourne: Oxford University Press.

The Dictionary of New Zealand English (1997) ed. by H. W. Orsman. Auckland: Oxford University Press.

The Macquarie Dictionary (1991) 2nd edn. by Arthur Delbridge, J. R. L. Bernard, D. Blair, P. Peters and S. Butler. Sydney: The Macquarie Library.

The New Zealand Oxford Dictionary (2005) ed. by Tony Deverson and Graeme Kennedy. South Melbourne: Oxford University Press.

Thomas, Alan R. (1984) 'Welsh English', in Peter Trudgill (ed.) *Language in the British Isles*, 178–94, Cambridge: Cambridge University Press.

Thumboo, Edwin (ed.) (1988) *Literature and Liberation: Five Essays from Southeast Asia*. Manila: Solidaridad Publishing House.

Times-Chambers Essential English Dictionary (1997) 2nd edn. Chambers Harrap & National University of Singapore.

Todd, Loreto (1974) *Pidgins and Creoles*. London: Routledge.

Todd, Loreto (2000) 'Where have all the Celtic words gone?', *English Today* 63: 6–10.

Tottie, Gunnel (2002) *An Introduction to American English*. Oxford and Malden, MA: Blackwell.

Tottie, Gunnel (forthcoming) 'How different are American and British English grammar? And how are they different?' In Günter Rohdenberg and Julia Schlüter. Cambridge: Cambridge University Press.

Trudgill, Peter (ed.) (1984) *Language in the British Isles*. Cambridge: Cambridge University Press.

Trudgill, Peter (1984) 'Standard English in England', in Peter Trudgill (ed.) *Language in the British Isles*, 32–44. Cambridge: Cambridge University Press.

Trudgill, Peter (2001) 'Received Pronunciation: sociolinguistic aspects', *Studia Anglia Posnaniensia* 36: 3–12.

Trudgill, Peter and J. K. Chambers (eds.) (1991) *Dialects of English: Studies in Grammatical Variation*. London: Longman.

Trudgill, Peter and Jean Hannah (2002) *International English: A Guide to Varieties of Standard English*, 4th edn. London: Arnold.

Tuleja, Tad (1994) *The New York Public Library Book of Popular Americana*. New York: Macmillan.

Turner, George W. (1994) 'English in Australia'. In Robert Burchfield (ed.) *The Cambridge History of the English Language*, vol. v, 277–327.

Watts, Richard and Peter Trudgill (2002) *Alternative Histories of English*. London: Routledge.

Webster, Noah (1789) *An Essay on the Necessity, Advantages and Practicality of Reforming the Mode of Spelling*. An appendix to *Dissertations on the English Language*. Boston.

Webster, Noah (1828) *An American Dictionary of the English Language*. Springfield, MA: Merriam & Co.

Wekker, Herman (1996) 'Creole words'. In Jan Svartvik (ed.) *Words*, 91–104.

Wekker, Herman (1996) 'The English-based creoles of Surinam', *English Today* 48: 33–8.

Wells, J. C. (1982) *Accents of English*. 3 vols. Cambridge: Cambridge University Press.

Wells, J. C. (2004) *Longman Pronunciation Dictionary*. London: Longman.

Whitelock, Dorothy (1967) *Sweet's Anglo-Saxon Reader in Prose and Verse*, 15th edn. Oxford: Clarendon Press.

Winchester, Simon (2003) *The Meaning of Everything: The Story of the Oxford English Dictionary*. Oxford: Oxford University Press.

Wolfram, Walt and Natalie Schilling-Estes (1998) *American English: Dialects and Variation*. Malden, MA: Blackwell.

Wrenn, C. L. (1977) *The English Language*. London: Methuen.

Index of People

(**Note**: This index covers the main text, but not the Notes section.)

Index of Topics

(**Note**: This index covers the main text, but not the notes section.)

Pronunciation

We have tried to use a system of phonetic transcription which is not biased towards a particular kind of speech, but this is not easy since British and American English, the two varieties we are mainly dealing with, differ more in pronunciation than in any other respect. To make things simple, we consider only one accent from each national variety: **Received Pronunciation** (or RP, see pp. 125–8), which is commonly used as a standard accent for the learning of British English pronunciation, and **Network English**, also called **General American** (abbreviated GA, see pp. 81–2), which has a somewhat comparable status in the United States. It is also convenient to use these two well-documented national varieties for reference when discussing other regional varieties of English in the world.

Phonetic symbols are enclosed in slant lines / /. Where necessary, we use the vertical bar I to separate RP and GA pronunciations (with the British pronunciation on the left and the American pronunciation on the right). Full length of a preceding sound is indicated by a colon: *sea* /siː/.

clerk /klɑːk I klɜːrk/
dance /dɑːns I dæns/
law /lɔː I lɒː/
limousine /lɪməˈziːn I ˈlɪməziːn/
advertisement /ədˈvɜːtɪsmənt I ædvɜˈrtaɪzmənt/

In phonetic transcriptions primary word stress is indicated by ' before the stressed syllable: *analysis* /əˈnæləsɪs/. Secondary word stress is indicated by ˌ before the syllable: *commentary* /ˈkɒməntəri I ˈkɑmənˌteri/. Outside phonetic transcriptions, word stress is often conveniently indicated by underlining: h<u>a</u>rass, har<u>ass</u> (see p. 40).

In words like *middle* transcribed as /ˈmɪdᵊl/, the raised ᵊ indicates that the schwa is optional, i.e. pronounced by some speakers, but omitted by other speakers. In words like *nurse* where the RP vowel is /ɜː/, GA has a rhotacized schwa transcribed as /ɜrː/.

General American intervocalic /t/, in words like *butter* and *better*, is not articulated as a voiceless stop (as in RP) but as a voiced tap. When American English is specifically discussed, as when comparing GA and RP (pp. 163–6), the GA pronunciation is represented as /ɒ/ (following *An Introduction to American English* by Gunnel Tottie, pp. 16–17).

Key to phonetic symbols

The transcription system largely follows *Longman Pronunciation Dictionary* by John Wells.

Consonants		Vowels	
/p/	<u>p</u>en	/ɪ/	b<u>i</u>d
/b/	<u>b</u>ack	/e/	b<u>e</u>d
/t/	<u>t</u>ea	/æ/	b<u>a</u>d
/d/	<u>d</u>ay	/ɒ I ɑː/	<u>o</u>dd
/k/	<u>k</u>ey	/ʌ/	b<u>u</u>d
/g/	<u>g</u>et	/ʊ/	g<u>oo</u>d

/tʃ/	chur<u>ch</u>	/iː/	s<u>ea</u>
/dʒ/	ju<u>dge</u>	/eɪ/	d<u>ay</u>
/f/	<u>f</u>at	/aɪ/	h<u>igh</u>
/v/	<u>v</u>iew	/ɔɪ/	b<u>oy</u>
/θ/	<u>th</u>ing	/uː/	tw<u>o</u>
/ð/	<u>th</u>is	/əʊ ǀ oʊ/	sh<u>ow</u>
/s/	<u>s</u>oon	/aʊ/	n<u>ow</u>
/z/	<u>z</u>ero	/ɪə ǀ ɪᵊr/	h<u>ere</u>
/ʃ/	<u>sh</u>ip	/eə ǀ eᵊr/	f<u>air</u>
/ʒ/	plea<u>s</u>ure	/ɑː/	f<u>a</u>ther
/h/	<u>h</u>ot	/ɔː ǀ ɒː/	l<u>aw</u>
/m/	<u>m</u>ore	/ʊə ǀ ʊᵊr/	c<u>ure</u>
/n/	su<u>n</u>	/ɜː ǀ ɜʳː/	n<u>ur</u>se
/ŋ/	lo<u>ng</u>	/ə/	<u>a</u>bout
/l/	<u>l</u>ight	/i/	happ<u>y</u>
/r/	<u>r</u>ight		
/j/	<u>y</u>et		
/w/	<u>w</u>et		

In text illustrations from older periods of the language and regional varieties there occur some additional sounds:

/ɛ/	approximately as in French *père*
/ɔ/	approximately as in German *Sonne*
/o/	approximately as in French *eau*
/y/	approximately as in French *du*
/ç/	voiceless palatal fricative, as at the beginning of *huge*
/ɬ/	voiceless alveolar lateral fricative, as in Welsh *Llanelli*
/x/	voiceless velar fricative, as in German *ach* and Scots *loch*
/ʔ/	glottal stop, produced by bringing the vocal chords tightly together, blocking off the air-stream, then releasing them suddenly; a 'catch in the throat', as used in the popular London pronunciation of *t* in *butter*.